Chicago's North Michigan Avenue:
Planning and Development 1900–1930

CHICAGO ARCHITECTURE AND URBANISM

A series edited by

Robert Bruegmann

Joan Draper

Wim de Wit

David Van Zanten

JOHN W. STAMPER

CHICAGO'S NORTH MICHIGAN AVENUE

PLANNING AND DEVELOPMENT, 1900-1930

THE UNIVERSITY OF CHICAGO PRESS

Chicago and London

Works in Chicago Architecture and Urbanism are supported in part by funds given in memory of Ann Lorenz Van Zanten and administered by the Chicago Historical Society.

John W. Stamper is associate professor in the School of Architecture at the University of Notre Dame.

The University of Chicago Press, Chicago 60637
The University of Chicago Press, Ltd., London

Library of Congress Cataloging-in-Publication Data
Stamper, John W.
    Chicago's North Michigan Avenue / John W. Stamper.
      p.   cm. —(Chicago architecture and urbanism :)
    Includes bibliographical references and index.
    ISBN 0-226-77085-0
    1. Architecture—Illinois—Chicago. 2. Architecture, Modern—20th century—Illinois—Chicago. 3. City planning—Illinois—Chicago—History—20th century. 4. Michigan Avenue (Chicago, Ill.)
5. Chicago (Ill.)—Buildings, structures, etc. I. Title. II. Series.
NA735.C4S83   1991
720'.9773'1109042—dc20   90-43226
                                                                CIP

C O N T E N T S

A C K N O W L E D G M E N T S

The subject of this book, the planning and architecture of Chicago's North Michigan Avenue, grew out of a study undertaken in 1982 with the encouragement of David Van Zanten at Northwestern University. This initial study focused on plans for the avenue in the 1909 Chicago Plan by Daniel Burnham and Edward Bennett, and on plan proposals published in 1918 for the North Central Business District Association of Chicago. My research soon expanded into a larger analysis of the numerous proposals for the avenue done previous to the Burnham Plan, and finally to a study of the more than thirty significant commercial, residential, and hotel buildings constructed on the avenue in the 1920s.

I would like to thank David Van Zanten as well as Carl Condit and Henry Binford, also of Northwestern University, for their support and guidance in this project. I would also like to thank Emily Harris of the Landmarks Preservation Council of Illinois who first introduced me to the wealth of available information on North Michigan Avenue; Meredith Taussig and Roy Forrey of the Chicago Landmarks Commission; Linda Hanrath, the librarian of the William Wrigley, Jr., Company; Terry Erickson of Ragnar-Benson Construction Company, who gave me a rare and insightful tour of the Wrigley Building; and Harold Reynolds, a former employee of Holabird and Root, who kindly told me about his work as an architect in the 1920s.

The staff of the Chicago Historical Society was of invaluable help, particularly Wim De Wit, Sabra Clark, and Lynn Laufenberg of the Department of Architectural Collections, and Archie Motley of the Department of Archives and Manuscripts. Of equal generosity in time and assistance were the staffs of the Chicago Municipal Reference Library, the Chicago Public Library, the Burnham Library of the Art Institute of Chicago, the Northwestern University Library, and the New York Historical Society.

Two people who enthusiastically read and commented on the text in its early stages were Kathy Roy Cummings

ACKNOWLEDGMENTS

and Robert Bruegmann. I also wish to thank my typists, Debbie Banik, Brenda Fitzwater, and C. J. McCracken. Finally, I want to thank my wife Erika Pistorius Stamper for her many hours of proofreading and for her unwavering support and encouragement.

N orth Michigan Avenue, known in the 1920s as Chicago's "Upper Boul Mich," is one of the city's most prestigious commercial corridors, containing some of its most significant architecture and urban planning features. It exemplifies the business and economic conditions of two important eras in the city's building history. The first is that of the 1920s, while the second began in the mid-1950s and continues today more or less unabated. The focus of this book is the building boom of the 1920s and the planning of the avenue that occurred in the previous two decades. It was during this period that the character and economic base of the avenue was established.

The avenue as it appeared in 1930 (figures I.1 and I.2), at the beginning of the Great Depression, was the result of many years of economic investment, speculation, planning, and political persuasion, and represented many changes in attitude toward architectural design and theory. Planning was begun in the 1880s with numerous proposals being put forth by architects, planners, and politicians, and there were several unsuccessful attempts made by the Chicago City Council and the Board of Local Improvements to build the new north-south connecting link around the turn of the century. The necessity of the avenue was affirmed in Burnham and Bennett's Chicago Plan of 1909, and its final form was proposed in a plan of 1918 commissioned by an organization called the North Central Business District Association.

While the planning and construction was going on, there was a considerable amount of real estate speculation taking place along the path of the new avenue as investors recognized the potential commercial value of the onetime wholesale trade area along the river and the residential area north of the river. The new avenue was the subject of an extensive marketing campaign promoting it as a major location of fine shops, offices, hotels, clubs, and apartments, and before the new bridge was even opened in 1920 three major buildings—the Crerar Library, Drake Hotel,

Figure I.1
View of North Michigan
Avenue in 1933 with
Wrigley Building on the
left, Tribune Tower on the
right. Courtesy of the
Chicago Historical Society.

and the Wrigley Building—were already under construction. As developers eagerly sought prime commercial property outside the overpriced Loop, they bought up the old warehouse buildings and the once stately mansions with the idea of getting in on the ground floor of the city's newest real estate gold mine. They were enthusiastically supported in this endeavor by banks and financiers who saw the future of the city moving northward. A location on the city's new North Michigan Avenue in the 1920s became a guarantee for financial backing and success.

There was a substantial desire on the part of the avenue's developers to maintain a high quality of land use and building design, although they found themselves at odds with planners who sought to limit the heights of buildings to ten stories, or about 100 feet. New zoning allowances that permitted buildings of 264 feet with towers of virtually

Figure I.2
View of North Michigan
Avenue looking south from
the Bridge Plaza; 333
North Michigan Avenue
Building at the left; Lon-
don Guarantee and Acci-
dent Building at the right.
Reprinted from Chicago
Board of Local Improve-
ments *(Chicago, 1931).*
With the permission of the
Chicago Architectural Pho-
tographing Co.

unlimited height radically challenged the planning visions
held by the avenue's earliest proponents and resulted in a
diverse urban mixture of low-rise and high-rise structures.
Taken individually, many of these buildings are among the
finest examples in the country of Beaux-Arts Classicism,
Gothic Revival, and Vertical Style Modernism, designed by
such leading architects as Daniel Burnham, John M. Howells and Raymond Hood, Alfred S. Alschuler, Andrew Rebori, and the firms of Graham, Anderson, Probst and
White, and of Holabird and Root. Taken as a whole, however, they pose some difficult problems, especially in terms
of urban context and design compatibility. An analysis of
these issues reveals much about urban development in the
United States during this period, illustrating the many de-
terminants at work in the building industry: property ownership, financing, zoning laws, design theory, advertising,

and building management. This study will attempt to explain the connecting links between these factors and architectural form, mediations which are themselves historically formed; in the case of each architect and each building they are historically specific.

The portion of Michigan Avenue under study corresponds to the planning proposal for the widening of the avenue made by Burnham in 1909 and to the actual project for its improvement in 1918–20. It begins at Randolph Street at the northern boundary of Grant Park, and extends northward across the river, past the Water Tower to Oak Street and Lake Shore Drive, encompassing a total of seventeen blocks (figure I.3). Although the actual change in address from north to south occurs at Madison Street, the most significant change in Michigan Avenue is at Randolph, where it breaks spatially from buildings on one side facing the park to a corridor lined with buildings on both sides.

There is currently no published literature that deals with the development of North Michigan Avenue as a whole. Its history must instead be pieced together from many diverse sources, ranging from general histories of architecture and books on Chicago to newspaper and periodical articles and archival material. There are a number of key books which must form the basis of any architectural analysis of Chicago. The first is Frank A. Randall's *History of the Development of Building Construction in Chicago* (1949), which includes factual information on nearly all of the buildings in this study. The second book, tracing the economic history of Chicago's real estate development, is Homer Hoyt's *One Hundred Years of Land Values in Chicago* (1933). Finally, Carl Condit's *The Chicago School of Architecture* (1964), along with *Chicago 1910–29; Building, Planning and Urban Technology* (1973) and its companion volume *Chicago 1930–70*, discuss many of the important buildings on North Michigan Avenue, concentrating on structural, economic, and urban factors in their design.

The literature of the planning of North Michigan Avenue is extensive, particularly as it relates to the Chicago Plan and the establishment of the Chicago Plan Commission. While many of these publications will be dealt with in Chapter 1 of this book, it is useful to mention at this point, in addition to *The Plan of Chicago* (1909) by Daniel H. Burnham and Edward H. Bennett, *Wacker's Manual for the Plan of Chicago* (1912) and *What of the City? America's Greatest Issue: City Planning* (1919), both by Walter D. Moody, the most prolific publicist of the Plan.

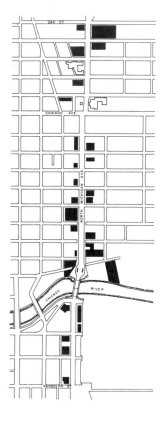

Figure I.3
Plan of North Michigan Avenue from Randolph Street to Oak Street, with principal buildings constructed between 1918 and 1930. Drawn by author.

In addition to these references, the majority of the original information for the present book came from three sources. The first was based on a methodical search of the deed records of the property on North Michigan Avenue covering the period from 1871 to 1930. These records, housed in the Cook County Tract Records Office, contain detailed and specific information on all property transactions for each building lot on the avenue. From this it was possible to reconstruct the history of the ownership of each parcel as well as to gain information about mortgage holders, trust owners, and leaseholds. The second source of information was articles in the real estate section of *The Economist* and of *Real Estate and Building News*. Published weekly in Chicago, these magazines contain a thorough ongoing documentation of real estate activity in the city, their articles including information on the buyers and sellers of property, financial arrangements, brokers, attorneys, as well as descriptions of the properties and buildings. The third major source of information was the Sunday real estate sections of the *Chicago Tribune*, information which could only be obtained by systematically scanning the newspaper on microfilm. There is a tradition in the *Chicago Tribune* of publishing impressive drawings of major building projects and giving detailed information about the developer, his architect, and his plans for the building, its financing, and its management. In some cases, these were published only with the intention of helping the developer gain financial support or potential tenants. Many were announced but never built.

EARLY DEVELOPMENT OF MICHIGAN AVENUE AND PINE STREET

During the early decades of the nineteenth century, what is now North Michigan Avenue was part of the old Green Bay Road and was little more than a collection of wooden buildings on a trail along the shore of Lake Michigan. Appropriately enough, the first structures in Chicago, the Jean Baptiste Point DuSable house and Fort Dearborn, were located on this trail. Jean DuSable, the city's first settler, built his house on the north side of the Chicago River (figure I.4) in 1779, the present site of the Equitable Building plaza. Fort Dearborn (figure I.5) was built on the south side in 1804 on the approach to the present Michigan Avenue Bridge.[1] The first plat of the city to include Michigan Avenue was the Fort Dearborn Addition in 1839, a seventy-

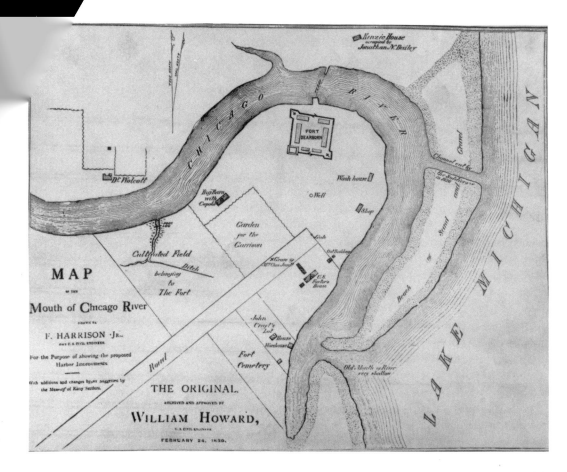

Figure I.4
Map showing sites of Kinzie
House (DuSable House)
and Fort Dearborn. Cour-
tesy of the Chicago Historical Society.

Figure I.5
Fort Dearborn, south side
of the Chicago River, 1803.
Courtesy of the Chicago
Historical Society.

five-acre tract south of the river, extending to Madison
Street and from the lakefront to State Street (figure I.6).[2]
Originally part of the fort's military reservation, this land

was vacant in the late 1830s except for a few wooden structures, including a house owned by early Chicago settler Jean Baptiste Beaubien.[3] At the time of its platting, Michigan Avenue lay only a few yards from the shoreline. The intervening property, along with the site of the present Chicago Cultural Center on the west side of Michigan Avenue between Randolph and Washington streets, was reserved for use as a public park.[4]

During the period from 1850 to 1860, Chicago's population grew from nearly 30,000 to over 100,000.[5] It was by then a thriving Midwestern town, spurred on by canal building and the railroads, with increasing business and rising rents and land values. Michigan Avenue became a warehouse and wholesale district, while the river frontage was developing primarily as a dock and industrial area with tanneries, distilleries, flour mills, and an iron works.[6] Most notably, the McCormick Reaper Works was built on the north side of the river, just east of the present Michigan Avenue Bridge. A hospital was built on the south side of the river, at the approximate location of the original Fort Dearborn.

In 1852, the Illinois Central Railroad purchased the lakefront area between Randolph Street and the river, and soon began filling in the lake about 1000 feet to the east to make a large tract for a passenger terminal, train sheds, and freight yards.[7] At the same time, it obtained the right to construct a wooden railroad trestle in the lake running parallel to Michigan Avenue and connecting the new station with its tracks coming up from the south (figure I.7). The City of Chicago had granted the right-of-way in the lake to the railroad because it was in need of stabilizing the shoreline to save it from flooding that had threatened Michigan Avenue itself.[8] The original Fort Dearborn property and the landfill extensions made by the railroad would eventually become the site of the Illinois Center development, its first buildings designed by Mies Van der Rohe. The railroad right-of-way in the lake would be gradually surrounded by even more landfill and would become part of Grant Park.

Figure I.6
Fort Dearborn Addition to Chicago, 1835. Redrawn by author from the Cook County Tract Records.

McCORMICKVILLE, STREETERVILLE, AND THE GOLD COAST

Development on the north side of the Chicago River had centered initially around the DuSable house and a complex

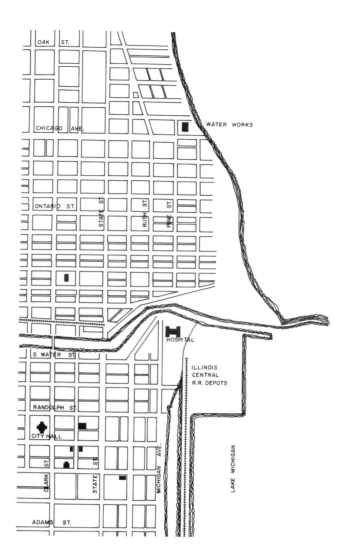

Figure I.7
Map of Chicago in 1855.
Redrawn by author from
map in collection of Chi-
cago Historical Society.

of buildings that grew up around it serving as a trading post for nearby Indian settlements. The area was subdivided and the land platted in 1834 as Kinzie's Addition to Chicago by Robert Kinzie and John Kinzie, Jr.[9] The subdivision consisted of fifty-four blocks extending north from the river to Chicago Avenue and from the lake to a line about fifty feet west of State Street (figure I.8).[10] What would later become North Michigan Avenue was called Pine Street. The area north of Kinzie's Addition, extending from Chicago Avenue to what is now Division Street, was platted in 1836.[11]

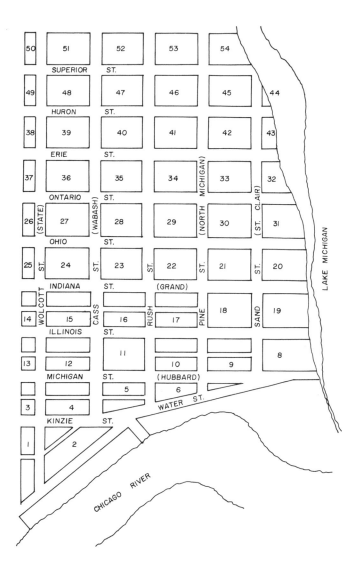

*Figure I.8
Kinzie's Addition to Chicago, 1834. Redrawn by
author from the Cook
County Tract Records.*

It was not long until a number of Chicagoans built their homes in Kinzie's Addition, many of them large mansions surrounded by landscaped grounds, some a full block in extent.[12] The most notable improvement to the area was the construction in 1867–69 of the Water Tower and Pumping Station (figure I.9) at the intersection of Pine Street and Chicago Avenue, a site then fronting directly on the lakeshore.[13] These buildings were designed in the Gothic Revival style by William W. Boyington, one of Chicago's earliest architects. Built of rough-faced, yellow limestone and decorated with turrets and crenellations, they housed the

Figure I.9
*Water Tower and Pumping
Station, corner of Pine
Street and Chicago Ave-
nue, 1867–69; W. W. Boy-
ington, architect.*

machinery necessary to pump water from an intake crib two miles out in Lake Michigan.[14]

Development of Kinzie's Addition along with the lake-front area south of the river was rudely brought to a halt in the Fire of 1871, which started on the city's West Side and burned the entire downtown area before crossing the river to the North Side. It destroyed the McCormick Reaper Works, the grain elevators, lumberyards, and residences beyond. It gutted the Pumping Station, though the Water Tower was spared, as was the Illinois Central freight house on the south side of the river. In all, 2100 acres were burned, nearly three-and-a half square miles, and 17,450 buildings were destroyed. The estimated loss was $190,000,000. The destruction of the North Side as a whole was nearly complete, with not more than 500 houses left out of some 14,000.[15]

The period immediately after the Fire of 1871 was spoken of among real estate people as the "great speculation years."[16] Between March and October of the succeeding year sales of city real estate amounted to over $45,000,000, and during the subsequent two years real estate trade was unsurpassed in the history of Chicago. Besides the large

investments of outside parties, primarily investors from the
East Coast, there was also a significant increase in the
amount of money deposited in savings and loan institutions,
thus resulting in vast sums of available mortgage money.[17]
The North Side became pitted in a clear competition with
other parts of the city, especially the South Side, to attract
socially accepted residents and high quality construction
and development. In 1873 real estate operator Henry C.
Johnson wrote a pamphlet in defense of the Near North
Side to encourage people to move to the area, and he pre-
dicted that the South Side eventually would be abandoned
as a first-class residential area.[18] He pointed out the advantages of the North Side, including wide streets, high
ground, good drainage, the lakeshore, and Lincoln Park,
which he described as the "only useful park in Chicago."
He also pointed out that there was fresh air, free of the
taint of the slaughterhouses which were the unfailing enemy
of the South Side, and he suggested that the property on
the North Side was cheaper than elsewhere in the city.[19]
Johnson acted not only out of a desire to attract new residents, but also to provide further encouragement to bankers who might have been hesitant to loan money in the area
for expensive residences.

There were about a hundred large residences and mansions built in the district in the first five years after the
Fire, the grandest being that of Cyrus McCormick, a Second Empire–style mansion at the corner of Rush and Erie
streets.[20] Other members of the McCormick family soon
built houses nearby, in fact, so many that the area became
known familiarly as "McCormickville." Probably the most
significant house built on Pine Street itself in the nineteenth
century was that of Perry H. Smith, a white marble-clad
structure with a slate-covered mansard roof and a prominent central tower (figure I.10).[21]

The area north and east of McCormickville is virtually
all landfill. In the nineteenth century, the pronounced
curve in the lakeshore at Oak Street did not exist. Instead,
the water's edge fell off gradually in a northwestward direction from the mouth of the river to the Pumping Station,
and finally to Oak Street at a point lying just west of the
axis of Pine Street (figure I.11). Many years of breakwater
construction, infilling, and developing were required to at-
tain the lakefront's present configuration, a process carried
out by the Lincoln Park Board of Commissioners in conjunction with prominent lakefront property owners. This
landfill area, encompassing nearly 120 acres, is known to-

Figure I.10
Perry H. Smith House,
northeast corner of Pine
and Huron streets, 1887;
G. R. Gilsdorf, architect.
Courtesy of the Chicago
Historical Society.

day as "Streeterville," so-named because of claims to the property made throughout the 1890s and early 1900s by George Streeter, an itinerant boat captain and land speculator.[22]

The area north of Streeterville, which became known as the "Gold Coast," centered around the castellated lakefront mansion of Potter Palmer, the founder of P. Palmer and Co. dry goods store, later to become Marshall Field and Company. He had also been the developer of much of State Street in the Loop during the 1860s and 1870s.[23] After building his house in 1882–84, and working with the Lincoln Park Board of Commissioners to build Lake Shore Drive as a northern extension of Pine Street, he developed the area with other large houses and nearly 300 apartments.[24] He then turned his attention to the area around the northern part of Pine Street, the last remaining undeveloped tract between his mansion and downtown Chicago, purchasing in the 1890s nearly all of the street's frontage between the Water Tower and Oak Street (figure I.12).[25] He built apartments and townhouses there until his death in 1902, after which his wife and their two sons, Honoré and Potter, Jr., managed the estate and made some modest

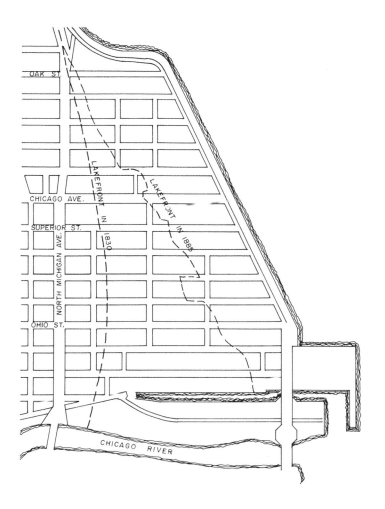

Figure I.11
Map of Streeterville show-
ing location of shoreline in
1830 and in 1885. Re-
drawn by author from Chicago Tribune *(10 May 1894*
and 10 August 1895).

attempts at further development. In the 1910s and 1920s, however, they became interested in other, larger-scale real estate ventures and sold off their Pine Street holdings to competing developers.[26]

The three neighborhoods, McCormickville, Streeterville, and the Gold Coast all overlapped near the north end of Pine Street. It was only fitting that the Fourth Presbyterian Church should be built here, on the west side of the street, between Walton Place and Delaware Place.[27] Constructed in 1912–14, it was attended mostly by residents of these neighborhoods, the church representing the spiritual aspirations of many of those who developed and speculated in property on the North Side. It was designed by Ralph Adams Cram, one of the country's leading exponents of the Gothic Revival and architect of St. John the Divine Cathedral in New York. Featuring lancet-arched openings, a

122-foot spire, carved sculpture and tracery, and stained-glass windows by Boston artist Charles Connick (figure I.13), its most important contribution was to the urban setting of the future North Michigan Avenue with its open courtyard bordered on the west and south by a Sunday School building and Parish House (figure I.14). The entrance facade of the church is connected to the Parish House by a lancet-arched pergola that fronts the street and provides an effective screen that both defines the courtyard and visually extends the public space into the realm of the church.

While the neighborhoods along the northern portion of Pine Street developed as exclusively residential areas before and after the turn of the century, that along the river developed as an industrial and warehouse district. The McCormick Reaper Works at the foot of Pine Street was replaced by the James S. Kirk and Company soap factory (figure I.15), a five-story brick building marked by a tall smokestack. The sprawling buildings of the Manitou Steamship Company stood to the east, and to the west were the large brick buildings of the George Bullen Company and the Northwestern Storage Company.[28] South of the river, Michigan Avenue to Randolph Street was lined with wholesale store buildings and industrial and warehouse structures (figure I.16) serving primarily as storage buildings related to the network of shipping canals and railroad spurs east of Michigan Avenue.

All of this was a great contrast to the mansions of McCormickville and Lake Shore Drive which stood as monuments to their wealthy builders. The real estate market had followed along the lines of utility, with industrial uses clustering along the river in order to take advantage of the shipping facilities, while residential development sought out the higher, cleaner, and quieter ground further north. This area was not destined to retain its exclusive residential character for long, however, as the competitive demand for property during the course of the next two decades transformed much of McCormickville into the city's fastest growing office and commercial district, and the Lake Shore Drive and Streeterville areas from neighborhoods of single-family mansions and townhouses into areas of high-rise apartments and hotels. The city paid a price for this unbridled development in the loss of elegant structures such as the Perry Smith House, the Cyrus McCormick House, and eventually the Potter Palmer mansion, as commercial

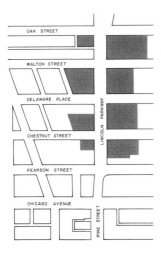

Figure I.12
Map of Potter Palmer
holdings on North Michi-
gan Avenue, 1902. Drawn
by author.

Figure I.13
Fourth Presbyterian
Church, southwest corner
of North Michigan Avenue
and Delaware Place, 1912–
14; Ralph Adams Cram in
association with Howard
Van Doren Shaw, archi-
tects. Courtesy of the Chi-
cago Historical Society.

Figure I.14 Fourth Presbyterian Church Parish House. Reprinted
from Architectural Record *(September 1914), copyright (1914) by*
McGraw-Hill, Inc. All rights reserved. Reproduced with the per-
mission of the publisher.

*Figure I.15
View of north side of Chicago River in 1916. Reprinted from Rand McNally and Co.,* One Hundred and Twenty-Five Photographic Views of Chicago *(Chicago, 1916).*

Figure I.16 Sprague, Warner and Company Building, northwest corner of Randolph Street and Michigan Avenue, c. 1895. Reprinted from G. W. Engelhardt, Chicago: The Book of the Board of Trade and Other Public Bodies *(Chicago, 1900).*

skyscraper towers became the standard economic entity and architectural image. The primary reason for this development occurring precisely where it did was the construction of the North Michigan Avenue Bridge and the widening of the avenue from Randolph Street to Oak Street. This work did not take place until the late 1910s, but it proved to be one of the most important public improvements ever undertaken in the City of Chicago.

THE URBAN
IMPERATIVE:
PLANNING
AND PUBLIC
IMPROVEMENTS

T he idea for transforming Michigan Avenue and Pine Street into a major commercial boulevard was talked about as early as the 1880s. It was a slowly evolving proposition that was initially developed and promoted largely by the city's commercial and industrial elite, those who stood to profit most by speculating in real estate on the new avenue. Once the idea was firmly established by the Chicago Plan of 1909, political support was quick in coming, primarily as an effort to appease and retain the allegiance of the city's commercial establishment. Support for the plan, however, was not unanimous, as many of those property owners and tenants directly affected objected to the demolition of their buildings. Storeowners resisted losing an established location for their business. Factory and warehouse owners resisted giving up their sorely needed space. They all objected to the proposed means of financing the project. Direct government involvement was needed to carry it out, the city exercising its power of condemnation to acquire the property needed for widening the avenue, issuing municipal bonds, and imposing special tax assessments to raise funds for the improvement.

This government participation was made possible by the support of a succession of mayors, both Democrat and Republican. Virtually all of them encouraged the planners and developers involved, and they supported various measures—city ordinances and bond issues—to make it possible. Some were more successful than others in accomplishing the various steps necessary in carrying out such a large endeavor, and all were quick to take credit any time results were forthcoming.

EARLY PLANS FOR A NORTH-SOUTH CONNECTING LINK

The earliest proposal for improving Michigan Avenue, suggested in the first years of the 1880s, called for widening Pine Street from the Water Tower to Grand Avenue, then turning west to Rush Street and south across the existing Rush Street Bridge to Michigan Avenue.[1] In 1888 another plan was proposed, this one for leaving Rush Street as it was and widening Michigan Avenue between Randolph Street and the river.[2] Property owners, however, claimed that if Michigan Avenue was widened, the increased business and traffic would make it more crowded than it already was. They suggested that it might be better to build a bridge-like structure over Michigan Avenue from Randolph Street to the river, leaving the lower level for heavy wagons and deliveries and creating a new upper-level roadway for carriage and pedestrian traffic.[3]

Another idea, this one for a subway tunnel under the river connecting Pine Street and Michigan Avenue, was proposed in 1892 and was incorporated into a plan for a lakefront park proposed by Daniel H. Burnham in 1896.[4] For Michigan Avenue he envisioned a subway tunnel to be located east of the avenue itself and to run under the Chicago River, coming up at Pine Street (figure 1.1). This was not to be like any already made, he stated, "but a thing of beauty, decorated with mural carvings and statues in full relief."[5] It would have been entered from a drive beginning at Madison Street, traveling eastward to a monumental fountain, and then northward where it would begin its descent. It would pass under a large arch opposite Washington Street, then under Randolph Street, and finally under the river.

Burnham presented his idea to members of the Commercial Club in October of 1896, and to the Merchants Club in 1897.[6] While it was an interesting proposal, nothing came of it at the time because of the economic panic that followed the World's Fair. Nobody would provide financial support for the idea, but the primary consequence of Burnham's presentations was the bringing together of a number of prominent citizens, all large property owners, along with representatives of the different park boards for the pur-

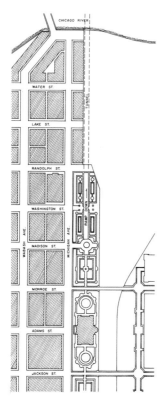

Figure 1.1
Proposal for North Michigan Avenue Tunnel, 1896; Daniel Burnham, architect. Redrawn by author from Chicago Tribune *(11 October 1896).*

pose of presenting a large-scale improvement that would make Chicago celebrated among the cities of the world.[7] Burnham was someone they respected. He had already played an important role in focusing world attention on Chicago with his planning efforts for the Columbian Exposition, and he would soon emerge as the most important figure in the planning of North Michigan Avenue.[8]

The proposal for a subway tunnel under the river was kept alive by John B. Hayes, chief clerk of the Board of Local Improvements, who in 1899 took the idea to the *Chicago Tribune*. He later made his own sketch of the proposal which the *Tribune* published. The idea of "a great spacious subway" gained further prominence as Mayor Carter H. Harrison, Jr., spoke of it in a message to the City Council early in 1904.[9] Mayor Harrison, who served from 1897 to 1905 and again from 1911 to 1915, recognized the importance of the Gold Coast development around Potter Palmer's mansion, and he was aware of the need to make it more accessible to the Loop, especially considering the fact that some of his largest campaign contributors lived on North Lake Shore Drive.[10]

Its function as a connecting link between the Gold Coast and the Loop became the overriding factor in promoting the idea of an improved avenue. The Loop was becoming one of the most vital urban areas in the country. Defined by the converging circuit of the city's elevated railway system, it was the center of Chicago's commerce and finance. State Street was the city's principal commercial street; LaSalle Street was internationally known for its financial institutions; Randolph Street was a mecca for theater goers; and Wells Street was an important wholesale merchandising district. The intersection of State and Madison streets was one of the busiest street crossings in the world, while the value of State Street property was the highest in the city.[11] An avenue connecting this commercial center with the Gold Coast became one of the mayor's primary political objectives.

In May of 1904, the *Chicago Tribune* published an article declaring Michigan Avenue and the Rush Street Bridge unfit to handle the volume of traffic passing over them each day. It was reported that an observer for the *Tribune* took a count of the traffic during a twelve-hour period and found that an average of 1000 persons and more than 300 vehicles crossed the bridge each hour. During the day, carriages and automobiles were bottled up repeatedly, and pedestrians were forced to hurdle over skids put across the

Figure 1.2
Rush Street Bridge in 1890.
Reprinted from Paul T.
Gilbert and Charles L.
Bryson, Chicago and Its
Makers *(Chicago, 1929).*

sidewalks by the wholesale houses for loading and unloading.[12] The Rush Street Bridge (figure 1.2), the traffic link across the river at this location since 1884, had become grossly inadequate. It was a swing-type bridge, thirty-six feet wide, with seven-foot-wide sidewalks, across which an estimated 50 percent of all north-south traffic in the city passed.[13] The intersection at the south end of the bridge was recognized as one of the most dangerous in the city. Upon crossing the bridge toward the south, either a sharp right turn to South Water Street or a sharp left turn to Michigan Avenue had to be made, a negotiation that often led to accidents.[14]

The *Tribune* recommended widening Michigan Avenue and building a new bridge over the river rather than building a subway tunnel beneath it. The cost of the improvement was estimated initially at approximately $2,000,000. It was suggested that the transformation of Michigan Avenue into a major north-south connecting link would drive out the unsightly wholesale businesses and bring in their place retail stores catering to the avenue traffic, thus enhancing the value of the property tremendously.[15] The Chicago Real Estate Board, which itself voted to support the project, urged that it proceed as quickly as possible while the price of the property was still relatively low.[16]

Shortly after the *Tribune* article, the Chicago City Council voted to take the lead in the movement to establish the new connecting link. At the request of Mayor Harrison, a joint committee of the City Council and the two park boards was formed to study the feasibility of the proposal. Included on this committee were Colonel Robert R. McCormick, a great nephew of Cyrus H. McCormick and future owner of the *Chicago Tribune*, along with members of the City Council and park boards, a number of realtors and businessmen, as well as two architects, Ernest R. Graham and Jarvis Hunt.[17] In January 1905, this joint committee approved plans for a connecting link for an estimated cost this time of $4,500,000. Of this sum, the committee sanctioned an expenditure for the purchase of land and buildings fronting on Michigan Avenue and Pine Street totaling $3,934,534. Details of the proposal were published in the *Tribune*, complete with a map (figure 1.3) and a list of all the structures to be demolished on the east side of Michigan Avenue from Randolph Street to the river, and on the west side of Pine Street from the river to Chicago Avenue (table 1.1).[18] The committee's plans for the project were presented to the City Council in February, and soon a motion was passed ordering the Board of Local Improvements to prepare and submit to the council an ordinance for condemning the property on Michigan Avenue and Pine Street for the widening of the avenue and the construction of a bridge.[19] This work was begun though the ordinance did not materialize during Harrison's term, and the project was abandoned, at least temporarily.

DANIEL BURNHAM AND THE 1909 PLAN OF CHICAGO

The proposal for the connecting link came to life again in 1906 when Daniel Burnham and Edward H. Bennett were commissioned to produce the Plan of Chicago, a project initiated and paid for by the Merchants Club, which later merged with the Commercial Club.[20] Early on in the preparation of the Plan, Burnham abandoned his initial idea of an underground tunnel, favoring instead an overhead bridge to be raised above the existing grade to clear cross traffic on the east-west streets and the railroad tracks north of the river (figure 1.4).[21] His new plan called for a ramp in front of the public library that would lead to an elevated

Figure 1.3
Plan of North Michigan Avenue widening project, 1905. Redrawn by author from Chicago Tribune *(6 January 1905).*

Table 1.1
**Buildings proposed to be demolished for widening
North Michigan Avenue** (*Chicago Tribune*, 6 January 1905)

Street no.	*Building*
	Buildings between Randolph Street and the river
151–53	J. and B. Moos, 5 stories
155–57	Arbuckle Brothers, 5 stories
161–63	Sprague, Warner and Company, 4 stories
165–67	Hamburger Company, 4 stories
175–77	Kimbark Block, 5 stories
185–87	E. L. Mansure Company, 5 stories
201–3	Thomson and Taylor Company, 7 stories
205–7	J. H. Bell and Company
215	W. F. McLaughlin and Company, 4 stories
217–19	Diamond Match Company, 4 stories
229	Nittich Hall and Company, 4 stories
301–13	Bowyer Block, 4 stories
317–21	R. J. Ederer, 4 stories
325–29	Curtiss-Williams Company, 4 stories
333–43	Vacant property and Goodrich Docks
	Buildings between the river and Ohio Avenue:
401–551	Dock and factory property; rows of two- and three-story brick flats and boarding houses
	Buildings between Ohio and Ontario streets:
128 Ohio	Large 3-story brick residence of Carrie Mears
127 Ont.	Two brick residences, one owned by the estate of B. F. Adams, the other by Mrs. John F. Newell
	Buildings between Ontario and Erie streets:
626–36	Vacant lot owned by Newberry estate
127 Erie	Prendergast flats, 4 stories
	Buildings between Erie and Huron streets:
662	Henry Sheldon House
668	Dr. S. J. Walker House
674	Mrs. William M. Scudder House
678	Leverett Thompson House
680	Charles Dyer House
	Buildings between Huron and Superior streets:
706	Perry H. Smith House owned by A. Cowles
712	Mrs. Elizabeth Bennett House
714	Sydney F. Andrews House
716	Willis S. McCrea House
	Buildings between Superior Street and Chicago Avenue:
126 Sup.	½ block north of Superior Street
702–6	Row of small brick buildings
748	Kinzie Apartment Building

street from Randolph to a plaza at the river. Here the axis of the avenue would shift east and lead across the river to a second plaza where the axis would again shift eastward to Pine Street.

In November of 1907, Burnham met with Mayor Fred A. Busse, who served from 1907 to 1911, to discuss what he called "The Grand Plan," the only one offering a permanent solution. Mayor Busse agreed to the plan at the meeting, and he ordered the Board of Local Improvements to resume work on it at once. He said "It is the only plan which offers the relief sought."[22] The current estimated cost of $5,000,000 would be raised by special tax assessment on the property fronting the avenue.[23]

Burnham's commission to produce the Chicago Plan was significant for the Michigan Avenue improvement because the proposal was now included within the context of a comprehensive city plan. The World's Columbian Exposition had demonstrated the benefits and results of large-scale planning in the best Beaux-Arts tradition, and it had become apparent that an overall plan of similar character was the best way to guide the city's future growth and development.[24]

The ideas proferred by Burnham and Bennett coincided directly with those sweeping the nation as part of the City Beautiful movement, the country's first attempt at self-conscious, nationwide urban planning. The Columbian Exposition had immensely strengthened, quickened, and encouraged aesthetic efforts in municipal life throughout the country. It had given tangible shape to a desire that was arising out of the larger wealth, increased travel, and the provision for the essentials of life.[25] Other expositions reinforced the trend: the Trans-Mississippi and International Exposition of Omaha in 1898, the Tennessee Centennial Exposition of the same year, the Pan American Exposition at Buffalo in 1902, and the Louisiana Purchase Exposition of 1904 in St. Louis.[26] Along with these was a seemingly mushrooming number of campaigns for comprehensive city planning projects calling for the regularity and monumentality of building design and the fusion of naturalistic park systems with Classicistic civic centers.[27] Among them were a competition for Copley Square in Boston; a public building group in Cleveland; the McMillan Plan for Washington, D.C.; and Philadelphia's Benjamin Franklin Parkway, to mention only a few.[28]

The importance of Michigan Avenue in the Chicago Plan was stated in chapter 6 of the report in relation to the

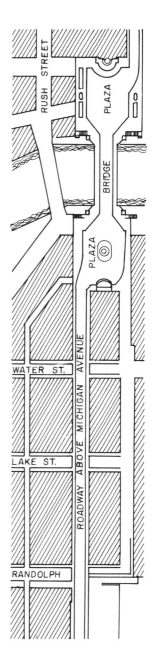

Figure 1.4
Proposal for Michigan Avenue improvement, 1907; Daniel Burnham, architect. Redrawn by author from Chicago Tribune *(5 March 1907).*

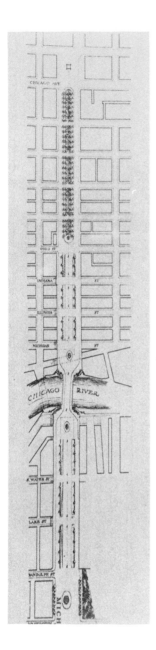

Figure 1.5
Plan of North Michigan Avenue, Plan of Chicago (1909); Daniel Burnham and Edward H. Bennett, architects. Reprinted from The Plan of Chicago (New York, 1970).

central business district of the city. It was asserted that within the next few years the boundaries of the Loop would be extended as far as Chicago Avenue on the north. Michigan Avenue was seen as becoming the major connecting link of the city's North and South sides as well as the most desirable avenue for office buildings, hotels, clubs, theaters, music halls, and shops. Burnham wrote, "So desirable has this thoroughfare become that extensions of it to the north or the south must enhance the value of the abutting real estate, because of the increased opportunities such extensions will create for continuing the building of structures of the highest class."[29] Burnham stated in the most direct terms possible the importance of Michigan Avenue and that its integrity as a major thoroughfare had to be maintained.

His plan for Michigan Avenue had by this time been transformed into a more refined version of his 1907 proposal, calling now for a continuous movement of traffic over the bridge, whose axis was angled slightly to the northeast similar to the proposal published by the *Tribune* in 1905 (figure 1.5). Burnham's vision for North Michigan Avenue is best depicted in a perspective rendering by New York artist Jules Guerin, a view northward from the public library to the Water Tower (figure 1.6). It can be compared to a photograph of the Champs Elysées in Paris (figure 1.7), one that was available to Burnham and Bennett while they prepared the Plan and later printed in a booklet publicizing the Plan.[30] As in the Paris scene, Guerin depicted buildings with uniform cornice heights, in this case seven stories, with mansard roofs lined with dormers. Each building filled out an entire block with light courts in the center, and there was little variation in stylistic details. On the east side of the avenue, north of Randolph Street, Guerin depicted a more distinctive, neoclassical style building, two blocks in length, intended to be a new terminal for the Illinois Central Railroad. He divided the avenue itself into three sections, a four-lane central thoroughfare flanked on either side by secondary lanes for stopping and turning. These lanes were divided by tree-lined islands with pylons at Randolph Street. Ramps to the lower level were indicated along the divider on the west side. This three-lane division corresponded to the organization of the Champs Elysées. Also like the Champs Elysées was Guerin's portrayal of the boulevard seemingly stretching to infinity.

The influence of Paris in Burnham's design for North Michigan Avenue can be ascribed to his travels to Europe in 1896 and 1901.[31] He was particularly interested in the

Haussmannization of the city, writing, "The task which Haussmann accomplished for Paris corresponds with the work which must be done for Chicago."[32] The grand boulevard and axial pattern of urban streets with squares and circles expressed a sense of rationalism and hierarchy. It also represented man's power and control which was similar to that found in industry, business, technology, and science.[33]

Within weeks of the completion of the Burnham Plan, while it was in the hands of various members of the Com-

Figure 1.6
Aerial view of North Michigan Avenue, looking toward Michigan Avenue Bridge from Randolph Street, with Chicago Public Library at left; Jules Guerin, renderer. Courtesy of the Chicago Historical Society.

Figure 1.7
Champs Elysées, Paris, c.
1905. Reprinted from
W. D. Moody, Wacker's
Manual for the Plan of Chi-
cago *(Chicago, 1912).*

mercial Club, opposition to the widening of Michigan Avenue that had been present from the beginning now
strengthened. The Chicago Board of Realtors, for instance,
at first wholeheartedly in support of the project, now came
out against it, objecting to the proposal for elevating the
street and to the means of assessment to pay for the project.[34] In June of 1908, the board appointed a committee to
closely watch the progress on Burnham's proposal for a
"boulevard on stilts." The board felt that the elevated
roadway would depreciate property values north of Randolph whereas a surface-level boulevard would enhance
values.[35]

One of the most persistent individuals to oppose the
boulevard link was George Packard, a prominent lawyer
who had been the assistant attorney for the Columbian Exposition.[36] Now serving as the president of the Michigan
Avenue Improvement Association, made up of Michigan
Avenue property owners, he published two small booklets
in 1908, *Argument on the Boulevard Link* and *The Boulevard Link,* in which he criticized the boulevard widening
plan as "decidedly obnoxious to public interests as well as
directly destructive of private rights."[37] He criticized the
Burnham Plan because of its "salient potency" which must
be "watched and guarded that it does not become an instru-

ment of tyranny and oppression in its disregard of private rights and individual property."[38]

What particularly incensed Packard was the concept of an elevated street. He wrote:

> The germ of the elevated street, I care not when and how it was conceived, had gotten into this committee, and reason and protest were in vain to eradicate it. Its virus extends through every single plan or miscalled compromise that has emanated from the Commercial Club committee. It is a supreme instance of the tyranny of a single subservient idea side-tracking and obscuring a great purpose.[39]

Packard argued instead for a surface-level boulevard and a single deck bridge, which he thought would better enhance the area and make it more conducive to the construction of important new buildings, and that it would better lead to the avenue becoming a major shopping district. Packard felt the Burnham proposal, on the other hand, would not lead to an enhancement of the area. He wrote further:

> For if this Burnham Plan goes through, it means merely a runway flanked only by circumambient air with a background on one side of decaying four-story rookeries, and on the other side the spectacle of freight yards and tracks. I should think that even the millionaire in his auto would hardly appreciate the benefit of that outlook.[40]

Packard also asserted that his plan for a single level boulevard would save from one-third to one-half of the Burnham proposal.

PUBLICIZING THE PLAN

In order to counter the opposition to the Burnham Plan in general and, more specifically, to the proposal for raising and widening Michigan Avenue and the construction of a new bridge, an extensive campaign was undertaken to gain political and public support. Leadership for this cause was taken up within the Commercial Club by Charles Wacker, a prominent Chicago businessman and real estate developer, whose first necessity was to assure the backing of the city administration in order to have a political base from which to work.[41] The Commercial Club passed a motion for

11

the creation of a City Plan Commission in April of 1909.
The recommendation was made to Mayor Busse, who readily agreed to the proposal.[42] He made his first appointments
to the Plan Commission in November 1909, including the
appointment of Charles Wacker as chairman.[43] The purpose of the commission was to serve as an advisory body,
to act as the intermediary between the city authorities and
the people and as a safeguard against unwise city development. This 328-member group included many of the most
active members of the Commercial Club as well as Chicago
aldermen and others representing a broad range of civic
interests.[44]

At first the commission's resources were limited. The
members of the Commercial Club were appealed to, and in
a few weeks nearly $100,000 was pledged. Already they had
contributed $85,000 for working quarters, technical ser-
vice, and publication of the Burnham Plan.[45] Wacker appointed as managing director Walter D. Moody, who had
been heading the Chicago Commercial Association. Moody
was a professional organizer, one of the new breed of executives who made careers out of managing civic organizations, and he assumed much of the daily responsibility for
running the commission.[46] Once funds were available, the
commission began to use all the means available to make
the Plan known: the press, the lecture platform, stereopti-
con slides, and printed reports and bulletins of the Plan
Commission itself. There was even a motion picture, *A Tale
of One City*. This educational program, financed for the
duration of the campaign in large part by the Commercial
Club, was the means by which the Plan Commission established good relations with the press and public alike.[47]

The Plan Commission's first step in its city-wide educational work was the publication in 1911 of a ninety-three
page booklet, *Chicago's Greatest Issue: An Official Plan*,
an abridged version of the original Chicago Plan book.[48] It
argued that by properly solving Chicago's problems of
transportation, street congestion, recreation, and public
health, the city could grow indefinitely in wealth and commerce. As a direct repudiation of those opposing the North
Michigan Avenue improvement, it defended the city's plan
to raise the avenue and construct a double deck bridge,
stating:

> There is to be a gradual grade the entire width of
> the street from building line to building line, start-
> ing from Randolph Street, reaching a maximum

height of 16 feet at the river crossing, then a grad-
ual descent to Ohio Street. This grade will be no
more perceptible than is Jackson Boulevard at the
river. The grades suggested are less than those existing on Fifth Avenue in New York. Imagine
standing at the intersection of Randolph Street
and Michigan Avenue and being able to follow
with the eye the straightened course of that magnificent widened thoroughfare direct to Lincoln
Park, where it would end in the lake at the intersection of Bellevue Place.[49]

The book went on to claim that the completion of the north-
south boulevard system with this connecting link would give
Chicago the most significant thoroughfare in the world.[50]

A publication that dealt exclusively with Michigan Avenue was Charles Wacker's *Argument in Favor of Michigan
Avenue Boulevard Link*, released in 1913, containing copies of the complete set of working drawings and specifications for the construction of the bridge. As a forward it
included the transcript of a presentation Wacker made to
the Board of Local Improvements urging the adoption of
the plan for building the new bridge. Wacker cited the
heavy traffic on the existing bridge, the need for a raised
street to separate the east and west traffic from that of
Michigan Avenue, and the fact that Michigan Avenue was
destined to carry the greatest amount of traffic of any street
in the city. He indicated further that the planned improvement was not just for the benefit of automobile owners or
to facilitate the passage of pleasure vehicles but to help all
commercial and industrial interests in the city.[51] He went
on to argue against the various other proposals that had
been suggested. He wrote of the recommendation for a
tunnel:

> Where is there a sanitary board on earth that
> would permit the construction of a tunnel six feet
> underground and nearly a mile long, to be used by
> countless numbers of pedestrians and in summer
> by open vehicles of all sorts?[52]

In response to those proposing a surface level boulevard he
wrote:

> Imagine Michigan Avenue widened on the surface,
> connecting with Pine Street by a single level
> bridge, with 10,000 vehicles a day crossing it at
> eight intersections—coal wagons, trucks, produce

carts and all manner of slow-moving, unsightly heavy truck vehicles. Add to that the North Western tracks north of the river crossing at grade, and what sort of a street would you have?[53]

Wacker attempted to further disarm critics of the elevated grade by saying:

> There is no longer any talk about the plan creating a "street on stilts." Such talk was never made except to divert attention from the real issue. The street when completed will carry the upper level from building line to building line, and the grades at the north and south approaches to the upper level will be almost imperceptible to anyone passing the street. All shops, stores, and buildings of whatsoever nature will have their entrances, shop windows, etc., on the upper, or boulevard level. The lower level will be used for shipping and receiving purposes.[54]

Several other books and pamphlets were published, at the rate of one or two a year, to win support for the various projects of the Chicago Plan. Probably the best known was Moody's *Wacker's Manual for the Plan of Chicago* (1912), which was published by the Board of Education and used as a textbook to train the city's youth to become responsible in matters of city planning. Other examples include *Fifty Million Dollars for Nothing* (1912) which demonstrated how the people of Chicago could obtain 1300 acres of lakefront parks; and *Chicago's World-Wide Influence* (1914), which served to keep the effort alive by demonstrating how the Plan was regarded by the rest of the world.

Another convincing factor that helped support the Plan Commission's efforts was the transforming effect of the automobile. Chicago's already severe traffic problem was getting steadily worse, a problem augmented by the thousands of new automobiles being sold in the city each year. The number of automobiles in Chicago would rise from 12,926 in 1910 to 89,973 in 1920. From 1920 to 1930 the number would rise 400 percent to 409,878. A twofold increase in the number of motor-driven trucks would be seen in the same time period, while the number of horse-drawn vehicles would be conversely reduced by one-half, from 20,391 to 9,351 in 1930.[55]

The automobile would become both a convenience and a status symbol, though at the same time it would pose new dangers in the urban realm. Businessmen, lawyers, doctors, not to mention the middle class, would buy them and would compete with one another in their luxury and number. Cars would begin to displace public transportation to get to and from work, for shopping, or to visit friends.[56] The ability to continue to move freely into and out of the Loop and to reach the ever expanding regions of the city was of critical importance. The idea of a broad, straight Michigan Avenue traversing the Near North Side was increasingly recognized as the way to ease traffic conditions off the adjacent, narrower north-south streets.

THE WIDENING OF NORTH MICHIGAN AVENUE

The City Council passed an ordinance for the widening of North Michigan Avenue and Pine Street and for the construction of a new bridge in 1913, two years after the beginning of Wacker's promotional campaign.[57] The bill was promptly signed by Mayor Harrison, and a commission was appointed by the court to determine the value of the land and buildings to be acquired and to apportion the exact amount of benefit to each piece of property in the zone of assessment. A Michigan Avenue bond issue was then approved in the next general election by one of the largest majorities ever given a public improvement project in Chicago.[58]

Once the proposal and its bond issue were passed, the next hurdle the city faced was the acquisition of property to allow for the widening of the street. It needed a strip of land and buildings on the east side of Michigan Avenue between Randolph and the river (figure 1.8), and from the west side of Pine Street between the river and Chicago Avenue. This strip was nearly a mile in length and between sixty-four and seventy-five feet in width. It would necessitate the acquisition of fifty-one parcels and would require the complete demolition of thirty-four buildings and the partial demolition of thirty-three others.[59]

A series of lawsuits was initiated beginning in February 1916, the city using its power of condemnation to obtain the property from those owners who proved uncooperative.[60] Lawyers for the property owners sought to obtain good deals for their clients, while lawyers for the city attempted to acquire the property at the lowest possible cost. One of the most celebrated cases was that of James S. Kirk, owner of the James S. Kirk and Company soap factory. He went to court arguing that he should receive from the city

Figure 1.8
View of North Michigan
Avenue during the widen-
ing project. Dashed line indicates line of original west
curb of Pine Street. Re-
printed from Chicago
Board of Local Improve-
ments (Chicago, 1931).
With permission of the Chicago Architectural Photo-
graphing Co.

$2,000,000, four times higher than the city valuation. At the end of a three-month trial, he was finally awarded only $470,000, nearly a quarter of it going to pay legal fees.[61] Walter Moody wrote later:

> We have come to learn that the good of the few must give way to the good of the many, just as we learned in the Great War that individual interests must give way to national interests. They favor the property owners rather than the city as an induce- ment to the property owner to assist in the making of public improvements. It was never intended that these advantages and benefits to the private individual should encourage him to hold up the city, or that, failing in this he would refuse to part with his property and fight the city to the highest courts for the exaggerated value he set upon it.[62]

By 1918 the city had acquired all of the property nec- essary, and work was begun in April of that year when the current mayor, William H. Thompson, presided over a ceremony to tear down the wall of a building at 311 North Michigan, the first to be demolished. Over 5000 people attended as Thompson, along with Michael J. Faherty, president of the Board of Local Improvements, and Charles Wacker took part in the ceremonies. This was followed by an automobile parade down the avenue and a banquet complete with speeches in praise of the project by the mayor, Faherty, Wacker, and others.[63] Daniel Burnham, the man most responsible for the project's initiation, had died in 1912, not living to see even the passage of the ordinance making the project possible.

The mayor, who served from 1915 to 1923 and again from 1927 to 1931, used the occasion of the banquet to denounce his political opponents.[64] He wanted to make it clear that it was his administration that deserved the credit for beginning the much needed project. He thanked those at the banquet for participating in the parade, referring particularly to the display of posters on the sides of their automobiles reading, "Michigan Boulevard link under way after years of waiting," "Mayor Thompson put it over," and "Mayor Thompson started Michigan Avenue boulevard link today." Charles Wacker also gave an address at the banquet, stating that the initial construction work on the Michigan Avenue extension marked the beginning of "the most important era in the entire history of Chicago, because it is the fundamental improvement of the Chicago Plan."[65] Compared to other north-south streets like Wabash, State, Dearborn, Clark, and LaSalle, described by him as being congested with streetcars and heavy traffic, Michigan Avenue with its connecting arteries

> is alone the great, unencumbered natural highway. Its continuous length of forty-five miles is choked and menaced by the narrow gap between Randolph Street and Chicago Avenue, which will now be eliminated. No street improvement is comparable to it, and none ever undertaken will produce anything like a commensurate amount of benefit.[66]

The bridge and new avenue took two years to complete, opening to traffic in May of 1920.[67] The final cost of the improvement was estimated to be $14,900,000, an amount more than seven times higher than the initial *Chicago Tribune* estimate in 1904. Funding for the project was provided by three public bond issues and two special tax assessments. The largest, amounting to $5,400,000, was required for the purchase of land and buildings. The upper-level structure of the avenue cost $5,300,000, the bridge $2,400,000, and paving and lighting $1,800,000.[68]

The final design of the bridge had been determined in 1911–12 by the city's chief engineer, Thomas G. Pihlfeldt, who was assisted by Edward H. Bennett, then working as the architect for the Chicago Plan Commission.[69] As proposed in the Chicago Plan, the bridge (figure 1.9), 340 feet long and ninety-two feet wide, is a double-decked trunnion bascule bridge that rises in the center, pivoting about a fixed axis at each end by the force of a counterweight and electric motors. It has the advantage over the swing-type bridge in that it does not require a center pier, thus affording an unobstructed channel. The Michigan Avenue Bridge was the first in Chicago to have two levels for car and truck traffic, and it was also the first to have a split span, that is, it has two parallel leaves so that the east or west half can be raised for repairs while the other half continues to function.[70]

The design for the Michigan Avenue Bridge was unique for its overriding aesthetic appeal. Pihlfeldt and Bennett looked to French precedents, designing four monumental house towers clad with Bedford stone and topped by Mansard roofs. Flanking the bridge abutments are grand staircases leading down to the river. A rendering of the bridge from the period (figure 1.10) announced that its construction "marks the first step in making this gateway as famous as the Place de la Concorde in Paris."[71]

The successful completion of the avenue and bridge project accomplished many functional goals for the city. It made the Near North Side much more accessible from the Loop and allowed the traditional central business district to more readily expand beyond the river. It led to the change of the old North Michigan Avenue district from a section of dilapidated warehouse buildings to one of new office buildings and stores, and the conversion of Pine Street into a wide avenue of new office buildings, apartments, hotels, and exclusive shops.[72]

The avenue was enhanced further in 1926 with the opening of Wacker Drive, extending westward from Michigan Avenue along the south side of the river. This area, originally South Water Street, had been the traditional center of the city's produce market for fruit, garden, and poultry business. As on the old Michigan Avenue, trade was carried out to a large extent in the street itself, causing se-

NEW GATEWAY OF THE GREATER CHICAGO

Figure 1.9
North Michigan Avenue
Bridge, 1918–20; Thomas
G. Pihlfeldt, engineer; Ed-
ward H. Bennett, archi-
tect. Courtesy of the Art
Institute of Chicago.

Figure 1.10
Michigan Avenue Bridge
Plaza, view toward the
south, 1921. Reprinted
from American Architect
(11 May 1921), copyright
(1921) by McGraw-Hill,
Inc. All rights reserved.
Reproduced with the per-
mission of the publisher.

Figure 1.11
Wacker Drive improve-
ment, 1925; Edward H.
Bennett and Edward S.
Campbell with the Board
of Local Improvements.
Reprinted from Chicago
Board of Local Improve-
ments *(Chicago, 1931),*
with permission of the Chi-
cago Architectural Photo-
graphing Co.

rious obstruction to traffic and making the sidewalks practically impassable. Dilapidated buildings lined the street
with canopies hung out over the sidewalks under which
trucks were parked and where the trading took place.
Charles Wacker had justly charged, "South Water Street
today is an economic waste; a burdensome charge on all the
people; a drawback to Chicago progress; an obstruction to
its prosperity; and a conflagration danger to the whole
Loop district."[73]

Work on the project was begun in January of 1925,
with all of the buildings being demolished and a two-level
reinforced concrete road structure built (figure 1.11), its
river elevation penetrated by a series of openings to the
lower level. Its massive piers are clad in rusticated ma-
sonry, and a balustrade tops the narrow horizontal bands
that mark the edges of the upper deck.[74] The upper level
connects with the Michigan Avenue Bridge Plaza and is 110
feet wide while the lower level, which passes under Michigan Avenue, is 135 feet wide.[75] The project succeeded in
changing the unsightly frontage on the south side of the

river into one of the city's finest avenues and opened up building sites for new office structures.[76]

The North Michigan Avenue and Wacker Drive improvements would not have been possible if the city had limited its efforts only to these areas. They were, in fact, part of a comprehensive municipal improvement program aimed at augmenting virtually every area of the city to some degree. The goal was to expand the crowded confines of the Loop not only to the north but to the west and south as well. Similar, though less dramatic, improvements were made to Roosevelt Road, LaSalle Street, Ogden Avenue, and Damen Avenue. In all, more than 100 miles of streets were opened and widened, more than 2000 miles of streets and alleys paved, 913 miles of sewers added, and the city's first subway was planned between 1915 and 1930.[77] These projects created employment on a scale hardly seen before in Chicago. They entailed training new building crews, masons, carpenters, decorators, and bridge builders. They meant the importation of building materials and the establishment of new docks and warehouses. The increased economic activity generated by these vast programs of improvements proved to be an integral part of one of Chicago's greatest periods of urban development.

THE NORTH CENTRAL BUSINESS DISTRICT ASSOCIATION PLAN

Throughout the period of the planning and construction of Michigan Avenue and its related improvements there arose the question of just how the property along the new avenue would be developed. Jules Guerin's aerial perspective of Michigan Avenue for the Chicago Plan had shown a uniform line of eight-story buildings fronting on the street. The realization of the concept was a difficult matter, however, since many different property owners were involved. There were a number of questions raised about the character the avenue should assume and about the desirability of creating a symbolic gateway on the north side of the bridge.

A group that dealt with these issues was the North Central Business District Association, founded in 1913 originally to promote the construction of the bridge and the widening of the avenue. The group's list of directors included Ogden McClurg, president of the A. C. McClurg Publishing Company; Arthur L. Farwell, who owned considerable frontage on Michigan Avenue; William N. Pelouse, of the Pelouse Manufacturing Company; and Potter Palmer, Jr.,

21

representing the Palmer estate.[78] This group of business-men and property owners took it upon themselves to study and make proposals for the development of the property along the avenue from just south of the river to Chicago Avenue. Early in 1918, acting with the approval of the Chicago Plan Commission, the association invited a number of architects to make recommendations for the architectural treatment best suited for establishing the character of the avenue. A committee of architects was formed for the project, including Edward H. Bennett; Coolidge and Hodgdon; Graham, Anderson, Probst and White; Holabird and Roche; Jarvis Hunt; Marshall and Fox; George W. Maher; Mundie and Jensen; Perkins, Fellows and Hamilton; Andrew Rebori; Schmidt, Garden and Martin; and Howard Van Doren Shaw.[79]

This project was an attempt to influence the architectural character of the avenue, setting standards of architectural treatment that would go hand in hand with restrictions on the kind of businesses for which the buildings could be used. The owners of the valuable property along the street hoped to permanently maintain its position as a high-quality commercial street, preserving it from the deterioration and demoralization that often overtakes some downtown sections in rapidly growing American cities. The results of the architects' committee were submitted to the North Central Association in November 1918, with four principal recommendations: (1) restricting the height of the buildings to ten stories, (2) the use of a uniform continuous balcony line between the third and second floors (figure 1.12), (3) the vacating of alleys crossing Michigan Avenue, (4) and the vacating of North Water Street.[80] These recommendations generally followed Burnham and Bennett's plan for uniformity, continuous elevations, and spatial definition of the avenue. The goal was to direct the development of North Michigan Avenue toward a uniformly designed commercial corridor based on European precedents, in this case by the prescription of street-oriented urbanism.

The most notable difference between this plan and that of Burnham and Bennett was the proposal to treat the plaza area just north of the bridge as a gateway to the avenue with taller buildings and possibly a triumphal arch spanning the avenue. The committee pointed out that the buildings proposed in the Burnham Plan for the north bank of the river were too limited and irregular to achieve the potential posed by the location.[81]

Typical of the designs proposed is one by Andrew Rebori recommending the construction of two slender, round towers with buttresses and a cupola at the top, generally in the Gothic Revival style (figure 1.13). Two smaller but similarly articulated towers attached to lower rectangular and trapezoidal-shaped buildings were proposed for the plaza south of the river. Another Rebori proposal called for two towers north of the river attached to massive ten-story block-like buildings with continuous arcades on their river and street sides (figure 1.14). A third proposal called for two slender square eighteen-story towers connected across the width of the street by a monumental three-bay arched gateway surmounted by a large victory statue in a horse-drawn chariot, with the inscription "Liberty World's Peace" in the entablature (figure 1.15). Representing the utmost in civic virtue and pride, this design suggested a Roman triumphal arch motif, based on examples such as the Arch of Constantine in Rome and the Arc de Triomphe in Paris.

In conjunction with the design proposals, the committee made recommendations for land use that generally reflected the ideals of the North Central Business District Association members. It was recommended, in general, that

Figure 1.12
Proposal for North Michigan Avenue, view south from Water Tower, 1918; Architects' Committee for the North Central Business District Association. Reprinted from American Architect *(11 December 1918), copyright (1918) by McGraw-Hill, Inc. All rights reserved. Reproduced with the permission of the publisher.*

*Figure 1.13
Proposal for North Michigan Avenue, 1918; Andrew Rebori, architect. Reprinted from* American Architect *(11 December 1918), copyright (1918) by McGraw-Hill, Inc. All rights reserved. Reproduced with the permission of the publisher.*

office buildings, banks, hotels, and high-grade shops were the preferred use over automobile showrooms, saloons, warehouses, and industrial buildings like those that predominated on South Michigan Avenue beyond Twelfth Street.[82] By May 1918, an agreement defining the restrictions for the use of avenue frontage from the river to Chicago Avenue was drawn up and a committee set to work obtaining signatures from property owners. A total of about 3800 feet of frontage was involved, covering all the property on both sides of the avenue to a depth of seventy-five feet. The agreement was to remain in force for twenty years.[83]

It was reported in *The Economist* in December of 1919 that the efforts of the North Central Business District Association to secure the agreement from the owners was successful and that developers could now convert North Michigan Avenue into an "Upper Fifth Avenue." The committee succeeded so well that practically every foot of ground along the avenue was bound by the agreement, thus encouraging all high classes of business to locate there without fear of having some undesirable business next door.[84] This voluntary agreement thus helped to limit the occupancy and uses of buildings to those businesses that would enhance rather than jeopardize the avenue's character.

While the North Central Business District Association would be successful in controlling the occupancy of buildings on North Michigan Avenue, it would not be so fortunate concerning the buildings' size and height. The vision shared by the association and by Daniel Burnham of uniform cornice heights held to a comfortable ten stories, except of course for those by the river, would be undermined by the coincident movement underway in the City Council to draft an ordinance for a city-wide zoning law. Chicago had had a building code ordinance in effect since 1898, at first limiting heights to 130 feet.[85] In succeeding years, this

Figure 1.14
Proposal for North Michigan Avenue, 1918; Architects' Committee for North Central Business District Association. Reprinted from American Architect *(11 December 1918), copyright (1918) by McGraw-Hill, Inc. All rights reserved. Reproduced with the permission of the publisher.*

amount was variously set at 200–260 feet, depending upon the rate of construction and the relative success of special interest groups in having ordinance amendments passed. By 1919, the limit stood at 260 feet with the additional provision that a tower could rise 400 feet so long as it occupied only 25 percent of the lot area.[86]

In 1923, Chicago passed its first comprehensive zoning ordinance, establishing five districts for the city based on use. Each of these districts was limited to specific uses such as residential, commercial, or manufacturing, and each had a distinct volume and height restriction. In direct contradiction to the recommendations of Daniel Burnham and the North Central Business District Association, North Michigan Avenue came under the jurisdiction of the fifth-volume district, the one allowing the greatest height. Instead of buildings being limited to 100 feet, they could rise to a maximum of 264 feet under the new ordinance (figure 1.16). The biggest change from the old building code brought about by the zoning ordinance was the elimination of the 400-foot height limit for towers. Now, any tower covering no more than 25 percent of the lot area could rise to virtually any height, the only provision being that its total volume would not exceed one-sixth of the main building block.[87] This meant that the larger the lot area, the higher the tower could rise.

The failure of the city to impose stricter limits on North Michigan Avenue represented a tragic clash of economic, political, and architectural interests. This dealt a major blow to the planning efforts of the previous two decades and would result in exactly the opposite effect for the avenue than that envisioned by its planners. Rather than an avenue of continuous-height buildings, it would develop with an incongruous mixture of low-rise and high-rise structures symptomatic of a dilemma over the need for economic return on investment and the maintenance of civic conscience. North Michigan Avenue property owners would become caught up in a struggle between rationalizing their desire to comply with the recommendations of the North Central Business District Association and their rightful ability to meet the maximum limits of the zoning ordinance. Some would choose one or the other extreme, others would compromise. As this dilemma played itself out during the 1920s, North Michigan Avenue's transformation would see the construction of some of Chicago's most significant individual works of architecture, yet at the same time this would result in a highly inconsistent pattern of urban design.

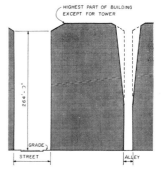

Figure 1.16
Illustration of Zoning Law.
Redrawn by author from
the Chicago Zoning Ordi-
nance.

COMMERCIAL
ARCHITECTURE
OF THE
EARLY 1920s

onstruction of new buildings on North Michigan Avenue began even before the widening project was complete. The John Crerar Library, located at the northwest corner of Michigan Avenue and Randolph Street was the first. It was followed by the Wrigley Building, north of the river, then several smaller commercial structures, and finally the London Guarantee and Accident Company Building. The first of these was built while the problems of postwar social and economic adjustments were still being felt. Uncertainty about the future and a lack of mortgage funding had caused a sharp decline in the real estate market in 1918 and 1919.[1] For a time, the government had clamped down on new construction, practically forbidding any building operations not directly related to defense work.[2]

By 1920, construction activity was resuming in the city, and bank credit for real estate purposes began expanding at a substantial rate. Real estate experts were talking about the dawn of the greatest building boom in America's history. The *Chicago Tribune* reported in August of 1922 that the first seven months of the year were the biggest in Chicago's building history, surpassing any previous year's record.[3] By the end of 1922, Chicago spent more than $227,000,000 on new construction, nearly twice the previous record of $113,000,000 set in 1916.[4]

JOHN CRERAR LIBRARY

The John Crerar Library was prominently located at Randolph Street, the southern-most entrance to the newly widened North Michigan Avenue (figure 2.1). Demolition of the former Sprague, Warner and Company Building located on the site was begun in 1919, and the new building was opened in 1920, a sixteen-story limestone-clad structure. It was designed to house both a library and commercial space, each having to be expressed architecturally on the facade but within a unified design (figure 2.2).

The building was made possible by John Crerar, who had grown wealthy in the railroad supply business during the 1870s and 1880s.[5] He had given his library collection, mostly technical in nature, to the city along with an endowment of over $2,500,000 after his death in 1889.[6] The library's board of directors established a building fund and be-

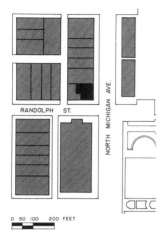

RANDOLPH ST.

NORTH MICHIGAN AVE.

0 50 100 200 FEET

Figure 2.1
John Crerar Library, northwest corner of Michigan Avenue and Randolph Street site plan, 1919–20; Holabird and Roche, architects. Drawn by author.

Figure 2.2
John Crerar Library, view from Grant Park. Courtesy of the Chicago Historical Society.

gan searching for a site, initially hoping to build in Grant Park.[7] In 1902, the Chicago City Council passed an ordinance entitling the library to build there, but it was forced to abandon the idea in the face of a number of lawsuits concerning the propriety of building in the park. The site at the northwest corner of Michigan and Randolph was settled upon in 1912, before Michigan Avenue was widened, and the firm of Holabird and Roche was commissioned to design the building the following year.[8] The intervention of World War I postponed the beginning of construction until 1919, by which time the widening of the avenue was well under way.

This was the first of many large commissions William Holabird and Martin Roche would receive for buildings on North Michigan Avenue. It established their reputation on the avenue for architecture suited to the particular needs of the client both functionally and symbolically. They had attained early success in Chicago with their designs for the Old Colony (1893) and the Marquette buildings (1894), and shortly before being commissioned to design the Crerar Library they were engaged in the design of the University Club (1910) and the Monroe Building (1912), both on South Michigan Avenue at Monroe Street.[9]

Their solution for the Crerar Library was essentially to place the library reading rooms and stacks on top of a standard office tower. The two uses were differentiated on the exterior primarily by a change in the size and treatment of the window openings. The lower floors were designed with paired rectangular windows contained within recessed bays, while the library's reading room floors were marked by grand arched windows above groups of tall triple-pane windows. The eastern half of the library portion facing Michigan Avenue was divided into two floors, each containing reading rooms with high ceilings. The western portion was divided into four floors, containing the library offices and cataloging areas.[10]

In plan the building was nearly square, covering an area of eighty-five feet by seventy-eight feet; with a projecting elevator and service core at the northwest corner (figure 2.3).[11] The south and east facades, facing the streets, were each divided into four bays, the piers and spandrels clad with Bedford limestone. The remaining two facades were clad partially in limestone and partially in brick, anticipating the construction of adjacent buildings of equal height that would mask their utilitarian appearance. The first three levels contained rental commercial and office

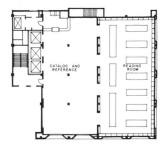

FOURTEENTH FLOOR PLAN

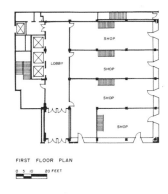

FIRST FLOOR PLAN

0 5 10   20 FEET

Figure 2.3
John Crerar Library plans. Redrawn by author from American Architect (25 August, 1920), and from plans in Holabird and Roche Architectural Drawing Collection, Chicago Historical Society.

space, floors four through ten contained stacks for the storage of books, and the eleventh through the fourteenth floors contained the library's reading rooms and offices. The building was, in the truest sense of the word, a vertical library, with each floor having a specific function or purpose.

The 200-foot-high building was constructed in eighteen months for a total cost of $1,350,000.[12] It was designed to house 650,000 volumes and seats for 400 readers. Because it was a reference library, used primarily by professional and business people, its location in the business district was particularly appropriate. At the same time, it became an effective transition between the Loop and the newly widened North Michigan Avenue. Standing at the corner of Grant Park, its two principal facades were best seen in dramatic perspective from the southeast, where it showed itself as a corner anchor for the line of buildings to the north and the west. Though it was taller than the buildings recommended by Burnham and the architects of the North Central Business District Association, it fit well in its site. It had a reasonable presence within the setting of Grant Park, and it was a good complement to the long and low Chicago Public Library located on the south side of Randolph Street.

WRIGLEY BUILDING

While the Crerar Library was under construction, the Wrigley Building (figures 2.4 and 2.5), the second of North Michigan Avenue's important skyscrapers, was begun on the west side of the avenue just north of the Chicago River. William Wrigley, Jr., commissioned Graham, Anderson, Probst and White to design this exuberant adaptation of the Spanish Renaissance in 1919, and he did so with a number of specific purposes in mind. First, it would have to be an eye-arresting building capable of drawing shoppers and businessmen over the new bridge; second, it would have to be a dramatic visual terminus for Michigan Avenue when viewed from the south; and third, it was to be an appropriate corporate advertisement for the Wrigley chewing gum empire.[13] The building's magnificent decorative design, combined with its prominent location at the northwest corner of the bridge plaza, made it an immediate success both as a symbol for the Wrigley Company and for initiat-

Figure 2.4
Wrigley Building, 400
North Michigan Avenue,
1919–22; Graham, Ander-
son, Probst and White, ar-
chitects. Reprinted from
Paul T. Gilbert and
Charles L. Bryson, Chicago
and Its Makers *(Chicago,*
1929).

ing the commercial development of North Michigan Avenue beyond the river.

Wrigley, like his building, was an exemplary Chicago success story. Moving to the city from Philadelphia in 1891, his first job was selling soap for his father's business, Wrigley's Scouring Soap Company.[14] He soon branched out into other areas, and within a year he began distributing chewing gum produced by the Chicago-based Zeno Manufacturing Company.[15] The key to his early prosperity was his development of the premium system, in which he offered gifts or other products as incentives for buying in large quantities. This was coupled with his massive advertising campaigns by which he succeeded to convert the Wrigley chewing gum business, with products like Juicy Fruit and Spearmint gum, into a national institution. By the end of World War I sales of the company reached over $27 million a year.[16]

In need of a permanent corporate headquarters, Wrigley entrusted realtor Bertram M. Winston with finding either a suitable building or a site on which he could build.[17] They made numerous inspections of potential sites early in 1918 and were strongly tempted by a building at the northeast corner of Michigan Avenue and Randolph Street, across from the Crerar Library and facing Grant Park to the south. The advertising possibilities of this prominently located site were tremendous, but the price for the land was too high. Wrigley then considered purchasing two buildings a block further north, at the corner of Lake Street. He acquired a one-third interest in one of these buildings as a speculation in connection with the widening of North Michigan Avenue but decided against it as the location for his new building.[18]

A few months later, Winston and Wrigley inspected the site on the north side of the river between the old Rush Street Bridge and the Michigan Avenue Bridge then under construction. From the roof of a dock warehouse on the site Wrigley could see that the property was on axis with Michigan Avenue to the south and that it would be a very prominent location for a new headquarters building.[19] He may also have thought of the wishes of his friend Mayor William Thompson, who anxiously wanted business to come up to this part of town in order to vindicate his strong support of the Michigan Avenue improvement project.[20] In deciding to buy this site, Wrigley was the first major businessman to relocate his company's headquarters on the north side of the river. While there was a certain degree of risk involved

Figure 2.5
Wrigley Building site plan.
Drawn by author.

in the undertaking, Wrigley suspected that a well-designed
building would dominate the neighborhood and act as a
magnet in drawing similar businesses to the area.[21]

Bertram Winston entered into negotiations in 1918 with
two trustees of the estate that owned the property. It was
an irregularly shaped site bounded by the north bank of
the river, Rush Street, North Water Street, and the elevated Michigan Avenue. All but Rush Street fronted the site
at a slight diagonal, thus accounting for its unusual shape.
The area of the property was a little over 11,000 square
feet.[22] Because of complexities in the site's ownership, negotiations dragged on for months until an agreement in
principle was reached, and the architect began to work on
the drawings. The final transaction was not completed until
February of 1920, long after construction had begun.[23]

In selecting the firm of Graham, Anderson, Probst and
White to design the building, Wrigley went to one of the
direct inheritors of the office of Daniel Burnham. Ernest
R. Graham had been a partner in Burnham's firm and a
founder of the office that took over his practice. The name
Graham, Burnham and Company was changed to Graham,
Anderson, Probst and White in 1917.[24] The most gifted architect in the firm was Pierce Anderson, a graduate of the
Ecole des Beaux-Arts, who had been instrumental in producing Burnham's city plans for Baguio and Manila in the
Philippines. Anderson served as chief designer of Graham,
Anderson, Probst and White, heading a drafting staff that
sometimes numbered as many as 200 men. Buildings to his
credit would include the Federal Reserve Bank Building
(1920), Union Station (1925), and the Straus Building
(1923), all indicative of his deft handling of historical stylistic traditions, the result of his Beaux-Arts training.[25]

Anderson's chief designer for the Wrigley Building was
Charles Beersman, who had also been trained in the
Beaux-Arts tradition, in this case at the University of Penn-
sylvania, then under the direction of the French-trained
Paul Cret. Afterward, Beersman had won the LeBrun fel-
lowship for a year of travel in Europe. He joined Graham,
Anderson, Probst and White in 1919, a few months before
the firm started to work on the Wrigley Building.[26]

They designed a sixteen-story building with an eleven-
story tower rising from the middle of the main facade. Two
levels are located below Michigan Avenue. Its wall surfaces
are clad with molded white terra cotta, ascending from
dark to light in five graded shades from the lower stories to
the top.[27] The ground levels, from the street to the river

Figure 2.6
Wrigley Building, detail of
lower stories. Reprinted
from Architectural Forum
(October 1921).

level, are clad with rusticated Indiana limestone (figure 2.6). The building's vertical articulation is organized in a traditional fashion on a base, shaft, capital motif. The commercial levels contain large rectangular openings with a vaulted entrance at the base of the tower, framed by twisted engaged colonettes (figure 2.7). Continuous piers and mullions rise from this point to a pair of cornices masking the fourteenth floor, special emphasis being given to this level because it housed Wrigley's own office. Two additional floors are located above and are topped by an elaborate cornice with a parapet and finials. Each window bay is capped by a seashell embedded in the entablature, and the piers are adorned at the top with eagles in flight and vine-covered vases.[28]

Figure 2.7
Wrigley Building, detail of
entrance. Reprinted from
Architectural Forum *(Octo-*
ber 1921).

The eleven-story tower (figure 2.8) rising above the entrance bay has three windows bracketed by thickened corner piers. These widened piers run uninterrupted through the full height of the building, making a secure frame for the tower and serving to divide the facade vertically into three parts. Transition to the tower is made by setbacks at the eighteenth floor. A clock face, twenty feet in diameter, is supported on the tower's four sides.[29] Two additional stories rise above, with heavily decorated walls, a cornice, and a dormer window. The composition is topped by a circular Corinthian temple, which is itself topped by a small cylindrical structure with pylons and a crocketed pinnacle. The whole composition is particularly impressive at night when fully illuminated by an extensive system of lights placed

Figure 2.8
*Wrigley Building, view of
Tower. Photo by author.*

along the opposite bank of the river. Power projectors
flood the structure with a brilliance accentuated by the
dazzling whiteness of the building itself.[30]

The plan of the Wrigley Building is irregular in configuration, made to fit the site's nearly trapezoidal outline.
The building's main facade on the bridge plaza is placed at
an angle to Michigan Avenue, with the tower facing diago-

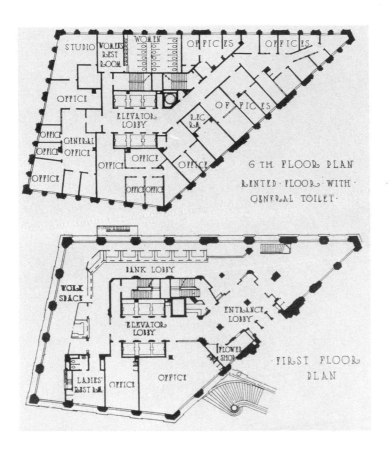

*Figure 2.9
Wrigley Building, plans.
Reprinted from* Architectural Forum *(October 1921).*

nally across the bridge and visible down the avenue from the south. This facade measures 135 feet in width, as does the north wall along Water Street. That on the river is seventy-five feet wide, that on Rush Street is eighty-eight feet.[31] The main entrance originally opened into a rectangular lobby (figure 2.9), one corner of which gave access to an elevator corridor with six passenger elevators, three on each side.[32] Offices and shops are located in spaces facing the river, while a banking lobby originally occupied the space on the north and west. Office layouts on the upper floors are fitted into the building's irregular outline like a jigsaw puzzle, with many resultant odd-shaped rooms and circuitous corridors.

The building's structure is a steel frame encased in concrete, with caissons going to bedrock. The main block of the building is 210 feet high, well within the city's building code allowance at the time of 260 feet, and the tower rose to 398 feet, two feet short of the allowable 400 feet for towers still in force in 1919.[33] In this case, such height for a

Figure 2.10
Giralda Tower, Seville,
Spain, 1159. Reprinted
from A. F. Calvert, Moor-
ish Remains in Spain.
(London and New York,
1906).

tower was also in keeping with the recommendations of the
North Central Business District Association, which called
for gateway towers at the river.

Beersman used as a basis for his design the Giralda
Tower of Seville Cathedral in Spain (figure 2.10).[34] One
Wrigley Company official said, "I think the architect had
seen the Giralda Tower in Spain and told Mr. Wrigley it
was his idea of a beautiful building."[35] It was unabashedly
derivative, and Beersman made no attempt to conceal the
source of his design. Though the Wrigley Building lacked
the Giralda Tower's lancet arches and overlapping grill-
work, it shared its ostentatious display of ornament on the
upper levels, the use of finials and urns, and the circular

temple at the top. Beersman was not the first American architect to adopt the Giralda Tower for his own purposes; McKim, Mead and White borrowed more directly from the Seville structure in their design of the tower for Madison Square Garden in 1891.[36]

The idea of a prominent tower jutting from a lower block had many immediate precedents in Chicago, the earliest of these being the Chicago Board of Trade Building of 1885 by W. W. Boyington, and Adler and Sullivan's Garrick Theater of 1891–92. But the most important for the Wrigley Building was the Montgomery Ward Building constructed in 1897–99 (figure 2.11) at the northwest corner of Michigan Avenue and Madison Street. It had a twelve-story main block with a central tower rising twenty-one stories to a steeply pitched roof supporting a cupola. Beersman saw this structure as the ideal symbol for a commercial enterprise and attempted to make an even bolder gesture that would overshadow the Ward Building in height and dignity.

The Wrigley Building was constructed in little more than a year, the foundation work having started in April of 1920. The total cost of the building came to over $8,000,000, an amount Wrigley paid in cash from his company's vast financial reserves.[37] When the building was completed in 1921, the old Rush Street Bridge was still in place, and while the Michigan Avenue Bridge was built, there were, as yet, no bridge houses, just metal platforms. Immediately north of the Wrigley Building were large, unsightly billboards (figure 2.12), elements standing in sharp contrast to the elegant new building.[38] The setting did not deter Wrigley and Winston from signing tenants for the building, however, as it was 100 percent rented by the time it opened.[39] Wrigley himself was instrumental in securing some of the tenants, a few of which were friends and business associates. Others, who were as yet undecided prospects, were convinced by Wrigley who talked to them about the advantages of the building, particularly of the advertising value of being in a building certain to be a landmark in the city, if not the entire country.[40]

So successful were his efforts that Wrigley decided almost immediately to expand by constructing a second structure, or annex, to the north (figure 2.13). In August of 1922 he acquired existing leases on the block bounded by Michigan Avenue, Rush, North Water, and Hubbard streets, which had an area about twice that of the original parcel.[41] He again commissioned Graham, Anderson, Probst and

Figure 2.11
Montgomery Ward Build-
ing, northwest corner of
Michigan Avenue and Mad-
ison Street, 1900; Richard
E. Schmidt, architect.
Courtesy of the Chicago
Historical Society.

White to design a structure that would be the same height
and architecturally consistent with the original building.
Announcing his plans on August 9, 1922, Wrigley stated:

> My decision to construct another building north of
> the bridge that will double our present capacity is

an expression of my personal faith in the future of Chicago. Chicago still lags behind New York in public improvements, but I hold out great hope for the future and am staking a little money on my belief.[42]

The addition of the annex was especially desirable from an architectural standpoint. The original south building, while striking, was relatively small and proportionally awkward. The north section added weight and solidity, perhaps even a bit of dignity. Constructed in 1923–24, the style and details of the annex are similar to that of the first building (figure 2.14). In the interest of uniformity, and to complement the Michigan Avenue Bridge Plaza, the east facade of the annex was set back to line up with the south building, thus leaving for the plaza a considerable area which could otherwise have been added to the building.[43] The main entrance of the new section, which rises to the third-story cornice line, is a modification of that in the

Figure 2.12
Wrigley Building in 1921.
Courtesy of the Chicago
Historical Society.

Figure 2.13
Wrigley Building with An-
nex. Courtesy of the Chi-
cago Historical Society.

main block. The two buildings are joined at the street level
by a plaza and colonnade over North Water Street and by
an enclosed third-floor walkway facing the bridge plaza. An
unusual skybridge was added at the fourteenth floor in
1936.[44]

In an effort to further beautify North Michigan Avenue, William Wrigley, Jr., in 1928 gave a fund for sculptural reliefs to be placed on the Michigan Avenue Bridge
houses. Wrigley and his son, Philip K. Wrigley, had both
served on the Chicago Plan Commission, and they shared a
considerable interest in the improvement of the city, with a
particular feeling of kinship for the riverbank and the

Figure 2.14
Wrigley Building Annex,
detail of parapet. Photo by
Author.

Michigan Avenue Bridge.[45] The sum of $100,000 was made available for the sculptural reliefs, with Wrigley paying for the two reliefs on the north plaza (figure 2.15). Those on the south were paid for by the Ferguson Trust, a fund administered by the Board of Directors of the Chicago Art Institute for the purpose of paying for public sculpture in the city.[46] The sculptures on the northern bridge houses were executed by the American sculptor James Earle Fraser. They depict "The Discoverers" Marquette, Joliet, LaSalle, and Tonti, who were the first explorers of the Chicago River (figure 2.16); and "The Pioneers" DuSable and Kinzie, Chicago's first permanent settlers. The southern sculptures, by Henry Hering, depict "Defense," the Fort Dearborn massacre of 1812; and "Regeneration," Chicagoans' efforts to rebuild the city after the Fire of 1871.[47]

ITALIAN COURT BUILDING

With the Crerar Library and Wrigley Building under construction at key points along the newly widened avenue, a number of smaller buildings and renovation projects soon followed. One of these was the Italian Court Building at the southeast corner of Ontario Street and Michigan Avenue

Figure 2.15
View of bridge houses on
north side of the river. Re-
printed from American Architect *(11 May 1921),*
copyright (1921) by
McGraw-Hill, Inc. All
rights reserved. Repro-
duced with the permission
of the publisher.

Figure 2.16
Bridge House, northeast
corner, 1928; James Earle
Fraser, sculptor. Reprinted
from Paul T. Gilbert and
Charles L. Bryson, Chicago
and Its Makers *(Chicago,*
1929).

Figure 2.17
Italian Court Building, 619
North Michigan Avenue,
1919–20; Robert DeGolyer,
architect. Courtesy of the
Chicago Historical Society.

(figure 2.17) about halfway between the river and Chicago Avenue. Two existing brick walk-up apartment buildings on the site were converted in 1919–20 by architect Robert DeGolyer for real estate developers Chester and Raymond Cook into a single shopping structure suggestive of a small European shopping quarter. The building's main attraction was an interior courtyard surrounded by an arcade, with shops, studios, and offices on three floors. The courtyard was paved with flagstone and had a fountain with a statue of Narcissus from Pompeii.[48]

The building was fully rented long before it was completed in the summer of 1920. One of the first tenants was William F. Castberg, a dressmaker, who moved here from the Loop so he would be closer to his rich clientele on the

Gold Coast. DeGoyler designed for him an elegant shop occupying two floors of the south building. Next to Castberg's was "LePetit Bazar," an antique shop which also contained the tearoom of the Home Delicacies Association, run by Mrs. Potter Palmer, Mrs. Marshall Field, and others from the list of social register ladies. Other popular shops in the building were Tatman's, which specialized in English glassware, the Shighisa Mori oriental shop, and the Italian Shop.[49]

The Cooks financed the building project with a mortgage from the Northwestern Mutual Life Insurance Company, one of several insurance companies and banks to extend loans to developers of North Michigan Avenue properties.[50] In fact, the availability of ample credit financing was one of the most important factors in the development of the avenue between 1920 and 1930 for those who, unlike the John Crerar Library executors or William Wrigley, lacked sufficient funds for a major building project. Investment in property through credit financing multiplied the effectiveness of available funds by enabling an owner to buy and develop properties that substantially exceeded the value of the funds invested.[51]

Mortgage financing generally involved a straight loan of approximately 60–80 percent of the appraised value of the land and building. This mortgage was made at the prevailing interest rate of 5–7 percent and for a period of from five to twenty years. Mortgage loans of this type were usually obtained through such channels as savings banks, life and fire insurance companies, land title insurance companies, and from estates whose funds were controlled by attorneys or real estate firms.[52] Of the more than thirty buildings constructed or renovated on the avenue in the 1920s, slightly more than half would be financed through mortgage financing.

LAKE SHORE TRUST AND SAVINGS BANK

One of the most distinguished of the smaller buildings on the avenue is the Lake Shore Trust and Savings Bank at the northeast corner of Michigan and Ohio Street (figure 2.18). Designed by Benjamin Marshall and Charles Fox in 1921, it is a Classical style building with Corinthian columns rising its full height of five stories and supporting a prominent entablature with dentilwork and a projecting cornice. The columns are three-quarters round, engaged to rectangular piers, and placed on a square base four feet

Figure 2.18
Lake Shore Trust and Sav-
ings Bank, 601 North
Michigan Avenue, 1921–22;
Marshall and Fox, archi-
tects. Photo by author.

high. The corner piers are smooth-faced limestone with an abbreviated capital. Window surfaces and spandrels are recessed the full depth of the columns.

The building's architects were at the same moment engaged in the design of the Drake Hotel, a sumptuous building in the Renaissance style located at the north end of Michigan Avenue at Oak Street. Born to wealth and gifted with a business sense equal to that of Daniel Burnham, Benjamin Marshall understood well how to create the spacious interiors and immodest elegance appropriate for North Michigan Avenue. Marshall lacked any formal education in architecture, having been apprenticed at an early age to several Chicago architects. He organized the firm of Marshall and Fox in 1905.[53] Like Marshall, Charles E. Fox had a minimal formal education in architecture, having obtained his architectural training as an apprentice in the office of Holabird and Roche.[54] The office of Marshall and Fox had been located in the former Perry Smith House before it was demolished for the widening of North Michigan Avenue.

The client of the Lake Shore Trust and Savings Bank was its board of directors, which included prominent members of the North Central Business District Association, men such as Colonel Robert McCormick, owner and editor of the *Chicago Tribune*; John Drake, owner of the Drake Hotel; Sheldon Clark, vice-president of the Sinclair Refining Company; and Bertram Winston, who had been instrumental in developing the Wrigley Building.[55] They had a

49

vested interest in the development of North Michigan Avenue, both in the character of its architecture and in its economic well-being. The bank's success was impressive, having opened in 1920 with only $300,000 in capital, an amount which grew to $10 million by 1926.[56]

PALMER SHOPS BUILDING

A third small building from the early years of the decade was the Palmer Shops Building at 942–50 North Michigan Avenue, on the west side of the street between Oak and Walton (figure 2.19). Designed in 1921 by Holabird and Roche, the structure was three stories with limestone walls articulated with pilasters and topped by a simple, smooth parapet with urns at either end. There were five separate shop entrances on the Michigan Avenue side, one of them occupied by the Martha Weathered Shop, which had the distinction of being the first women's apparel shop to locate on North Michigan Avenue.[57] Also in the building was the Women's Exchange, a restaurant and shop run by society women for other women who were in need of charitable assistance.[58]

Shortly after it was completed, the building was sold by its builders, Honoré and Potter Palmer, Jr., to Mrs. Edith Rockefeller McCormick, who was becoming at the time a major purchaser of North Michigan Avenue property. The Palmers themselves would spend much of the decade selling off their extensive holdings, making way for the development of such buildings as the Drake Hotel, the Palmolive Building, and the Michigan-Chestnut Building. Many of the residential buildings Potter Palmer, Sr., had erected would be replaced by the larger and more modern structures of the 1920s.[59]

Even upon selling their holdings, however, the Palmers continued to have some influence on the character of the avenue's development. All sales of their property were made under an "option contract" whereby the purchaser made a deposit, and before paying the remainder he was required to submit plans of the proposed building project for the approval of the estate. Restrictions on the building's size and use, which generally followed the recommendations of the North Central Business District Association, were enforced, thus helping to assure the development of high quality commercial and residential buildings in the area.[60] These restrictions could only be in force, however, when the Palmers sold the property, and could not be ap-

Figure 2.19
Palmer Shops Building,
942–50 North Michigan
Avenue, 1921–22; Holabird
and Roche, architects.
Courtesy of the Chicago
Historical Society.

plied to subsequent owners. Thus, the earliest buildings of
the 1920s generally followed the guidelines established by
the North Central Business District Association, while
those of later owners diverged dramatically by the end of
the decade.

LONDON GUARANTEE AND
ACCIDENT COMPANY BUILDING

The first major commercial structure on the avenue to compete in size and prominence with the Wrigley Building was
the London Guarantee and Accident Company Building
(figure 2.20) at 360 North Michigan.[61] Located directly
across the river from the Wrigley Building, and initiating
the development of the south side of the bridge plaza (figure
2.21), it was designed to serve as a headquarters for the
company's rapidly increasing business in the United States.
In the end, however, the company decided to locate in New
York rather than Chicago, leaving the building with only a
small branch office and the London Guarantee name.[62] It
thus became largely a speculative rental building with many
tenants.

The project was carried out by a group of English
investors, along with a Chicago attorney, John S. Miller,
who formed the Site of Fort Dearborn Building Corporation in 1921. Miller already owned the irregularly shaped
site at the southwest corner of the bridge plaza, near what
had once been a corner of Fort Dearborn and later the
location of the William Hoyt Company warehouse.[63] Rather
than obtaining a mortgage to finance the building, the

51

Figure 2.20
London Guarantee and Accident Building, 354 North Michigan Avenue, 1922–24; Alfred S. Alschuler, architect. Courtesy of the Chicago Historical Society.

group obtained a bond issue underwritten by Bonright and Company of Chicago and the Union Trust and Otis Companies of Cleveland. The total cost was estimated to be $4,916,500.[64]

The financing of building development through bond issues had been in use in the United States since the turn of the century, but it was not until the war had popularized the sale of Liberty Bonds that it became widely accepted in real estate finance. Developers were encouraged to plan large buildings, stores, office buildings and apartments, and loans based on bond issues were offered sufficient to pay for 100 percent of their cost or more.[65] The issuance of real estate bonds was carried out by large mortgage bond companies like Bonright and Company, which developed a highly specialized service to provide necessary construction and permanent mortgage loans through the underwriting of an issue of mortgage bonds which were established as a lien on the building and land. The mortgage loan obtainable through such sources was payable in installments over a period of from ten to fifteen years. The fact that the owner began to reduce the mortgage the first year after the building was completed further accounted for the availability of more liberal loans than were possible through ordinary mortgages.[66]

The growth of the real estate bond market is demonstrated by the statistics of one of Bonright and Company's competitors, the Chicago Trust Company, whose number of individual investors in bond issues rose from 500 in 1919 to over 6,000 in 1923.[67] A similar growth in demand was experienced by other Chicago mortgage companies, such that from 1925 to 1928 some $800,000,000 worth of mortgage bonds were issued. No other city in the country challenged Chicago's preeminence in the field.[68] About one-fifth of the buildings on North Michigan Avenue erected in the 1920s were financed by this means.

Newspaper advertisements for the London Guarantee Building bond issue stressed its location as being one of the most important in Chicago, directly opposite the Wrigley Building at the "New Gateway of the Greater Chicago."[69] It therefore had to be a significant design, one that would hold its own against the Wrigley Building. To produce this design, John Miller commissioned Chicago architect Alfred S. Alschuler, a graduate of the Armour Institute who had begun his career in the office of Dankmar Adler. In 1903 he had formed a partnership with Samuel A. Treat, and four years later established his own practice, specializing in commercial, department store, and industrial buildings.[70] He completed the plan of the London Guarantee Building in December of 1921, and the work of sinking its fifty caissons was begun the following month.[71] Construction was finished in 1924.[72]

The building's principal elevation, diagonally oriented to the northeast, faces the river and the Michigan Avenue Bridge. It has a shallow inward curvature in plan, which serves to enlarge the plaza area in front of its entrance.[73] The facade is adorned with a large triumphal arch motif at its base (figure 2.22) and a colonnade of eight smooth-shafted Corinthian columns beginning at the eighteenth floor and extending to the twentieth. The building is surmounted by a small circular temple-like structure composed of a ring of slender Corinthian columns alternating with molded piers and supporting a decorated dome and lantern (figure 2.23).[74] A major problem in designing the

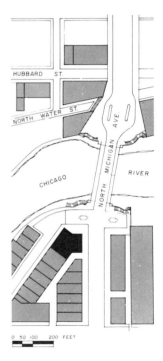

Figure 2.21
London Guarantee and
Accident Building site
plan. Drawn by author.

Figure 2.22
London Guarantee and Ac-
cident Building, entrance
detail. Reprinted from
American Architect *(27 Au-*
gust 1924), copyright
(1924) by McGraw-Hill,
Inc. All rights reserved.
Reproduced with the per-
mission of the publisher.

building was caused by John Miller's initial inability to acquire title to a twenty-four by fifty-five foot lot facing Michigan Avenue that was owned by the John W. Keough estate.[75] The position of this lot is indicated by the light court on the building's east side. After long and unsuccessful negotiations with the owner, Miller and Alschuler decided to use this area as a permanent light court and build around it in such a manner that it could be incorporated in the lower floors of the building if it were eventually acquired.[76] The two wings on either side of the court presented a difficult problem as their widths were twenty-four feet and forty-four feet. Alschuler made the top three floors of the two wings the same width by stepping back the wider wing (figure 2.24) at the eighteenth floor.[77] After construction of the building was started, Miller finally succeeded in obtaining a long-term lease for the small lot, and Alschuler de-

Figure 2.23
London Guarantee and Ac-
cident Building, detail of
roof temple. Reprinted
from American Architect
(27 August 1924), copy-
right (1924) by McGraw-
Hill, Inc. All rights re-
served. Reproduced with
the permission of the pub-
lisher.

signed a five-story structure compatible with the base of the main building to fill in the space.[78]

In contrast to the white-glazed terra cotta of the Wrigley Building, the exterior surface of the twenty-one-story London Guarantee Building is faced with gray Indiana limestone on the east, north, and west sides, while its south side is clad with brick. As with the Crerar Library, it was expected that the construction of new adjacent buildings to the south would soon hide this wall, something that unfortunately has not happened to this day.

The building's most significant interior space, prior to its remodeling in the 1960s, was the vestibule located just inside the entrance. Here was found a circular rotunda

Figure 2.24
London Guarantee and Ac-
cident Building, detail of
upper stories on east fa-
cade. Photo by author.

with its vaulted ceiling studded with hundreds of variously shaped medallions in gilt, greens, and reds, and an ornate chandelier hanging from the center (figure 2.25). Walls of travertine stone were enriched with flutings and carvings at the doors of shops opening off the rotunda on either side. The floor was Carthage marble with bold insets of green marble in geometric designs (figure 2.26). Two double doors of polished brass led to the lobby with a grand staircase leading to the second floor and two banks of elevators also with polished brass doors.[79]

Architect and critic Alfred Hoyt Granger wrote in 1933 that in designing this building for an English company, Alschuler "happily introduced the London tradition into the American scene."[80] This was no doubt part of Alschuler's thinking; however, it must be kept in mind that neoclassicism was not regarded as a foreign style in the United

Figure 2.25
London Guarantee and Ac-
cident Building, entrance
lobby. Reprinted from
American Architect *(27 Au-*
gust 1924), copyright
(1924) by McGraw-Hill,
Inc. All rights reserved.
Reproduced with the per-
mission of the publisher.

States. Instead, it was indigenous to America since the colonial era and was the basis of the City Beautiful movement
in the early 1900s. Magnificent, beautiful, and orderly displays of public architecture were intended to symbolize the
ideals of democracy and thereby inspire civic pride and national patriotism.

John Zukowsky writes in the exhibition catalog *Archi-*
tecture in Context: 360 North Michigan Avenue that
speeches by Thomas Condon of the London Guarantee

57

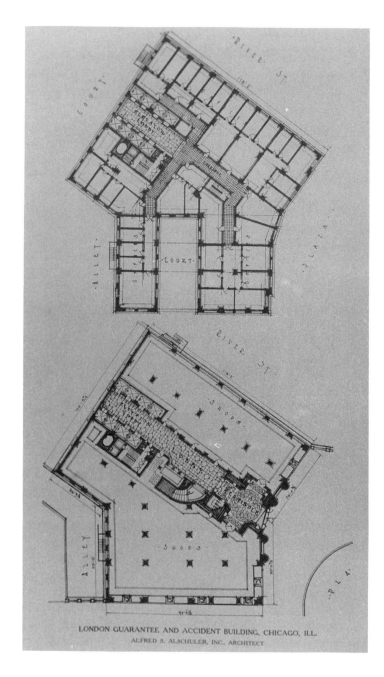

LONDON GUARANTEE AND ACCIDENT BUILDING, CHICAGO, ILL.
ALFRED S. ALSCHULER, INC., ARCHITECT

Company and writings of Alfred Alschuler indicate the extent to which they viewed this structure as a permanent
"civic contribution to Chicago's cityscape akin to the monuments of ancient Greece and Rome."[81] The Classical imagery in the building—Corinthian columns, Greek meander patterns, Roman eagles and lions, and the reclining

sculptures of the gods Ceres and Neptune—reinforces that association with the antique world. In addition, there was local imagery in the Fort Dearborn bronze relief over the central door, and corporate imagery in the griffons, urns, and coats of arms of the City of London found throughout the lobby and the exterior of the building. The cupola on top was intended "to balance the effect of the round temple on the Wrigley Building tower."[82] It reflects Alschuler's interest in this type of architectural element. In 1934 he wrote that he admired them on public buildings in Helsinki and Stockholm, particularly the Stockholm Town Hall of 1909–23. Thus, the cupola here is as much a formal device as an iconographic one.[83]

When the building was completed, its success as a rental property was immediate.[84] Rental brochures stressed its practical advantages in its proximity to business, with "wide avenues, broad views, the placid, flowing river, cherry sunshine and fresh air." And all of this was "away from the din, dirt and disorder of the Loop."[85] Images of the building and its urban environment were reproduced in countless postcards, newspaper ads, books, and magazine illustrations, demonstrating that it was an important addition to the Chicago skyline of the early 1920s. Further recognition came in the form of the gold medal for 1923, an annual award for outstanding architecture made by the Lake Shore Trust and Savings Bank.[86]

The construction of the Wrigley Building and the London Guarantee Building on the north and south sides of the Michigan Avenue Bridge Plaza began to give a new urban form to this important gateway to the newly opened avenue. They set a standard for urban expression of the corporate enterprise and established a context for the relative size and form of the buildings that would follow on the east side of the avenue, those that would eventually replace the still existing warehouse and factory buildings facing the river and the freight yards. The parameters of North Michigan Avenue were now established, with the Crerar Library marking its southernmost entrance, the Wrigley and London Guarantee buildings framing its jog at the Chicago River, the Water Tower and Pumping Station flanking its second jog at Chicago Avenue, and the Palmer Shops Building and the just completed Drake Hotel (see Chapter 5) marking its north entrance.

Of these buildings, only the Drake Hotel, at fourteen stories, conformed to the recommendations of Daniel Burnham and the North Central Business District Association.

All of the others were either considerably taller or lower than the suggested ten stories. Why did this occur? It was primarily due to the circumstances of the individual owners: the size of their respective properties, their programmatic needs, and the extent of the financial commitment for their building projects. Ultimately, it was these factors rather than the aesthetic ideals of its early planners that determined the character of the avenue. Burnham and the North Central Business District Association had failed to judge the extent to which the diversity of owners and developers of property on North Michigan Avenue would eventually build equally diverse buildings representative of the competitive nature of the real estate industry. They did have some influence on the development of the avenue, however, particularly in their effective control over building use, consistency in the placement of shopfronts facing the avenue, and in their formulation of the shared goal of making North Michigan Avenue the city's most prestigious commercial thoroughfare.

THE CHICAGO
TRIBUNE
TOWER

The Chicago Tribune Tower, the third major high-rise building to have a presence on the Michigan Avenue Bridge Plaza (figures 3.1 and 3.2) was begun while the London Guarantee Building was still under construction. Colonel Robert McCormick, editor of the *Tribune*, and a great-nephew of reaper inventor Cyrus McCormick, expressed his wish of providing "an administration building that would be an inspiration to its workers—a tower that would interpret in terms of architecture the *Tribune*'s purpose and ideals—one that would be a model for future generations."[1] Coupled with this was McCormick's vision of the paper's role in the social, political, and industrial development of Chicago as expressed symbolically by the new building. McCormick suggested that the *Tribune* was "truly part of Chicago and merged with its destiny would give to Chicago the utmost in civic development—the world's most beautiful modern building."[2]

The *Chicago Tribune* had published its first issue in 1847 in a building on the southwest corner of Lake and LaSalle streets in the heart of the Loop.[3] The paper was acquired in 1855 by a combative editor named Joseph Medill, who was best known as the founder of the Republican party.[4] An early admirer of Abraham Lincoln, Medill covered the 1858 Lincoln-Douglas debates and later helped secure Lincoln's nomination at the Chicago convention.[5] In 1861, the *Tribune* was incorporated, and two years later Medill became its editor-in-chief. After a brief foray into politics in the early 1870s, he returned to the paper, and for the remainder of the century he kept it literate, competent, Republican, and well informed on national and international issues.[6]

Figure 3.1
Tribune Tower, 435 North
Michigan Avenue, 1922–25;
John Mead Howells and
Raymond Hood, archi-
tects. Photo by author.

The *Tribune* moved its offices several times before erecting its own building in 1868 at the southeast corner of Madison and Dearborn streets.[7] It was first rebuilt after the 1871 fire and replaced again in 1902 by a seventeen-story building designed by Holabird and Roche, a model newspaper plant and office building that had been expected to adequately serve its purpose for decades (figure 3.3).[8] Within fifteen years, however, it was completely outgrown, and a search was on by 1919 for an appropriate location for a new facility, one that was close to the center of the city but not trapped in the growing congestion of the Loop.[9] Not only had the building become too small, but deliveries in and out of the Loop were difficult because of the traffic, a problem that would not be alleviated by simply moving to another Loop location.

It is not surprising then that Colonel Robert Mc-Cormick, who had become the paper's president in 1911, turned his attention to the Near North Side and the new North Michigan Avenue.[10] He had been interested in the area since his childhood, having grown up in McCormick-ville in an apartment building at the corner of Ontario and

Figure 3.2
Tribune Tower site plan.
Drawn by author.

Figure 3.3
Tribune Building, south-east corner of Madison and Dearborn streets, 1902; Holabird and Roche, architects. Reprinted from the Chicago Tribune, The WGN *(Chicago, 1922).*

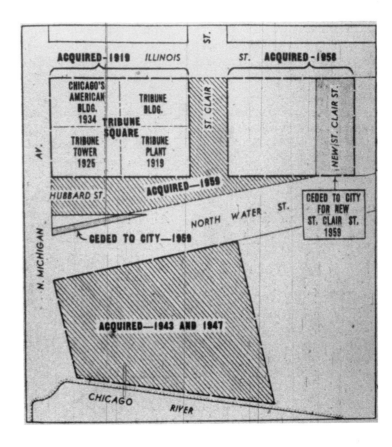

Figure 3.4
Chicago Tribune Building
site, North Michigan Ave-
nue between Illinois and
North Water streets. Re-
printed from the Chicago
Tribune *(6 December*
1961).

State streets. In 1904, while serving as a city alderman, he had personally escorted members of the City Council's committee studying the proposed Michigan Avenue improvement on a walking tour of the entire district lying north and south of the river.[11] He thus had a vested interest in the area having staked his political reputation on its potential development. When the opportunity arose, he was one of the first to buy property on the new avenue, purchasing in September 1919 a site at 435 North Michigan Avenue, the south half of the block bounded by Hubbard, St. Clair, and Illinois streets (figure 3.4). The property, fronting 100 feet on Michigan Avenue, was purchased in several parcels for a total cost of $477,000.[12] It contained a number of small factory and warehouse buildings and, as was the case with the Wrigley Building, the grade level of the site was about fifteen feet below the sidewalk of North Michigan Avenue. McCormick later wrote:

> It was quite a mental struggle to accept the present building site. It seems so remote . . . but we got

our south half of the block very cheap . . . nobody thinking a Loop enterprise would cross the river.

Our motive in coming here was not real estate profit, but the double level and the railroad tracks. We only built on the back end of our lot, not knowing what the future might hold.[13]

In 1919, *The Economist* reported that the *Tribune*

contemplates a huge structure at the northeast corner of North Michigan and Austin (Hubbard), including a great office building with a tower and a wireless station 400 to 500 feet high. This will be the most conspicuous point on the North Side as one crosses the new bridge which will soon span the river.[14]

The first building the *Tribune* constructed was not a tower but a six-story printing plant, located on the southeast quarter of the block. It was built by the Tribune Building Corporation, organized by McCormick and his cousin and fellow editor, Joseph M. Patterson, along with attorney Joseph B. Fleming and architect Jarvis B. Hunt.[15] Ground was broken for the new building later in 1919, and construction was completed the following year (figure 3.5).[16] The building's facades were quite utilitarian with a clear

Figure 3.5
Chicago Tribune *plant, 435 North Michigan Avenue, 1920–21; Jarvis Hunt, architect. Reprinted from* Chicago Tribune, The WGN *(Chicago, 1922).*

articulation of the structural bays and a complete lack of ornamentation. They would later be clad with limestone in a simplified Gothic style to match the new office tower.

McCormick took an active role in the building's design, especially on the proposed press layout, developing a system for which he eventually obtained a patent. The sub-basement of the new plant provided for newsprint storage, reel rooms, press units, and machinery for automatically carrying folded newspapers to the loading docks on the ground floor. The double-deck Michigan Avenue Bridge provided easy access for circulation trucks while the building's location on a railroad line was important since nearly all the newspaper's print from Canada was at that time shipped by rail. The *Tribune* would soon acquire an adjacent site directly on the river for a newsprint loading dock and warehouse, with a tunnel for utilities linking it to the plant.[17]

THE TRIBUNE TOWER COMPETITION

The design for the Tribune Tower to be built in front of the printing plant was, of course, the product of a famous international competition.[18] Announced on June 10, 1922, the *Tribune*'s stated purpose was the creation of a monument that would commemorate seventy-five years of achievement and would be an inspiration to the future for both the community and the newspaper. The *Tribune* exaggerated its description of the site of the proposed structure (figure 3.6) saying it was "among the most significant and inviting to be found in any of the great cities of the world."[19] To the south and west it overlooked the river and the commercial heart of Chicago; to the north and east it looked toward the vast stretches of the lake and shoreline parks and drives.[20] What the *Tribune* did not say was that it also overlooked decaying neighborhoods, rundown factory buildings, dilapidated grainaries, and miles of railroad tracks. On the contrary, the newspaper depicted the image of paradise, the ultimate vision of the City Beautiful. The *Tribune*'s directors saw it as "a site to respect, to adorn and to enoble," because it was a vital point in a tremendous metropolitan scheme, the possibilities of which were heroic.[21] They recognized it as a commercially strategic point in the enlarged Chicago then taking shape, and were confident that other significant structures would rise nearby.[22]

The competition program was prepared by Howard L. Cheney, an advisory architect for the *Tribune*. Drawn up

according to the rules of the American Institute of Architects (A.I.A.), the competition was to run for three months, from August to November 1922, and the winning entry would be selected by a jury of five people in conjunction with an advisory committee of six prominent business and political leaders. The brochure for the competition listed the prize money for first-, second- and third-place winners, along with the honorable mention awards.[23] It stated also that by terms of the city's municipal building code the building could rise to a height of 260 feet plus a tower of 140 feet, giving it a total height of 400 feet.[24] No mention was made of the proposals by Burnham or the North Central Business District Association. It was clear that the *Tribune*'s concern was not for the context of the avenue as a whole but for their building alone. The fact that it would be a high-rise structure filling the zoning envelope to its entirety was a foregone conclusion.

Figure 3.6
Aerial View of Chicago
Tribune Building site in
1922. Reprinted from Chi-
cago Tribune, The WGN
(Chicago, 1922).

The *Tribune*'s announcement of the competition received an overwhelming response from architects all over the world. By July 6 more than 500 architects had requested information about the contest. The acting Italian consul asked for thirty copies of the contest rules to be sent to architects in Italy.[25] Any architect could submit an application to enter provided he could show "sufficient evidence of education, ability and experience."[26] Besides the open invitation, the *Tribune* extended special invitations to ten architects of national recognition, including the firms of Holabird and Roche and D. H. Burnham and Company of Chicago, and John Mead Howells of New York.[27]

In calling for the most beautiful building in the world, the *Tribune* was not expecting a truly functional design with a complete plan layout. The competitors were asked not to submit meticulous specifications and details—all that would come later—but a design showing only the structure's south and west elevations and a perspective from the southwest.[28] Style was of utmost importance. The newspaper emphasized:

> It is unnecessary for the purposes of this competition to know the mechanical needs of the *Chicago Tribune* or to be concerned with the plans for developing and extending the various departments which will occupy the space in the new building. The purpose and desire of the Tribune in instituting this competition is to secure primarily a distinctive and beautiful exterior design.[29]

The emphasis of the formal and visual over the functional and technological aspect was an evident search for a standard of beauty for the American skyscraper.

During the course of the competition, from its inception to its conclusion, the *Tribune* continually published in its Sunday magazine pictures of buildings of acknowledged high quality of design ranging from Renaissance palaces, oriental tombs, and domed mosques to Christian churches and modern imitative collegiate buildings (table 3.1). Accompanying each presentation was the query, "Is this to be the type of architecture embodied in the *Tribune*'s new home?"[30] The first of these, published on June 18, contained an explanation of the paper's intent:

> Today the first of a series of pictures of the world's most beautiful and most famous buildings is published in this section. Other pictures of buildings both in this country and abroad in clas-

sic lands will be reproduced. Readers are asked to
study these carefully with a view to choosing one
after which the Tribune monument appropriately
may be modeled. If your idea of the Tribune monument is not exemplified in any of the pictures,
you are invited to submit your views indepen-
dently, that a consensus may determine just what
is Chicago's idea of the most beautiful building in
the world.[31]

Readers were asked to send their ideas to the architectural
editor, and their opinions would be taken under advise-
ment. This attempt to involve the public in the competition
process had the twofold purpose of educating the *Tribune*'s
readers about architecture and of promoting the newspaper itself. The *Tribune* was not indifferent to the advertising value the competition had for the newspaper; however, it stressed that beauty was the only object sought and
that it was really for the public benefit.[32]

It is probable that these pictures not only kept the public interested in the competition but also indicated to the
architects participating in it that the *Tribune* favored a historical style, possibly Gothic, over a modernistic approach.
The Woolworth Building, for instance, was featured twice
in the Sunday rotogravure section, once in June and again
in July.[33] The Harkness Memorial Tower at Yale, Mc-
Cormick's alma mater, was featured in August with the
statement:

> It must be a concrete expression of a great news-
> paper, not merely a big office building. It must ex-
> press the restless energy and surging power char-
> acteristic of a great newspaper.[34]

A picture of Amiens Cathedral, published in November,
was accompanied by an obviously admiring caption:

> With its flame-like tracery, its complicated pinna-
> cles, its glimmering niches, pierced parapets,
> dainty filigree work and sculptural lace, it was a
> marvel of imagination, dramatic sense and consu-
> mate craftsmanship.[35]

At the close of the competition on the first of November, 120 entries had arrived, though others, particularly
from abroad, continued to filter in throughout the month
until a total of 258 were received.[36] Howard L. Cheney arranged the drawings for judging in a large room on the second floor of the Lake Shore Trust and Savings Bank. The

Table 3.1 continued

Philadelphia City Hall
Hibernia Building,
   New Orleans

16 July 1922
   Florence Cathedral

30 July 1922
   Antwerp Cathedral

6 August 1922
   Bush Tower, New York

13 August 1922
   Hotel de Ville, Arras

20 August 1922
   Harkness Memorial
   Tower, New Haven

17 August 1922
   Koutub Tower of
   Victory, Dehli

17 September 1922
   Court of Honor,
   Columbia Exposition,
   Chicago

29 October 1922
   Palace of Justice,
   Brussels

19 November 1922
   Cathedral at Amiens

26 November 1922
   Kali Gopura,
   Steerungen, India

judging took place in two stages, with all of the designs first being reviewed by the committee of business and civic leaders.[37] This advisory committee reduced the 258 entries to twelve possible winners. These were then submitted to the final jury, composed of Robert McCormick and Joseph Patterson, along with Edward S. Beck, managing editor of the *Tribune*, Holmes Onderdonk, manager of *Tribune* real estate, and a single architect, Alfred H. Granger, who was appointed chairman.[38] On November 13, the first secret ballot was taken. The Howells and Hood invited design received first place, with second place going to Holabird and Roche. Third place went to a design by the San Francisco firm of Bliss and Faville. On November 27, the second ballot was circulated with the same result. On November 29, however, two days before the final vote was to be taken, Eliel Saarinen's entry arrived, which the jurors immediately realized must be included among the designs considered for final selection. The jury reassembled and voted the Saarinen design second place, with the Howells and Hood design still first, and the Holabird and Roche design moved to third. The Bliss and Faville design was removed from mention.[39] Alfred Granger later wrote that the final decision between the Howells and Hood design and that of Saarinen was debated for forty-eight hours before taking the final vote. Granger wanted the prize to go to Saarinen, but the other four members of the jury preferred the Howells and Hood scheme. The lone architect withdrew his objection, and the vote was unanimous.[40]

The Howells and Hood design (figure 3.7) was based on a thorough study of the formal features of a Gothic tower—the overall silhouette, the proportions of structural, decorative, and utilitarian elements, and the relations of these parts to the whole. The design motif was based on eight buttresses, and their sustaining piers carried from the ground to the summit. The most widely acknowledged model was the Tour de Beurre of the Cathedral in Rouen, France (figure 3.8), an example of the late Norman Gothic style.[41] Hood revealed in a letter of January 14, 1924, other sources of the design:

> I do not know as it is quite fair to the Butter
> Tower in Rouen to say that the Tribune Tower
> was taken from it. As far as I could go would be to
> say that we studied the silhouette of the Butter
> Tower very carefully, but at the same time the
> tower of St. André des Arts in Rouen, the tower of

St. Jacques in Paris, and the tower of St. Rumbold in Malines, Belgium, gave us a great deal of inspiration.

As far as the detail went, we studied very carefully the small church at Caudebec-en-Caux, St. Maclau in Rouen, the Church of Senlis, and the Cathedral at Albi. As you can see, Normandy and Belgium had a lot to do with the tower.[42]

The use by Howells and Hood of the Gothic style for the Tribune Tower and for the American Radiator Company Building the following year did not stem from any firmly held conviction of its validity in American skyscraper design, as Hood wrote in the *Architectural Forum*:

> To use two buildings as examples, they are both in the "vertical" style or what is called "Gothic," simply because I happened to make them so. If at the time of designing them I had been under the spell of Italian campaniles or Chinese pagodas, I suppose the resulting compositions would have been "horizontal."[43]

Hood felt that the skyscraper problem was still a relatively new phenomenon in American architecture, lacking any established traditions or strict formulas. He was quite happy with the prevailing mood in which everyone could try out whatever idea came into their head.[44]

Announcement of the awards was made at a dinner given on the evening of December 3, 1922, in the *Tribune* plant. Addressing the gathering of civic officials and architects, John Mead Howells said of their design:

> It climbs into the air naturally, carrying up its main structural lines and binding them together with a high open parapet. Our disposition of the main structural piers on the exterior has been adopted to give the full utilization of the corner light in the offices and the view up and down of the avenue.[45]

In attempting to characterize the building's design motif, he said,

> Our desire has been not so much an archaeological expression of any particular style as to express in the exterior the essentially American problem of skyscraper construction, with its continued vertical lines and its inserted horizontals. It is only

Figure 3.7
Project, Tribune Tower
Competition; John Mead
Howells and Raymond
Hood, architects. Re-
printed from Chicago Trib-
une *(2 December 1922).*

Figure 3.8
Tour de Beurre, Rouen,
France, 1202–20. Re-
printed from Arthur Kings-
ley Porter, Medieval Architecture: Its Origins and
Development *(New York*
and London, 1909).

carrying forward to a final expression what many of us architects have tried already under more or less hampering conditions of various cities. We have wished to make this landmark the study of a beautiful and vigorous form, not of an extraordinary form.[46]

In announcing the winners of the competition, the *Tribune* put great stock in the fact that John Mead Howells was the son of novelist William Dean Howells, former editor of the *Atlantic Monthly*. This association with an important figure in the literary history of the United States was thought to further legitimize the *Tribune*'s selection.[47] A graduate of the Ecole des Beaux-Arts, John Mead Howells had a great reputation in his own right as an architect, having designed notable university, bank, and apartment buildings, mostly on the East Coast.[48] Being one of the ten specially invited architects for the *Tribune* competition was a great honor for Howells and was a welcome acknowledgment of his standing in the profession. His partner in the competition, Raymond Hood, was also a graduate of the Ecole des Beaux-Arts and a former apprentice in the offices of Cram, Goodhue and Ferguson in Boston, and of Palmer and Hornbostel in Pittsburgh. He would later go on to design the American Radiator Building and the Daily News Building in New York.[49]

The design of the Tribune Tower was a collaborative effort between Howells and Hood. An early sketch by John Mead Howells (figure 3.9) suggests the genesis of the major features of the final design: the arched entranceway set within a simple base, vertical piers rising the height of the building, and an upper tower framed by flying buttresses. Sketches by Raymond Hood show the development of this concept, retaining the basic features but endeavoring to make a more unified form (figure 3.10). Hood also produced a series of detailed studies of the tower and the base and entranceway, all possessing the characteristic features of the final design.[50]

The *Tribune* was lavish in its praise of the winning design, claiming that Howells and Hood had given the *Tribune* "all that its heart was set upon." They gave it beauty and power, with the Gothic crown uttering the *Tribune* ideal: "The colossal flying buttresses which—both literally and spiritually—are the supreme note of the structure seem to us to utter a message of both challenge and guardianship." Best of all, the *Tribune* felt it would lift their new

*Figure 3.9
Design sketch, Tribune
Tower, 1922; John Mead
Howells, architect. Re-
printed from* Architectural
Record *(March 1926),
copyright (1926) by
McGraw-Hill, Inc. All
rights reserved. Repro-
duced with the permission
of the publisher.*

Figure 3.10
Design sketches, Tribune
Tower, 1922; Raymond
Hood, architect. Reprinted
from Architectural Record
(March 1926), copyright
(1926) by McGraw-Hill,
Inc. All rights reserved.
Reproduced with the per-
mission of the publisher.

home out of the category of commercial profit makers and make it an ornament and an inspiration to the city.[51] It was thought that the Howells and Hood design would set a new standard for skyscraper design, a towering symbol by which all others would be measured.

The design was generally well received by the public, though a few members of the architectural community expressed dissatisfaction. Their criticism was generally focused on the incongruity of cladding a steel structure with a Gothic facade and on the seeming artificiality of the buttresses as mere stage scenery with no structural purpose. The most liberal and vocal critics of the design were Chicago architects Thomas Tallmadge, Irving K. Pond, and Louis Sullivan.

Thomas Tallmadge, writing in *Western Architect*, acknowledged the design was "a work of great talent, in fact of such superlative talent that it is impossible to pick any technical flaw in it."[52] He went on, however, to describe its buttresses as highly artificial stage scenery with no useful function. He closed his argument by saying, "As for being the most beautiful building in the world—I doubt it."[53] Irving K. Pond, writing in *The Architectural Forum*, criticized the building in a general way referring to the use of superimposed features to catch the public fancy:

Figure 3.11
Project, Tribune Tower
Competition, 1922; Eliel
Saarinen, architect. Re-
printed from The International Competition for a
New Administration Build-
ing for the Chicago Trib-
une, 1922 *(Chicago, 1922).*

Spiritually, that rare compound of grace, charm
and mystery, is not achieved by setting up a
medieval cathedral tower upon a modern thoroughfare and grouping about it, seemingly, a clus-
ter of vertically elongated chapels.[54]

Louis Sullivan, who did not enter the competition, wrote a criticism of the winning design, ridiculing its "unnecessary gothic tracery" and the "meaningless flying buttresses that top the building but serve no structural purpose."[55] This criticism, published in the *Architectural Record,* contained a lengthy explanation of his theories of art based on American democratic idealism, which were then brought to bear on the winning entry. As with Tallmadge and Pond, he felt that if the Gothic buttresses and decorations at the top were removed, the real building "would reveal itself as a rather amiable, delicate affair with a certain grace of fancy."[56]

It was Eliel Saarinen's second-place design (figure 3.11) that received nearly universal praise from architects and critics alike. Thomas Tallmadge called it a work of unquestioned genius, and Irving Pond considered it the only structurally pure and thoroughly logical solution to the problem of the steel-framed skyscraper.[57] Louis Sullivan heralded it as "a voice, resonant and rich, ringing amidst the wealth and joy of life."[58] Sullivan saw in this design a logic of new order, the logic of living things, and he decried the competition jury for not voting it the first-place winner.[59] The building's simplicity and accentuation of basic structural patterns indicated a new direction in skyscraper design, one that would strongly influence the design of later buildings on North Michigan Avenue.[60]

The third-place entry by Holabird and Roche, like the winning design, had relied on the Gothic style, though its massing and handling of details was not as refined as the Saarinen or Howells and Hood designs (figure 3.12). The style was adequately suggested by a tall base with lancet windows and by a prominent central tower at the top with a colossal lancet window in each facade. As with their design for the John Crerar Library, the intervening office floors were treated with a simple vertical motif of continuous piers and recessed spandrels and with pronounced corner bays.[61] Thomas Tallmadge suggested that the project placed as high as third not because of design quality but because of the elegance of the renderings. He wrote,

> Had it been less dramatically and poetically presented, I feel sure it never would have attained its proud position as a prize winner. Even the authority of the great firm of architects who produced it cannot justify the huge Gothic mass, presumably of masonry, resting on the roof of a

Figure 3.12
Project, Tribune Tower
Competition, 1922; Hola-
bird and Roche, architects.
Reprinted from The International Competition for a
New Administration Build-
ing for the Chicago Trib-
une, 1922 *(Chicago, 1922).*

79

building not Gothic at all except in the detail of its lower story, and it must be confessed none too interesting in the arrangement and decoration of the shaft.[62]

FINAL DESIGN AND CONSTRUCTION

After the announcement ceremonies were concluded and the ensuing arguments subsided, the *Tribune* signed contracts with Howells and Hood to produce the construction drawings and specifications for the building. Robert McCormick continued to actively direct the entire operation, though Holmes Onderdonk was appointed to oversee the day-to-day details on a full-time basis.[63] Working with Howells and Hood were engineers Frank E. Brown and Henry J. Burt, while Holabird and Roche assisted in the preparation of the mechanical plans.[64]

Throughout the design development and production of the working drawings in Hood's office, models played an unusually large role in studying details and proposed changes. Hood's staff made a series of small-scale plaster models (figure 3.13), the first showing only the mass of the building and its relation to surrounding structures. The second, larger model carried the design into the realm of exterior architectural expression with the general lines of the building worked out in greater detail, and the windows and floor levels indicated. A third model at a still larger scale was then made, showing the architectural ornamentation. Finally, individual architectural details were studied at a still larger scale, especially concerning the play of light and shade, relative projections, and contours. When these study models were satisfactory to the architect, three-quarter and full-sized details were prepared from them by draftsmen.[65]

A change was suggested by the *Tribune* in the midst of the building's design development that could have resulted in a radical alteration of the original Howells and Hood proposal. It was precipitated when the Methodist Church of Chicago succeeded in obtaining a variance from the City Council to construct a new building in the Loop 556 feet high, 156 feet taller than the existing building code allowed.[66] This action resulted in a much publicized debate among city officials, builders, and architects, many predicting that Chicago's skyline would take on new heights, unprecedented even by New York. Charles Wacker stated

*Figure 3.13
Design models, Tribune
Tower, 1922–23; Raymond
Hood, architect. Reprinted
from* Architectural Forum
(September 1924).

that he was in favor of "anything within reason which will
develop beauty as well as usefulness in skyscrapers, at the
same time safeguarding surrounding property as to health
and sanitation."[67] Building Commissioner Charles Bostram
stated in opposition:

> If great height is deemed a necessity to beauty let's
> take off the lid. My own opinion, however, is that,
> when health, sanitation, Loop congestion, and the
> right of surrounding property owners is taken into
> consideration, the present occupation limit is
> about right.[68]

The *Tribune* not only supported the action of the City
Council in granting a variance to the Methodist Church,
but it promptly took steps to profit from the initiative,

Figure 3.14
Design sketches, Tribune
Tower, 1923; John Mead
Howells and Raymond
Hood, architects. Re-
printed from Chicago Trib-
une (27 December 1922).

sending Holmes Onderdonk to New York to consult with
Howells and Hood about increasing the height of their pur-
posed building. The architects quickly prepared a series of
drawings (figure 3.14), one with the winning design carried
to a height of 570 feet, and a second based on an altogether
new design carried to a height of 650 feet. The *Tribune*
expressed the conviction that such an increase in height
would greatly add to the beauty and spirituality of the
building, and it lobbied for a permanent change in the
heights allowed in the building code.[69]

In the end, even though the new city zoning ordinance
instituted in 1923 raised the allowable height limit, the
Tribune backed down. Stating that it sought "beauty and
majesty in architecture, rather than the breaking of height
records," the final plans of Howells and Hood called for
only a slight additional height amounting to four stories
more than originally planned.[70] This increase brought the
building's height to 450 feet, still the tallest building to be
erected on North Michigan Avenue until it was superceded
by the Medinah Club Building in 1928–29.[71]

Contracts for the construction of the building were awarded in May 1923 to the Hegeman-Harris Construction Company, a firm headed by John W. Harris. Construction of the steel-frame and limestone-clad building took two years and one month, at a cost of $8,500,000, financed in part by a mortgage from the Prudential Insurance Company.[72] The building opened in June 1925, with the *Tribune* occupying sixteen floors and renting out the remaining twenty.[73]

When built, the Tribune Tower represented everything Robert McCormick had desired in the way of a civic monument both for his company and the city, despite the criticisms of a few isolated architects. It is a sheer visual delight created in exciting and vivid forms. The main tower rises twenty-four stories, with a slight offset at the fifth floor and a larger setback on the building's east side at the twentieth floor. The twenty-fifth level is screened with Gothic tracery behind which rises an octagonal tower that diminishes in diameter in steps at the thirty-third and thirty-fourth floors. At the top is a lantern that serves as a mechanical and electrical penthouse.[74]

The main entrance to the building is emphasized by a recessed opening extending up to the building's third story (figure 3.15), its carved ornamentation suggesting the portal of a cathedral. At the fourth floor, over the entrance arch, is a series of richly carved niches with canopies which are repeated in a simplified form around the three street-level facades, forming a continuous decorative molding. The building's main vertical piers begin at these fourth-floor decorations and rise to the screened parapets and flying buttresses at the top (figure 3.16). As Carl Condit points out in *Chicago 1910–29*, these buttresses appear to receive the brunt of the central tower, though in reality there is no outward thrust exerted on them.[75] Wind bracing of the tower is achieved through the use of knee braces and diagonal bracing in both the horizontal and diagonal planes.[76]

In plan the building was laid out with two central banks of elevators entered on opposite sides from a ring corridor (figure 3.17). The first floor contains a large entrance lobby and was designed for rental spaces on the north and south sides, each with separate entrances through the outer chamfered corners. The *Tribune*'s company offices and the composing rooms are located on the lower floors, while the executive offices are on the twenty-fourth floor. McCormick

Figure 3.15
Tribune Tower, entrance
detail. Courtesy of the Chi-
cago Historical Society.

and fellow editor, Joseph Patterson, had their offices on this floor, with McCormick occupying a large office in the southwest corner and Patterson opposite him on the northwest corner. The octagonal tower contains a single elevator and two stairways in a core in its southeast quadrant, with open office space on the remaining three sides.

It was determined early on in the design development to build decorative cloistered halls for the elevators on each floor and to make the main lobby leading to the elevators lofty and dignified. The reason for this was the idea that it belonged in a communal sense to every tenant in the building. The space taken on the ground floor for a dignified entrance and an ample lobby was regarded as capitalized for the benefit of the rental floors above, and for every tenant in them.[77]

*Figure 3.16
Tribune Tower, parapet
detail. Courtesy of the Chicago Historical Society.*

An addition was built north of the Tribune Tower in 1934 to house the WGN radio station owned by the newspaper (figure 3.18). Done in the same Gothic style as the original building, it rises four stories in an L-shaped plan, creating a small courtyard just north of the tower. It was designed once again by John Mead Howells in association with Raymond Hood and his partner J. André Fouilhoux. Also involved was Chicago architect Leo J. Weissenborn.[78] A few years later, it was followed by an eleven-story addition to the east, effectively completing the development of the *Tribune* block.

Though it was not as prominently located as the Wrigley Building or even the London Guarantee Building, the Tribune Tower nevertheless had an important visual impact on the Michigan Avenue Bridge Plaza (figure 3.19). On

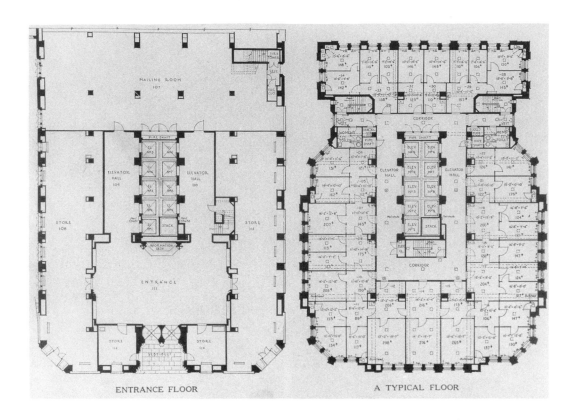

ENTRANCE FLOOR   A TYPICAL FLOOR

Figure 3.17
Tribune Tower plans. Re-
printed from Architectural
Forum *(October 1925).*

Figure 3.18
Tribune Tower Addition,
1934; John Mead Howells
with Hood and Fouilhoux
and Leo J. Weissenborn,
architects. Courtesy of the
Chicago Historical Society.

Figure 3.19
View of North Michigan
Avenue, with Wrigley
Building on the left and the
Tribune Tower on the
right. Courtesy of the Chi-
cago Historical Society.

crossing the bridge to the north, one's attention was drawn immediately past the Wrigley Building and to the Gothic crown of the Tribune Tower. It became a dominant element of North Michigan Avenue, lending it further prestige and creating yet another model to be emulated by other corporations considering a move from the Loop. It would be several decades before the property south of the Tribune, from Hubbard Street to the river, would be developed, but, even so, the ensemble of buildings fronting on the Michigan Avenue Bridge Plaza had by 1925 made it an effective gateway to the city's newest commercial district.

The final location and appearance of the Tribune Tower were as much a product of the city's growth and development as they were the concept of Robert R. McCormick, John Mead Howells, and Raymond Hood. While the publication of a newspaper is a commercial pursuit, Robert McCormick and the *Tribune* attempted to transcend commercial utility with a building that related traditional religious and educational institutions and ideals with their public-oriented enterprise. Though not everyone was happy with the building, its carefully designed appearance and attention to detail demanded the respect of the critics. In the end, the tower would have a direct impact on skyscraper design beyond its own period, and the competition it arose from was regarded as an accurate reflection of what was going on architecturally across the country in the early 1920s.

COMMERCIAL
ARCHITECTURE
OF THE
MID - 1920s

W hile the Tribune Tower was under construction, a number of other building projects were undertaken on the avenue. A second insurance company building was constructed, and a third planned though not built. Three other major commercial buildings were constructed, and two large-scale renovations were begun. The building boom that had started in Chicago early in the decade reached its peak in 1926, with a total value of new construction in the city that year reaching $366,500,000, compared with $79,100,000 in 1920.[1] This feverish spurt of new construction coincided with an increase of 80 percent in office rents and a rise in retail store rents from 100 to 1000 percent.[2]

By the middle of the decade, the transformation of the Michigan Avenue corridor was well under way. Commerce was encroaching upon the residential property of McCormickville, relentlessly pushing residents northward. As the city grew and expanded outward, the old population moved slowly away, to be replaced by more mobile, shifting, middle- and lower-class residents.[3] While business and industry were expanding across the river and up the streets of the Near North Side, and the old residential area deteriorated, the Gold Coast continued to develop as a fashionable apartment and residential district.

CENTRAL LIFE INSURANCE
COMPANY BUILDING

While the London Guarantee Company was the first major insurance company to build on Michigan Avenue, the Central Life Insurance Company was the first to build on the northern portion of the avenue, at the southwest corner of Michigan and Superior, near the Water Tower and Pumping Station (figure 4.1).[4] It was a pioneer in this part of the district, the first builder of a large office structure so far from the Loop. The site, at one time owned by Cyrus H. McCormick, measured only fifty-four feet in width on Michigan Avenue and sixty-eight feet on Superior Street.[5] Built in 1923–24, the building was designed by D. H. Burnham and Company, then headed by Daniel Burnham's sons, Daniel H. and Hubert Burnham. The two had been partners in their father's firm until his death in 1912. They were then partners in Graham, Burnham and Company

Figure 4.1
Central Life Insurance
Company Building, 720
North Michigan Avenue,
1922; D. H. Burnham and
Company, architects.
Courtesy of the Chicago
Historical Society.

Figure 4.2
Central Life Insurance
Company Building. Re-
printed from the Chicago
Tribune *(17 December*
1922).

until 1917, at which time they reestablished D. H. Burn-ham and Company.[6] Stylistically, they carried on the neo-classical and Renaissance forms their father had so brilliantly used since the Columbian Exposition.

The Central Life Insurance Company of Illinois was organized in 1907 in Ottawa, Illinois, its primary business being the sale of twenty-year term insurance. The company's founders included several judges, nearly all from the town of Ottawa. Judge H. W. Johnson was made president while Charles Nadler was named a vice-president. The company's early business had been concentrated in the rural areas around Ottawa, thought by the company's directors to be conservative and safe for the organization. Upon moving its headquarters to Chicago, it changed its business focus to the urban center, albeit in "a careful way."[7] The company grew steadily throughout the decade until its assets exceeded $7,000,000 and its insurance policies amounted to nearly $60,000,000.[8] Like the London Guarantee Building, this structure was meant to be a monument to the company's success in the insurance field.

The building rose sixteen stories on its narrow lot and contained the insurance company's offices on the upper floors, with rental offices on the intermediate floors and shops at the street level (figure 4.2). The first two levels were clad with rusticated limestone, while the third floor was heavily decorated with terra cotta details. The office floors rose uninterrupted from there to the fifteenth floor, which was again highly decorated and topped by a projecting cornice. Above was a penthouse featuring a prominent Palladian window motif.

The building was criticized at the time of its construction for the lack of any architectural treatment on the west wall. The *Chicago Tribune* stated:

> The west wall, overlooking one of the finest sections of the north side, unfortunately will not be the same as the north and east fronts, although it will loom up almost as conspicuously. It would seem that the owners should give the question consideration . . . This west wall won't be shut off from view for a great many years—in fact, never completely—and it would seem good business to make the building as attractive as possible from the west.[9]

It was now common practice, however, for designers of high-rise buildings on the avenue to concentrate their design efforts on the facades visible from Michigan Avenue and the side streets while leaving the rear walls unadorned, usually of yellow brick. As with the London Guarantee Building, it was generally thought that other buildings of similar height would eventually be erected behind these buildings, thus shielding undecorated walls from view. During the 1920s, however, this occurred very seldom on North Michigan Avenue, as buildings of such height were too scattered and property on the blocks to the east and west would continue to be developed with low-rise buildings or, at worst, cleared and left vacant for parking.

NATIONAL LIFE INSURANCE COMPANY PROJECT

One developer who tried unsuccessfully throughout the early and middle years of the 1920s to erect an office building on North Michigan Avenue was Albert M. Johnson, president of the National Life Insurance Company. His first plans called for a building to be located at the corner of Michigan Avenue and Erie Street, a twenty-story structure with a prominent corner tower.[10] Then, in January 1922, he revealed plans for a second office building of similar form to be located on the block bounded by Michigan Avenue, Chestnut, Rush, and Pearson streets (figure 4.3), the site occupied by the houses of John and Charles Farwell just north of the Water Tower.[11]

Publicized as Chicago's greatest office building, it was to be larger than the Continental Bank Building, covering an area of 67,000 square feet, with 214 feet fronting on Michigan Avenue and 327 feet on Chestnut. Its cost was to be $7,000,000.[12] Johnson stated,

> Our plan to build on such a large scale is to provide for future expansion and also to participate in the unmistakable trend to upper Michigan Avenue. The time is coming when great buildings will line the boulevard, making it one of the showplaces in the country.[13]

Johnson chose as the architect for his building the same firm that designed the Wrigley Building: Graham, Anderson, Probst and White. Their design consisted of a main block rising 260 feet and a prominent square tower rising to 400 feet at the building's southeast corner. Though not as lavishly decorated as the Wrigley Building, it nevertheless shared its impressive siting on the avenue, its gleaming

white terra cotta cladding, and its corporate grandeur. Because Michigan Avenue makes a jog in its path at Chicago
Avenue, the building's tower would have been visible the
entire length of the avenue from the bridge plaza, just as
the Wrigley Building tower is visible from Randolph Street
and beyond. There was an emphasis on verticality in both
the tower and the main block of the building with pronounced vertical piers rising uninterrupted to pointed
arched windows at the top. Small spires were to rise from
each corner of the building while a single large spire rose
from the center of the tower.

Apparently unsatisfied with the Graham, Anderson,
Probst and White design, Albert Johnson abandoned the
scheme shortly after its announcement and plunged into a
higher realm of architectural creativity by commissioning
Frank Lloyd Wright to produce yet another design for his
proposed office building. "I want a virgin, Mr. Wright—a

virgin!" he explained as the two met early in 1923 to discuss the project.[14] Agreeing to pay Wright $20,000 for studies for a new kind of skyscraper, Johnson decided that his structure should be something completely different from the Wrigley Building, that it should be a totally new and unique kind of corporate symbol.[15]

The life and career of Frank Lloyd Wright are well known already, but it should be noted that the 1920s were not happy or successful years for him; it was a time when he had few commissions and was plagued by extensive marital and financial difficulties.[16] He had finished his plans for the Midway Gardens in 1914, and from 1916 to 1922 he spent much of his time in Japan overseeing the construction of the Imperial Hotel. Upon returning to the United States, he undertook two large commissions, including a huge ranch complex near Los Angeles (1921) for Edward Doheny, president of the Pan-American Oil Company, and a summer colony for Lake Tahoe (1922–23), neither of which was built.[17] In 1924 Wright designed several concrete houses in California, four of which utilized the textile-block system he developed for the Mrs. George Millard House. Stylistically the forms of Wright's work in the 1920s drew from architecture of disparate sources: the International style, Mayan Revival, and the Southwest American Indian.[18]

Problems in his personal life greatly affected Wright's career during this period. Separated from his first wife, Catherine Wright, he suffered the additional tragedy in 1914 of the murder of his lover Mamah Borthwick. This was followed by a tumultuous relationship and marriage to Miriam Noel in 1924. The ensuing years were filled with lawsuits and countersuits between him and Miriam, so interrupting his practice that he built almost nothing during the great boom years of the late 1920s.[19] He made an attempt in 1924 to establish a creditable practice when he announced that after January 1, 1925, he would make his home in Chicago—where he was preparing an office at 19 Cedar Street to accommodate twelve draftsmen—and devote himself exclusively to commercial architecture.[20] But neither his Cedar Street studio nor his commercial practice materialized as his battles with Miriam Noel kept him broke and unsettled.[21]

At the time he designed the National Life Insurance Company Building in May of 1923 there was still cause for optimism in Wright's career, his California houses being yet a new direction in his creative outpouring. He designed

for Johnson an equally unique building composed of four intricately detailed office units set against a main tower-spine, with cantilevered floors and copper and glass curtain walls (figure 4.4).[22] Wright hoped to achieve an architecture especially suited to the country's institutions, values, and goals that in principle exalted freedom and individuality.[23] In doing so, he manipulated elemental geometric shapes into new arrangements challenging preconceptions about the appropriate form for high-rise structures. His extensive use of glass was an attempt to abandon the traditional box with punched holes. On the interior, his aim was to achieve a spatial quality that related to external space, a free-flowing space uninhibited by closed corners, in section as well as plan.

Wright published his plans for the National Life Building in the *Architectural Record* in October 1928, describing it as "a practical solution of the skyscraper problem."[24] He emphasized the building's copper and glass facades, designed to disappear in the sense that they were non-load-bearing, standardized sheet copper and glass screens, lacking any apparent weight or thickness. Windows were to be individual units in the screen fabric, opening singly or in groups at the will of the occupant. Vertical copper mullions were to serve as sunshades projecting as much or as little shadow on the glass as desired.[25] Supporting piers were to be set back from the walls, with the floors becoming cantilevered slabs (figure 4.5), and they were to become exposed buttresses on the upper floors where the walls stepped back. All interior wall partitions were to be movable, made up in sections complete with doors and ready to be set in place.[26] Stairways were to be located at the ends of the four projecting wings (figure 4.6), their location on the south facade being marked by projecting bays of continuous vertical copper panels ending in the upper floors in a series of Mayan-inspired geometric arrangements. The walls of the first two floors were to be plate glass for the maximum exposure of street-level shops.

Along with his revolutionary design, Wright proposed an equally radical construction system, that of prefabrication. Every element of the building, apart from its concrete structural frame, would have been produced in the shop and assembled in the field, a method he knew to be economically superior to conventional construction techniques. He wrote, "In this design, architecture has been frankly profitably, and artistically taken from the field to the factory—standardized as might be any mechanical thing whatever, from a penny-whistle to a piano."[27] He wrote further,

> My aim in this fabrication employing the cantilever system of construction which proved to be effective in preserving the Imperial Hotel in Tokyo, was to achieve absolute scientific utility by means of the Machine—to accomplish—first of all—a true standardization which would not only serve as a basis for keeping the life of the building true as architecture, but enable me to project the whole, as an expression of a valuable principle involved, into a genuine living—architecture of the present.[28]

Details of the building were Mayan in character similar to his Hollyhock House of the same period. Geometric patterns and extended verticals and horizontals all suggested

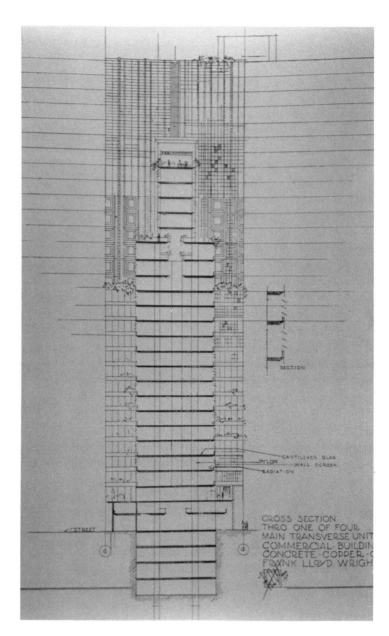

*Figure 4.5
Project, National Life Insurance Company Building
section. Reprinted from
Architectural Record (October 1928), copyright
(1928) by McGraw-Hill,
Inc. All rights reserved.
Reproduced with the permission of the publisher.*

Mayan influence. The building would have been an unconventional corporate symbol, its overt Mayan imagery and its juxtaposition of volumes being unlike anything else on the avenue, or in the rest of Chicago for that matter.

Frank Lloyd Wright was an avid critic of the skyscraper as it proliferated in Chicago and New York. He saw the typical urban commercial structure as causing undue congestion and blocking out light and air from the side-

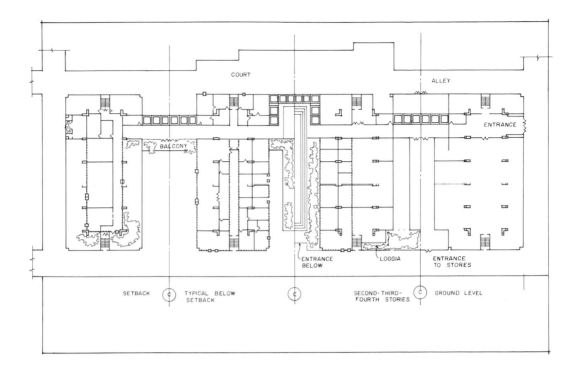

COURT ALLEY

ENTRANCE

BALCONY

ENTRANCE
BELOW   LOGGIA   ENTRANCE
TO STORES

SETBACK   ℄   TYPICAL BELOW
SETBACK   ℄   SECOND-THIRD-
FOURTH STORIES   ℄   GROUND LEVEL

walk, all for the purpose of greater individual profit. He wrote, "From a humane standpoint the super-concentration of the skyscraper is super-imposition not worth its human price."[29] He felt the only appropriate place for high-rise buildings was in a suburban or rural setting where they could be isolated on the landscape and cause a minimal disturbance to other buildings around them. His concept for the National Life Insurance Company Building, with its multiple glass-enclosed wings, was an attempt to mediate between the urban skyscraper tower and low-rise infill buildings by expanding horizontally, letting sun and light filter down to the street level.

Unfortunately for Wright and for Chicago, Albert Johnson was unable to arrange adequate financing for the project, and thus it was never built. This was a great disappointment to Wright and a profound loss of public achievement.[30] Had it been built, it would have dramatically changed the appearance of North Michigan Avenue both in terms of urban form and architectural style. It would have formed a wide crystalline backdrop for the Water Tower and would have been an effective termination point for that part of Michigan Avenue from the Wrigley Building to Chicago Avenue. It would have introduced a

Figure 4.6
Project, National Life Insurance Company plan.
Redrawn by author from Architectural Record *(October 1928), copyright (1928)* by McGraw-Hill, Inc. All rights reserved. Reproduced with the permission of the publisher.

new architectural style, one derivative not of European precedents but of Mayan and American Indian sources, a design statement that could have had a significant influence on subsequent architecture on the avenue.

Wright would utilize the idea for a cantilevered mid-rise building again in 1929 in a project for an apartment block for William Norman Gutherie's Saint Mark in the Bowery Church in New York. It was to have three octagonal towers with alternating vertical and horizontal facades, with cantilevered floors and copper and glass walls. This was followed in 1930 by a project for grouped apartment towers in Chicago and for the Elizabeth Noble Apartment House in Los Angeles. All were abandoned during the Depression. Although Wright secured fewer commissions in the 1920s than in the previous decades of his career, several of them, particularly the National Life Building, could well have turned around his career and made him once again an important contributor to Chicago architecture.[31]

BELL BUILDING

The Bell Building, at the northeast corner of Michigan and South Water Street (figure 4.7), was the first high rise to be built on the narrow strip of land south of the river between Michigan Avenue and the Illinois Central railroad yards.[32] It was built in 1924 by Herbert E. Bell, president of the Bell and Zoller Coal Company, for a cost of $3,000,000.[33] At the time of its construction, the twenty-three-story building occupied a conspicuous position because of the jog in the avenue at the bridge. Even though it was a block away from the bridge, it formed a termination point for the avenue from the north just as the Wrigley Building did from the south (figure 4.8).

It was located on the former site of the homestead of Jean Baptiste Beaubien, and just south of the original Fort Dearborn, a location rich in historical tradition. Bell had purchased the west portion of the property, containing a four-story brick building, in 1917. The lot measured 130 feet along Michigan Avenue and was seventy-five feet deep.[34] The following year, however, a sixty-three-foot-wide strip was taken by the city to widen the avenue, leaving him with only twelve feet of buildable area. At first he proceeded with plans to build a twelve-foot-wide building, but at the last minute he was able to acquire the adjoining property, and the way was made clear to erect the present structure.[35]

Figure 4.7
Bell Building, (Old Repub-
lic Building), 307 North
Michigan Avenue, 1924;
Karl Martin Vitzhum, ar-
chitect. Courtesy of the
Chicago Historical Society.

The architect of the Bell Building, German-born and educated Karl Martin Vitzhum, had worked for D. H. Burnham and Company in the early 1900s before starting his own practice in 1919.[36] His design for the Bell Building is in some ways a simplified version of the nearby London Guarantee Building, with a modified triumphal arch motif

Figure 4.8
Bell Building in 1925.
Courtesy of the Chicago
Historical Society.

at the entrance (figure 4.9), and smooth vertical piers rising through the office floors to support a double-story colonnade at the top. The first level and the mezzanine floor were divided into shop spaces, and a large restaurant was located in the basement. The building's base is clad with beige-colored granite, while the upper floors are clad with terra cotta.

MICHIGAN-OHIO BUILDING

The Michigan-Ohio Building, at the northwest corner of Michigan Avenue and Ohio Street (figure 4.10), was built in 1924 both as a rental office building and as an anchor location for a Thompson Restaurant, at the time a well-known restaurant chain noted for its white-tile decor and twenty-four-hour service. This was the first major real estate venture for the company's flamboyant president, John R. Thompson, Jr., who had inherited the restaurant business founded by his father and became its president at the

*Figure 4.9
Bell Building, entrance detail. Photo by author.*

age of thirty. He rapidly expanded the business until he
had a chain of 120 restaurants in forty-two states, all advertising with the slogan, "Thompson's Restaurants Must
Be a Good Place to Eat!"[37]

Thompson had negotiated for this Ohio Street site for
over a year before finally signing a long-term lease that allowed him to construct a new building. Initially, the lot
measured 100 by 75 feet. He commissioned Alfred Alschuler, who had just completed the London Guarantee Building, to design a six-story terra cotta-clad building, a rendering of which was published in the *Chicago Tribune* in
January 1924.[38] Shortly afterward, however, Thompson
was able to negotiate a lease for the adjacent lot to the west,
and he asked Alschuler to produce a new design for a building two stories taller and of a more distinct appearance.
The cost of the first design was to have been $500,000; that
of the second was approximately $800,000.[39]

*Figure 4.10
Michigan-Ohio Building,
612 North Michigan Ave-
nue, 1924; Alfred S. Al-
schuler, architect. Cour-
tesy of the Chicago
Historical Society.*

As built, it rises eight stories and contains shops and a restaurant on the first two floors with offices above. Clad with Indiana limestone, the shop levels were originally rusticated while the upper floors have a smooth-faced surface, with projecting quoins defining the corner bays. A round-arched doorway at the north end of the Michigan Avenue facade marks the entrance to the elevator lobby, an elegant space with marble walls and bronze trim.

A typical Thompson "white tiled armchair rapid fire food emporium" was located in the building's corner street-level space. Three other stores faced the avenue, and shops also occupied the second floor, with offices on the upper six. The top floor was arranged for studios and architects' offices. The building was completed and occupied in May 1925. Shortly afterward, Thompson either changed his mind about operating a rental office building or else he decided to take a quick profit, because he sold the building in the summer of that year to the Michigan-Ohio Building Corporation for $1,000,000.[40]

*Figure 4.11
Hibbard, Spencer, Bartlett
and Company Building,
northeast corner of Michigan Avenue Bridge Plaza,
1926; Graham, Anderson,
Probst and White, archi-
tects. Photo by author.*

HIBBARD, SPENCER, BARTLETT
AND COMPANY BUILDING

Although it did not front directly on North Michigan Avenue, the huge warehouse building on the north side of the
river, known before its demolition in 1989 as the Mandel
Building, was by its sheer size one of the avenue's most
imposing structures (figure 4.11). Built in 1926 for Hibbard, Spencer, Bartlett and Company, the structure
served as a warehouse for its wholesale hardware business.[41] Containing 900,000 square feet in fourteen stories
and one basement level, it was the largest in the country to
be devoted exclusively to hardware storage. It represented
a total investment in land and building of $6,000,000.[42]

Designed by the firm of Graham, Anderson, Probst and
White, the building was composed of brown brick walls articulated with pilasters framing recessed bands of windows,
and continuous horizontal limestone belt-courses highlight-
ing the top and bottom floors. There was no decoration on
the building's wall surfaces, though there were suggestions

105

of corner towers, calling to mind a medieval fortress. An unusual feature of the building was its trapezoidal site, causing the building to be skewed slightly from the north-south axis and its end walls to be at odd angles to the side walls. The building's south wall fronted directly on the river while the James S. Kirk soap factory originally stood between it and Michigan Avenue. It formed an effective backdrop for the Michigan Avenue Bridge Plaza, hiding from view the still unsightly industrial riverfront that extended out to the lake, and it further served as a strong counterbalance to the Wrigley Building and the Tribune Tower, giving better proportion to their dominant vertical lines.

LAKE-MICHIGAN BUILDING

The Lake-Michigan Building, at the southwest corner of Lake Street and Michigan Avenue, was built in 1926–27 by a corporation headed by Charles L. Schwerin and Frederick T. Hoyt (figure 4.12).[43] Designed to house offices and street-level shops, as with other buildings on the avenue, it was marketed as having an advantageous location, commanding a view of the lake, Michigan Avenue, and Grant Park, and it was pointed out that it was close to transportation, yet removed from the congestion of older sections of the city.[44] Schwerin and Hoyt selected as their architect Alfred S. Alschuler, who designed in this case a twenty-three-story building with an arched entranceway, continuous vertical piers, and intermittent decorative projecting spandrels.[45] The building's uppermost floor is stepped back, and the parapets are decorated with Mayan-inspired motifs that may have been influenced by Wright's design for the National Life Insurance Company Building.[46]

The two partners responsible for developing the Lake-Michigan Building were both veterans of Chicago real estate development. Charles L. Schwerin was the president of the Buildings Development Company of Illinois and of the Beedee Management Company, and he worked as an active promoter of Chicago real estate.[47] Frederick T. Hoyt was likewise a real estate manager and developer, who went into partnership with Schwerin in 1926 to develop not only the Lake-Michigan Building but also an apartment building at 1209 Astor Street.[48]

Their interest in the Lake-Michigan Building was of a purely speculative nature, having financed its construction with a mortgage bond issue underwritten by Lawrence

*Figure 4.12
Lake-Michigan Building,
(Harvester Building), 180
North Michigan Avenue,
1926–27; Alfred S. Alschuler, architect. Courtesy of
the Chicago Historical Society.*

Stern and Company and the First Trust and Savings Bank, and then hiring a series of professional management companies to operate it and keep it filled with tenants.[49] Among them were the General Motors Acceptance Corporation, the Lundoff Bicknell Contracting Company, and several advertising, architectural, and real estate firms.[50] In 1936, it became known as the Harvester Building when International Harvester became the sole tenant.

FARWELL BUILDING

The Farwell Building, at the northwest corner of Michigan Avenue and Erie Street, is an unusually good example of French-inspired architecture used to create an elegant setting for offices and exclusive shops (figures 4.13 and 4.14).[51] Built by Arthur L. Farwell in 1926–27, its intent

Figure 4.13
Farwell Building, 664
North Michigan Avenue,
1926–27, Philip B. Maher,
architect. Reprinted from
Architecture *(February*
1929) (Charles Scribner's
Sons, New York).

was to convey an element of prestige and suggest a sense of
cultural attainment. In particular it was meant to appeal to
the sensibilities of Chicago society and to provide a place
for fashionable display and social interaction. It was even
the home for a number of years of the famous Institute for
Psychoanalysis, directed by Dr. Franz Alexander. Com-
menting on the building and its location, Lloyd Wendt
wrote that "the lady who has just bared her psyche can go
across the street to Saks Fifth Avenue or to the new Helena
Rubinstein Salon."[52]

The building's owner, Arthur Farwell, was the son of John V. Farwell, who had built his mansion at the northwest corner of Pine and Pearson streets in the 1880s.[53] Arthur had been vice-chairman of the board of his father's wholesale dry goods store until 1925, when it was purchased by Carson Pirie Scott and Company.[54] From the proceeds of this sale along with a loan from the Northwestern Mutual Life Insurance Company he was able to finance a building project of this size. He already owned the property, having purchased it in 1912, and he owned other property on North Michigan Avenue, including the northwest corner at Ontario Street and the northeast corner at Superior Street.[55]

Farwell commissioned Chicago architect Philip B. Maher to design the building.[56] The son of noted Prairie School architect George W. Maher, he had studied at the University of Michigan and traveled extensively in Europe before establishing his own practice in an office just off North Michigan Avenue, at 157 East Erie Street. He gained his reputation by designing buildings for the Chicago Town and Tennis Club and the Glencoe Women's Club as well as numerous residences on the North Shore. His proximity to North Michigan Avenue and his success with the Farwell Building eventually led to a number of subsequent commissions for buildings on the avenue, including the Woman's Chicago Athletic Club, the Blackstone Shop, Jacque's Shop, the Malabry Court Building, and the Erskine-Danforth Building.[57]

His design for the eleven-story Farwell Building features prominent vertical piers clad with Indiana limestone, round-arched corner entrances (figure 4.15), and a stepped-back upper level topped by a Mansard roof form which was prefigured in Jules Guerin's 1909 rendering of North Michigan Avenue for the Chicago Plan. The Farwell Building, however, is distinctly different from these proposed structures because of its size. Rather than filling out an entire block like those buildings proposed by Guerin and Burnham, the Farwell Building is less than a quarter of a block in size. With the exception of a few buildings like the Drake Hotel and the Wrigley Building, multiple ownership of the properties on any given block made it virtually impossible to carry out the kind of large-scale structures proposed by Burnham or the North Central Business District Association. The Farwell Building was as good a compromise as could be expected under the circumstances.

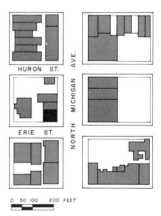

*Figure 4.14
Farwell Building site plan.
Drawn by author.*

Figure 4.15
Farwell Building, shop
front detail. Reprinted
from Architecture *(Febru-*
ary 1929) (Charles Scrib-
ner's Sons, New York).

The building was completed in October 1927, and it was fully rented within six months. It received the gold medal for design from the Lake Shore Trust and Savings Bank in 1928.[58]

John Bollenbacher, a member of the jury, stated:

> This building combines to a remarkable degree good architectural design, a well worked out plan, and a fine use of materials on the part of the architecture.
>
> It is also evident that the owner gave the architect the fullest cooperation and encouragement and deserves a great deal of credit. The design is distinctive and outstanding among the buildings submitted.[59]

MALABRY COURT AND ERSKINE-DANFORTH BUILDINGS

Of the other commercial office and shop buildings designed by Philip Maher on North Michigan Avenue, the Malabry

Figure 4.16
Malabry Court Building,
571 North Michigan Ave-
nue, 1926; Philip B.
Maher, architect. Re-
printed from Architectural
Record *(February 1928),*
copyright (1928) by
McGraw-Hill, Inc. All
rights reserved. Repro-
duced with the permission
of the publisher.

Court and Erskine-Danforth buildings were significant for
their reliance on carefully selected historical styles, one the
French Directoire, the other the Georgian Revival. Maher
was especially adept at handling a wide range of architectural styles, which he could use to create individual commercial settings according to the needs of a particular
client. Both of these projects were remodelings of already
existing structures, and both added greatly to the commercial ambience of the avenue.

The Malabry Court Building (figure 4.16) at 571 North
Michigan Avenue was developed in 1926 by Chester and
Raymond Cook, who had constructed the Italian Court
Building in 1919.[60] In fact, they purchased both sites the
same year. The site originally had three brick townhouses
that were three stories in height, with first-floor entrances
about five feet above ground level. These buildings extended approximately sixty feet back of the building line,
leaving sixty-seven feet at the rear of the lot undeveloped.

Property values made it expedient to utilize the entire
plot, so Maher constructed a new building in the rear area
and remodeled the front buildings for shops, three on each
floor. The new addition contained an art gallery on the first
floor and apartments on the upper two (figure 4.17). These

111

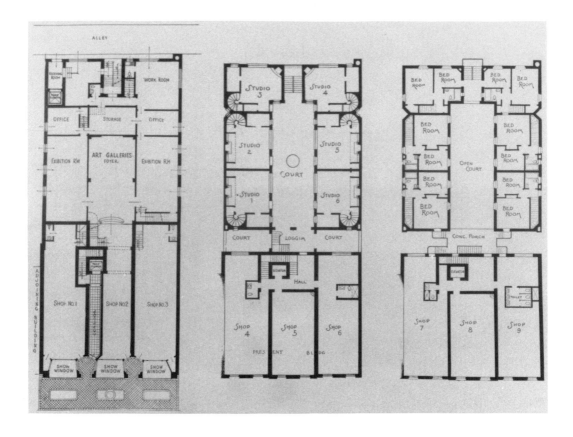

*Figure 4.17
Malabry Court Building
plans. Reprinted from Ar-
chitectural Record (February 1928), copyright (1928)
by McGraw-Hill, Inc. All
rights reserved. Repro-
duced with the permission
of the publisher.*

apartments were arranged around an open courtyard (figure 4.18), each with its own entrance and each containing
a studio-living space on the lower level with two bedrooms
upstairs. Each living room had a large window facing the
courtyard. Combining to create a general European effect
were wrought iron rails, grilles, lanterns, stone doorways,
and window planters.[61]

The French Directoire treatment of the facade was
achieved through the use of Indiana limestone, a slate roof,
wrought iron grills, large windows, and a well-balanced,
dignified ornamentation. The original intention had been to
retain the brick fronts, but the limestone was added instead
to give the structure a sense of newness. Large shop windows were installed on the ground floor, with two archways
providing entrances to the shops and elevator lobby.[62]
When Malabry Court was completed it too won a gold
medal from the Lake Shore Trust and Savings Bank for the
best remodeled building of the year on the Near North
Side.[63]

*Figure 4.18
Malabry Court Building,
courtyard. Reprinted from*
Architectural Record *(February 1928), copyright
(1928) by McGraw-Hill,
Inc. All rights reserved.
Reproduced with the permission of the publisher.*

Maher was commissioned to remodel a former coffee
warehouse at the southwest corner of North Michigan Avenue and Ontario Street for the Erskine-Danforth Corporation in 1928.[64] To make it suitable to house the company's retail furniture store he converted the four-story
brick structure into a five-story building and added limestone cladding on the first floor and red brick above, with
three elegant Palladian windows on the second floor (figure
4.19). The design followed a Georgian precedent, and it reflected the distinctive type of furniture made by the company, based on the Georgian and early American styles.[65]

Remodeling projects like the Malabry Court and
Erskine-Danforth buildings were quite common on the
Near North Side throughout the 1920s. It was a convenient
and relatively inexpensive way to take advantage of inflat-

Figure 4.19
Erskine-Danforth Build-
ing, 620 North Michigan
Avenue, 1928; Philip B.
Maher, architect. Photo by
author.

ing prices in a rapidly developing area of the city. Dilapidated buildings could be bought at low prices, renovated,
and held to a future date when surrounding development forced up their value. There were numerous Mc-
Cormickville mansions on Michigan Avenue, Rush Street,
and the cross streets that were remodeled mainly for small
and exclusive shops, as they had a special appeal to shoppers attracted by the intimate scale and decorative architecture. Each was done in a different style taking advantage of the advertising qualities of distinctive design motifs.
At 150 East Erie Street, for instance, was a converted residence with a quaint English facade; at 115 East Chicago
Avenue was a converted residence with a new Venetian
style facade. Further north, along Walton Place and Oak
Street, were a number of similarly remodeled buildings, all
suggesting a festive, European atmosphere.[66]

HOTEL, CLUB, AND RESIDENTIAL ARCHITECTURE

W hile commercial and office buildings predominated on North Michigan Avenue in the 1920s,
there were also residential, hotel, and club
buildings erected along its path, especially near
its northern end. This location was at the center
of the middle- and upper-class residential devel-
opments of Streeterville and the Gold Coast,
near Lincoln Park, yet close to the center of the city. Being
ideal for high density residential development, there was a
great demand for living space in the area. While the apartments and hotels provided luxurious living quarters, social
and athletic clubs provided places for social gatherings, living accommodations, and entertainment and exercise facilities.

At the time of the World's Fair of 1893, Chicago had
about fifty hotels, most of them located in the city's downtown area and on the South Side. More were built during
the 1910s and early 1920s, including the Blackstone, Stevens, Morrison, and Bismarck hotels, with an increase of
some 10,000 rooms.[1] There were few hotels located north
of the river, the Virginia and the Plaza being among the
largest. With the widening of North Michigan Avenue and
the rush to the Gold Coast, however, millions of dollars
were spent on erecting hotels on the North Side during the
1920s, this area alone gaining nearly 20,000 rooms. The
Drake Hotel, at the corner of Michigan Avenue and Oak
Street, was the first, followed by a series of residential and
resort hotels built in the same area and further north, beyond Lincoln Park, including the Edgewater Beach, Ambassador, Belmont, Belden-Stratford, Pearson, and the
Sheridan. By 1929, there were nearly 300 hotels citywide.[2]

These hotels were developed both in response to the city's growing tourist and convention trade and to a growing number of wealthy families who owned a suburban house and lived intermittently in a hotel when they wanted to be closer to downtown. The large apartment building was developed in direct response to the residential requirements of the rapidly expanding North Side population. A further impetus for this form of urban residential living was the growth of a new type of real estate ownership: the cooperative apartment where both the land and building were owned jointly by the tenants.[3] This arrangement combined all the housekeeping conveniences and economic advantages of apartment living with the satisfaction that accompanies private home ownership. Called "Home Clubs" in New York, they were organized with a certain amount of stock entitling the owner to a long-term lease. These leases were generally transferable only to parties acceptable to other members of the club.[4] As with the nineteenth-century mansions of the Gold Coast, the architect had to design both luxurious interiors and an impressive facade, but now for a collective ownership and numerous tenants with a wide variety of tastes. The apartment buildings and cooperatives of the district all exhibited similar characteristics, which became standard for this kind of construction. Facades were generally simple, dignified, and restrained, with ornaments restricted to the upper and lower stories and the mid-sections left largely unadorned. The entrances and lobbies at the street level were given the greatest architectural elaboration.

One of the earliest of the larger apartment buildings in the area was the Raymond Apartment Building at 920 North Michigan Avenue, designed by Benjamin Marshall in 1900. Rising eight stories, this structure was distinguished for its round-arched windows on the top floor and prominent bay windows on the north side.[5] Other nearby Gold Coast apartment buildings included 1100 and 999 Lake Shore Drive, along with 199, 209, and 179 East Lake Shore Drive, all designed by Benjamin Marshall (figure 5.1).[6]

A number of other architects also contributed to the apartment building boom of the area. Fugard and Knapp built 229 and 219 East Lake Shore Drive; Howard Van Doren Shaw designed a nine-story building at 1130 North Lake Shore Drive in 1910; William Ernest Walker designed buildings at 936 Lake Shore Drive and 942 Lake Shore Drive. Robert DeGolyer designed three apartment buildings in the area from 1916 to 1918, including 200 East

Pearson Street, 1242 and 1430 Lake Shore Drive, and 1120 Lake Shore Drive in 1924–25.[7]

Besides its commercial and residential character, the Near North Side was described in the December 1927 issue of the *North Central Journal* as "the city's great clubhouse district."[8] At least eighteen clubs were located there, taking advantage of the proximity to the Loop, the attractive surroundings, and the nearness to the lake. Most of the city's elite belonged to a club, many of them to several. They provided a place for men and women alike from different professions, businesses, and social positions to meet over lunch, carry on business while exercising, or to intermingle at balls and debuts.

Two of Chicago's famous women's clubs were built on North Michigan Avenue: the Illinois Women's Athletic Club at 820 North Michigan, and the Woman's Chicago Athletic Club at 626 North Michigan. These organizations became especially popular in the 1920s when women of families of great wealth took it upon themselves to construct club buildings either in the Loop or on the Near North Side.[9] Many of these had a philanthropic purpose, but all were principally concerned with fostering the social interaction of the city's wealthiest members of society.

Figure 5.1
View looking south at Oak Street and Lake Shore Drive, 1930. Reprinted from Paul T. Gilbert and Charles L. Bryson, Chicago and Its Makers *(Chicago, 1929).*

Figure 5.2
Drake Hotel, southeast
corner of Michigan Avenue
and Oak Street, 1919–20;
Marshall and Fox, archi-
tects. Courtesy of the Chi-
cago Historical Society.

DRAKE HOTEL

The first of two hotels built on North Michigan Avenue was
the Drake. Designed by Marshall and Fox for a site at the
avenue's northern end (figure 5.2), it was constructed at
the same time as the Wrigley Building.[10] Standing fourteen
stories and filling nearly a full city block, it was a sentinel
on North Michigan Avenue (figure 5.3) to complement the
Blackstone Hotel on South Michigan Avenue, which had
also been built by John C. and Tracy B. Drake, whose father had been one of Chicago's pioneer hotel managers.[11]
The Drake was designed to be one of the city's most lavish
and exclusive hotels, built to take advantage of the postwar
resumption of business and vacation travel. Located on the
east side of Michigan Avenue, it was built on land created
by the Lincoln Park Board in the 1890s that was part of
the extensive holdings of the Potter Palmer estate.[12]

The construction of a hotel at this location had been
anticipated for several years, a number of proposals having
been announced only to be thwarted by a lack of capital.
As early as 1911 the Palmer estate contemplated building a
hotel on the site, but in the following year it began negoti-

ating to sell the site to hotel operator George H. Gazley who proposed the construction of a hotel building in the French Renaissance style designed by Holabird and Roche. This structure was to be ten stories high, its plan in the shape of a U enclosing a raised terrace that would provide tennis courts, promenades, and a tea garden. The interior decorations were to be modeled after the palatial architecture of late seventeenth-century England, "rich, dignified, and homelike."[13] Gazley never actually purchased the site, however, and negotiations with the Palmer estate eventually broke off when it became evident he could not raise the funds necessary to carry out the project.

The site was finally sold in 1916 to the Drake brothers, who stated that Chicago was to have the finest and most up-to-date hotel in the world, rivaling that of anything in New York City.[14] The Drake brothers' plans for the building were interrupted by World War I, but in 1919 they established the Whitestone Hotel Company, organized under a complex, though exemplary, financing scheme arranged by S. W. Straus and Company in which capital to design and construct the building was provided for by issues of stock and mortgage bonds.[15]

The Drakes estimated that the earning power of the hotel would be as great as any metropolitan hotel of its size ever constructed. The area of the property, 400 by 216 feet, was more than six times larger than that of the Blackstone Hotel, while the cost of the land was less. With 800 rooms, the capacity of the Drake was over double that of the Blackstone. It was estimated that when fully occupied with 1100 guests the daily income would be $4,400 for rooms alone. Added to this would be an equal amount from restaurant and shop rentals, thus making a daily earning power of nearly $10,000. It was further estimated that expenses of maintenance and operation would cost less than half of this, and that it would take no more than 60 percent of capacity to produce earnings sufficient enough to pay the interest and dividends on the securities.[16] The company prospectus pointed out that the Blackstone had always paid the dividends on its preferred and common stock even through the war period when the hotel business was greatly affected by a nearly complete halt of all social functions.

So attractive was the financial package for the new hotel, estimated to cost $5,000,000, that all of the stock certificates and bonds were bought up immediately by a few of the Drake brothers' closest friends, including members of the Armour, Swift, McCormick, and Palmer families, as

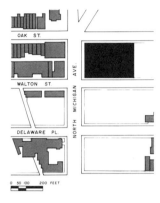

*Figure 5.3
Drake Hotel site plan.
Drawn by author.*

well as the building's architects, Marshall and Fox. Tracy Drake was the company's president and John Drake served as treasurer, while architect Benjamin Marshall was vice-president and his partner, Charles Fox, was secretary.[17] Marshall and Fox took an ownership position in the company in lieu of a standard architecture fee, with the promise of sharing in the hotel's future profits.[18]

The first design proposed by Marshall and Fox in 1919 (figure 5.4) called for a twelve-story building, U-shaped in plan similar to that of Holabird and Roche's initial project.[19] It was changed shortly afterward, however, to an H-shaped configuration, with both the north and south elevations recessed back in the center above the third floor. This configuration provided a maximum number of rooms with views to the north and south. Further, it was raised to fourteen stories, a height still consistent with the Burnham Plan and the North Central Business District proposals. While the building's height was consistent with the earlier plans for the avenue, the deep recesses in its upper floors marked a sharp contrast to the perimeter block buildings with internal courtyards preferred by Burnham and Rebori.[20] It was thought that rooms with a view only to an inner courtyard would be of little value compared to rooms with a view to the street or the lake.

The building's main entrance is located on Walton Place rather than North Michigan Avenue. This design de-

Figure 5.4
Project, Drake Hotel,
1919; Marshall and Fox,
architects. Reprinted from
the Chicago Tribune *(27*
April 1919).

Figure 5.5
Drake Hotel, west facade.
Photo by author.

cision, which would be shared later by the Allerton Hotel, allowed for easier vehicular access to the building's front door. It made it possible for cars to stop at the curb directly in front of the hotel without blocking Michigan Avenue traffic. It also served to relate the hotel more to the residential district adjacent to Michigan Avenue rather than directly to the commercial thoroughfare itself.

The building's facades are articulated in a tripartite division with a three-story base, unadorned intermediate floors, and decorated upper floors. The base has alternating rectangular piers and shop windows at the street level, while round-arched windows rise through the second and third floors, suggesting a double-story *piano nobile* (figure 5.5). On the north side, facing Oak Street, a two-story grand ballroom is marked by Tuscan Doric columns framing large rectangular windows. The windows of the twelfth floor are highlighted by capping pediments, and those of the thirteenth are divided by decorative panels with urns, shields, and scrollwork. The building's fourteen-story center portion features pediments and decorative panels that occur one level higher than those of the flanking wings. The whole building is topped by a projecting dentiled cornice.

Marshall and Fox placed all of the building's most important public spaces—the lobby, restaurant, lounge, meeting rooms, and ballrooms—on the second and third floors. All were lavishly and elegantly decorated with Classical columns, wood paneling, and lush carpeting. A series of shops organized along interior corridors were placed at the street level. None of them are accessible from Michigan Avenue itself but only from inside the hotel.[21]

When built, the Drake was one of the truly grand hotels of the city. Perched on the lakefront at the point where the city's most fashionable residential area joined its newest commercial avenue, the Drake became a focal point for both districts. Though almost inhospitable in its severity, the exterior of the Drake symbolizes the solidity and respectability patrons had come to expect of a first-class hotel; it was an effective transitional element between North Michigan Avenue and the Gold Coast.[22]

ALLERTON HOTEL

The Allerton Hotel, the second hotel to be constructed on North Michigan Avenue, was of an entirely different character. Located at the northeast corner of Michigan Avenue and Huron Street (figures 5.6 and 5.7), it was designed to be a residential club to cater to young, single men and women in a home-like atmosphere, aiming for a market that complemented the wealthy convention goers, tourists, and weekend shoppers accommodated by the Drake. This building, the first outside of New York for the Allerton Company, was part of a chain of "club hotels" built to provide living quarters along with the privileges of a club, featuring lounges, writing and reading rooms, dining rooms, a game room, gymnasium, and handball courts.[23] William H. Silk, vice-president and managing director of the Allerton Company, sent out brochures to Chicago businessmen in 1923 accompanied by a cover letter encouraging them to house their junior associates in the Allerton Hotel, stating, "A man's living environment largely determines the quality of his work."[24] The company was selling not just living quarters but also an appropriate social setting for young professionals. The goal was to persuade businessmen that

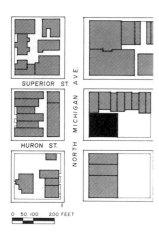

Figure 5.6
Allerton Hotel site plan.
Drawn by author.

Figure 5.7
Allerton Hotel, 701 North
Michigan Avenue, 1923–24;
Murgatroyd and Ogden in
association with Fugard
and Knapp, architects.
Courtesy of the Chicago
Historical Society.

those who lived comfortably and economically in their hotel
would be more successful in their jobs.

In New York the Allerton hotels were located in the
heart of the city's shopping and business districts. Four
were built in the late 1910s, designed by New York architect Arthur Loomis Harmon in the characteristic style of
Medieval architecture of Northern Italy.[25] In the early
1920s, the Allerton Company replaced Harmon with the
firm of Murgatroyd and Ogden, who designed for it the
Fraternity Clubs Building (figure 5.8) and the Barbizon
Hotel (figure 5.9), as well as the Allerton Hotel in Cleveland, Ohio, and this one in Chicago.[26] The principal of the
firm, architect and engineer Everett Murgatroyd, continued as the chief architect for the Allerton Company
throughout the 1920s and perpetuated the use of the Northern Italian style first used by Harmon.[27]

Figure 5.8
Fraternity Clubs Building,
New York, 1924; Murga-
troyd and Ogden, archi-
tects. Reprinted from Architectural Forum *(July*
1924).

The company had decided to locate their Chicago Allerton Hotel on North Michigan Avenue in 1922, purchasing the northeast corner of Michigan and Huron.[28] The site
at that time contained a single townhouse that was demolished to make way for the new building. The company announced it would build a twenty-story structure to accommodate 750 guests (figure 5.10), with the total cost of the
project to be $4,000,000. It was to be financed by a mort-
gage bond issue underwritten by S. W. Straus and Company, which had financed one of the Allerton Company's
hotels in New York in a similar way.[29] For supervision of
the building's construction, the Allerton Company selected
the Chicago firm of Fugard and Knapp, which had become
proficient in the design of period-style Gold Coast apartment buildings.[30]

*Figure 5.9
Barbizon Hotel, New York,
1926–27; Murgatroyd and
Ogden, architects. Re-
printed from* Architectural
Forum *(May 1928).*

The building as constructed rises twenty-five stories
rather than the originally planned twenty. It initially contained 1010 rooms, a number that has been reduced by
subsequent remodelings.[31] As with the Drake Hotel, a
three-story limestone-clad base fills the entire site, while
the building's shaft is H-shaped in plan to maximize the
amount of outside wall surface and window area. The
building rises in this configuration to the twentieth floor,
where the corner wings become octagonal in shape to form
tower-like crowning features. The central portion of the
building rises beyond as a separate tower and is topped by
a hipped roof and a cupola. The massing and design of the
building is similar to Murgatroyd and Ogden's designs for
the Fraternity Clubs Building and the Barbizon Hotel, but
with a shorter, less dominating central tower.

*Figure 5.10
Project, Allerton Hotel,
1922; Murgatroyd and Og-
den, architects. Reprinted
from the* Chicago Tribune
(2 July 1922).

The building's three-story base has an arcade motif consisting of broad pilasters and lancet arches with window motifs and corbeled sills and arches (figure 5.11). At the main entrance, which as with the Drake Hotel faces south rather than onto Michigan Avenue, the arcade motif is open to form a grand loggia. The building's upper-wall sur-

Figure 5.11
Allerton Hotel, detail of
lower floors on south side.
Reprinted from Architectural Forum *(May 1925).*

Figure 5.12
Allerton Hotel, view of
lobby. Reprinted from Architectural Forum *(May*
1925).

127

faces, clad in red brick, are articulated by pilasters and further punctuated by a pattern of projecting headers giving the building a rustic quality. Other features of the Northern Italian style are seen in corbeled cornices, striping, and, at the top, overhanging balconies supported by arched brackets.[32]

The architectural treatment of the interior, now altered from the original, was done in various styles, depending on the room's use and location. A two-story main stair hall, in the Renaissance style with large arches framing the upper level (figure 5.12), gave access to the second-floor hotel lobby (figure 5.13). The main lounge, located off the west end of the lobby, was done in a Tudor style inspired by Hever Castle in Kent, England.[33] The main dining room, located in the southeast corner of the same floor, had rough stucco walls and a vaulted ornamented ceiling divided into two parts by a heavy beam supported on piers at the center of the room.[34]

The ground floor of the building served a twofold purpose, one to provide a restaurant and barbershop primarily for the hotel residents, and the other to provide for six shops facing Michigan Avenue. The shops, all with two levels, took advantage of the building's prime shopping location and thus provided added revenues to the owners, over and above the income of the hotel rooms themselves. In addition to this was the Tip Top Tap, a popular bar on the building's uppermost floor.

When the building opened in 1924, weekly rates were advertised at from $10 to $20, depending on the size and location of the room. It became a popular location for young college graduates, especially those who had been affiliated with fraternities and sororities during their college years. Like the Allerton Company's Fraternity Clubs Building in New York, it became a place where they could make their transition to the professional world while at the same time maintaining their social ties to their Greek-lettered college friends.[35] The building eventually became a residential headquarters for 102 colleges and universities and twenty-one national Panhellenic fraternities and sororities, with ten floors for men, seven for women, and four for married couples. In addition to the private rooms and apartments, it provided a series of common club rooms, all located on the twenty-third floor.[36]

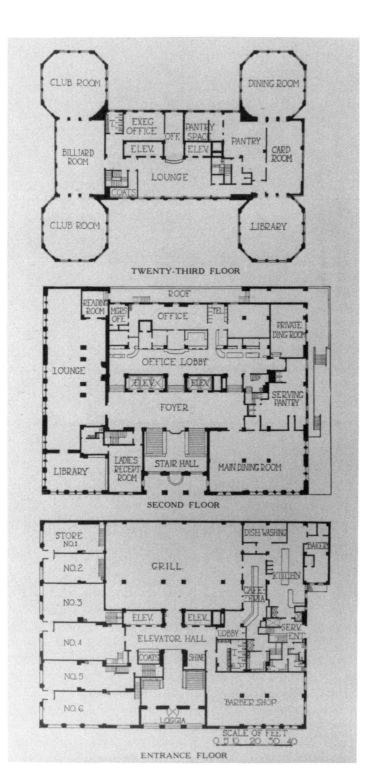

Figure 5.13
Allerton Hotel floor plans.
Reprinted from Architectural Forum *(May 1925).*

Figure 5.14
900 North Michigan Ave-
nue Apartment Building,
1925–27; Jarvis Hunt, ar-
chitect. Courtesy of the
Chicago Historical Society.
Photo by Glenn E. Dahlby.

900 NORTH MICHIGAN AVENUE APARTMENT BUILDING

Although North Michigan Avenue was closely tied to the Gold Coast, only one apartment building was constructed on the avenue itself in the 1920s, that at 900 North Michigan Avenue (figures 5.14 and 5.15), just south of Benjamin Marshall's Raymond Apartment Building. Built in 1925–27, it was one of Chicago's earliest cooperative apartments.[37] Unique in combining a commercial ground floor, rental apartments, and luxury cooperative apartments, it represented a type and style of building significant in Chicago's history. It was a "storefront with apartments" brought to its most urban and sophisticated conclusion.[38] The building's architect, Jarvis Hunt, had considerable experience in the design of expensive buildings for wealthy clients, including Robert R. McCormick's first building on North Michigan Avenue for the *Chicago Tribune*. Hunt was a nephew of both the painter William Morris Hunt and architect Richard Morris Hunt. He had first come to Chicago in 1893 to design the Vermont state building for the Columbian Exposition, and he became known for his ability to provide elegant surroundings for his clients both in exterior imagery and interior space and furnishings.[39]

The 900 North Michigan Avenue Apartment Building was constructed by a building corporation formed in 1925 in which only residents of the building could be corporate shareholders.[40] Stock was sold on the basis of the number of square feet to be occupied by the apartment, and the assessments were prorated on the basis of the amount of stock owned. The tenant owners held all of the cooperative's stock so that there was no outside ownership.[41] The original co-owners numbered among Chicago's leading citizens—corporate heads, doctors, and lawyers—most of whom were Presbyterian and Republican and belonged to the best clubs, especially the Chicago Club and the Saddle and Cycle Club.[42] Included among them were the building's architect, Jarvis Hunt, and Cyrus McCormick, Jr., son of Cyrus Hall McCormick and a vice-president of International Harvester.[43]

The building corporation bought the site from Honoré Palmer in August 1925 and immediately obtained a mortgage from the Continental Illinois National Bank.[44] Construction began the following year. The building stood nine stories and had one basement level. Its north wall was supported on rock caissons and the rest of the building on wood piles, the difference being the fact that the building's foundations were designed by engineers Liebermann and Hein to support a proposed future addition that would bring it to twenty stories plus a tower.[45] The building's owners resided on the upper six floors which were divided into thirty-six single and duplex apartments, each one left unfinished so that they could be completed to the taste and needs of the individual residents. On the second and third floors were thirty-three rental apartments. Whereas the apartments for the co-owners had four to twelve rooms, the rental apartments had just two to four. The income from the rentals, plus that from the retail on the first floor, all but covered operational and maintenance expenses in the early years of the building's life. Every room in the apartment suites had a view—in some cases of the avenue, in some cases of the courtyard.[46]

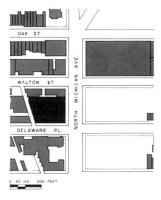

Figure 5.15
900 North Michigan Avenue Apartment Building site plan. Drawn by author.

Figure 5.16
900 North Michigan Ave-
nue Apartment Building,
facade detail. Photo by
author.

The building's exterior possessed a sense of refined elegance brought about through a subtle and restrained use of materials and color (figure 5.16). The lower four floors were clad with rusticated limestone while the upper floors were brick trimmed with limestone. It was U-shaped in plan above the base, with a south-facing raised courtyard that had a fountain, flagstone paths, and formally arranged evergreens. From an urban viewpoint, the building was a perfect complement to the Drake Hotel and the Fourth Presbyterian Church (figure 5.17). Like the Drake, its Michigan Avenue facade filled out the block and its main entrance

Figure 5.17
View of west side of North
Michigan Avenue looking
south from Oak Street,
1955. Courtesy of the Chi-
cago Historical Society.

was on the south, facing the side street for easier access. The raised courtyard looked onto the Fourth Presbyterian Church and beyond to the Water Tower. Apartments on the upper levels enjoyed splendid views of the lake and the Loop.

The building was never enlarged to twenty stories as originally planned because of the Depression, and as new apartment buildings erected in Streeterville slowly blocked its views to the lake, its prestige steadily diminished. It was demolished in 1984 to make way for the new 900 North Michigan Avenue Building housing Bloomingdale's, a building which attempted to repeat its form as a base for a gigantic fifty-eight story tower.

ILLINOIS WOMEN'S ATHLETIC CLUB

The Illinois Women's Athletic Club was constructed in 1926–27 at 820 North Michigan Avenue, on Tower Court, just west of the Water Tower (figures 5.18 and 5.19).[47] Practically everything in the new building was planned for women, not only the club itself but even the shops, studios, and offices on the lower floors.[48] Journalist Laura Mae Corrigan wrote in *The Woman Athlete* in 1927:

> The Herculean courage shown by the women pioneers in this movement who conceived the idea,

133

moulded the plan and put into execution the building of a beautiful 17-story clubhouse merits comment. A few years ago it would have been considered impossible for women to raise the money necessary for such a huge project. In making their dream a reality, these leaders have shown such a dynamic force that it is certain they will never suffer their community to stand still.[49]

The Illinois Women's Athletic Club had been founded in 1918 by Mrs. William Severin, a part owner of the Women's Federal Oil Company and an active political supporter of Mayor Thompson.[50] During the war, she was active in Liberty Bond work and in urging women to buy American goods. Thus holding a position of leadership in the women's community, Mrs. Severin was well suited to undertake the establishment of a women's club. Helping her in this endeavor were club treasurer Mrs. Leona A. Krag, who was head of the domestic service department at Armour and Company, and Miss Grace Merchant, one of the club's several directors and treasurer of Hales and Company, grain dealers. Another club luminary was Mrs. Medill McCormick, wife of Medill McCormick, a former *Tribune* executive who was later elected to the U.S. Senate.[51]

Before constructing its own building, the club had occupied a series of quarters in its early days, first in the Century Building, moving later to the Stevens Building, and finally purchasing the old Parmalee Prentice residence on the site of the present building.[52] The lot measured 63 by 144 feet.[53] The site was thought to be unusually attractive for a club, given its location in the North Michigan Avenue commercial district. South of the site was a four-story building and beyond was a group of once-fashionable graystone houses.

The club selected the firm of Schmidt, Garden and Martin to design the building in 1922, though construction did not begin until 1926. German-born Richard E. Schmidt had studied at M.I.T. in the mid-1880s before establishing his practice in Chicago in 1887. His talented design partner, Hugh M. G. Garden, had worked for such notable Chicago architects as Henry Ives Cobb and Shepley, Rutan and Coolidge as well as Louis Sullivan before going into partnership with Schmidt.[54] The third member of the office, Edgar D. Martin, was an engineer who remained only until 1925, when the firm name was changed to Schmidt, Garden and Erikson.[55]

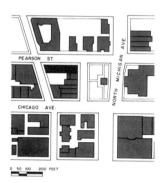

Figure 5.18
Illinois Women's Athletic Club site plan. Drawn by author.

Figure 5.19
Illinois Women's Athletic
Club, 820 North Michigan
Avenue, 1926–27; Schmidt,
Garden and Martin, archi-
tects. Reprinted from Paul
T. Gilbert and Charles L.
Bryson, Chicago and Its
Makers *(Chicago, 1929).*

A proposal for the building was published in the *Chi-*
cago Tribune in 1922 showing an Italian Renaissance-style
high rise with rounded-arched windows on the upper floors

and a projecting dentiled cornice that topped a low pedimented parapet on the front (figure 5.20). As built, however, the round-arched windows were replaced by projecting Gothic bay windows, and the cornice was replaced by a straight parapet with Medieval corner towers and finials. Rising seventeen stories, the building is a tall and narrow structure extending the length of the block from Tower Court to Rush Street. The first two floors were originally devoted to specialty shops, above that, from the third to the ninth were offices, and the upper eight floors, from the tenth to the seventeenth, were used for club purposes.[56] The initial estimated cost was $1,250,000, but the final cost at the building's completion was $3,500,000.[57] It was the tallest building erected to date this far north on Michigan Avenue.

The building's location on the Near North Side and its location on North Michigan Avenue were two important factors contributing to the prestige of the institution it

Figure 5.20
Project, Illinois Women's Athletic Club, 1922; Schmidt, Garden and Martin, architects. Reprinted from the Chicago Tribune *(11 June 1922).*

housed. Adding to its high character was its Gothic style, somewhat reminiscent of the University Club downtown, at Michigan and Monroe. Advertising literature of the club emphasized the building's location and appearance stating, "This beautiful 17 story, newly erected building, a monument to Chicago's largest Women's Club, rises majestically in plain sight of all those traveling on Michigan Boulevard."[58] The first private club building for women to be erected on the avenue, it was a further recognition of prestige and social prominence for this area of the city.

WOMAN'S CHICAGO ATHLETIC CLUB

The second women's club to be erected on the avenue was for the Woman's Chicago Athletic Club, built at 626 North Michigan in 1926–28 (figure 5.21).[59] This modern version of an elegant French Second Empire style building, designed by Philip Maher, was an appropriate symbol of the club— an ultramodern society establishment whose members were from the city's wealthiest families. Having been the oldest athletic club for women in the nation, it was particularly important to have a building of unusual grace and refinement. Established in 1898 by a group headed by Mrs. Philip D. Armour, its first president, the club was the setting for debuts, balls, and wedding parties as well as exercise, afternoon tea, and private socializing. It also raised $500,000 a year for the indigent sick.[60] Before its move to North Michigan Avenue, the organization had been housed in the Harvester Building at 606 South Michigan.

The site on North Michigan Avenue at Ontario Street, measuring 109 by 75 feet, was selected by the club's current president, Mrs. William Pelouze, whose husband was a member of the Chicago Plan Commission and the North Central Business District Association.[61] The club entered into a ninety-nine-year lease with its owner, John V. Farwell, brother of Arthur L. Farwell, who wrote into the lease certain stipulations for the design of the building that would make it easy to convert to offices at a later date, should the Woman's Club ever move.[62] These required, for instance, that the entrance to the club be on Ontario Street; that the ground floor, except for the entrance, foyer, elevator corridor, and elevators be developed into shops fronting on the avenue; and that the swimming pool be located in the basement.[63] Maher followed these requirements, placing the pool in the basement, shops on the first floor, and a lounge, library, and meeting rooms on the sec-

137

*Figure 5.21
Woman's Chicago Athletic
Club, 626 North Michigan
Avenue, 1926–28; Philip B.
Maher, architect. Photo by
author.*

ond, the main dining room on the third, special baths and exercise rooms on the sixth, and a grand ballroom on the seventh. This ballroom, measuring seventy by forty-six feet, had an adjoining room along the south side whose windows could be opened to create a sort of porch. A soft feminine elegance pervaded all of the rooms, with pastel colors, molded lines of the furniture, and frosted glass with curvilinear designs derived from the 1925 Paris Exposition des Arts Décoratifs.[64]

The building's exterior equally reflects Maher's taste for French-inspired design (figure 5.22). Rising nine stories, with walls of smooth-faced Bedford limestone, the building has a central portion topped by a mansard roof and flanked by lower wings. Large round-arched windows

Figure 5.22
Woman's Chicago Athletic
Club. Reprinted from the
Chicago Tribune *(25 Sep-*
tember 1927).

are located at the second and seventh floors, and the otherwise sober wall surfaces are decorated with carved heads
of rams, garland-festooned horns, and fierce winged animals perched in arched niches near the roof. Even though
the building is abundantly decorated, it shares with
Maher's building for Arthur L. Farwell at Michigan and
Erie Street a simplified French-like elegance.

MEDINAH CLUB

The last of the club buildings to be constructed on North
Michigan Avenue was the Medinah Club (figure 5.23), located at 505 North Michigan, just north of the Tribune
Tower.[65] Built exclusively for members of the Shriners, it
contained lounges, dining rooms, handball courts, a swimming pool, gymnasium, and bowling alley as well as 600
rooms for the use of members and their guests. All of these
spaces were contained in an exuberant forty-five story
structure combining Oriental and Art Deco-inspired design

Figure 5.23
Medinah Club, 505 North
Michigan Avenue, 1927–29;
Walter Ahlschlager, archi-
tect. Courtesy of the Chi-
cago Historical Society.

motifs and topped by a tower with a minaret and pear-shaped dome. It was designed by Chicago architect Walter Ahlschlager with engineer Frank A. Randall.

The directory of club members, limited to 3,500, was an exclusive list of well-known men in both commercial and professional circles, many of whom contemplated living in the building.[66] To become a member, one had to be nominated to the ancient Arabic Order of the Nobles of the Mystic Shrine. The organization also owned the Medinah Temple Building at Wabash and Ontario streets, and the Medinah Country Club, and it ran a home for handicapped children, the Illinois Masonic Hospital, and the Illinois Masonic Orphan's Home. These institutions all represented certain aspirations of the club members just as the new Medinah Club Building was "not only a monument to Shrinedom and Chicago" but was also a monument to each of the club's 3,500 members.[67]

The organization purchased the site, which measured 100 by 150 feet, in 1925 for a cost of $1,000,000.[68] The presiding officer of the Medinah Club responsible for initiating the project and buying the land was Thomas J. Houston, a past potentate of the Masons and owner of the T. J. Houston Insurance Company.[69] The building committee responsible for financing and carrying out the project was headed by Urbine J. Herrmann, a friend of Mayor Thompson and vice-president and manager of the Cort Theatre Company of Chicago as well as an owner of Boston's American League baseball club. An adventurous man with many interests, Hermann was also a member of the MacMillan Arctic Expedition in 1925.[70]

The assignment given the architect for the new building was to create the general atmosphere and tone of the Middle Ages in a setting like that of a fortress—staunch and secure, capable of successfully warding off invading foes.[71] There was an invited competition, though Chicago architect Walter Ahlschlager seems to have been the leading candidate from the beginning, his preliminary design for the building being published in the *Chicago Tribune* even before he was formally selected (figure 5.24).[72] The image he created borrowed decorative motifs from many countries: Egypt, Assyria, Persia, France, Italy, the Nordic countries, and Turkey.[73] Ahlschlager was well suited for the eclecticism of this design, having grown up in a prolifically creative family, the son of architect Frederick Ahlschlager.[74] The senior Ahlschlager had established his reputation in Chicago in the 1880s and 1890s with designs for several churches, stores, and warehouses, specializing peculiarly enough in the design of bakery buildings. In his own practice, Walter Ahlschlager received such major commissions as New York's Beacon and Roxy theaters (1925–27), and a large Art Deco style complex in Cincinnati, which included the Starrett Netherland Plaza Hotel, Carew Tower, and the Mabley and Carew Department Store (1929).[75]

Ahlschlager's preliminary design of 1925 for the Medinah Club called for a thirty-four story building rising in stepped-back stages to a central tower to be topped by a bulbous dome.[76] A second, more detailed perspective drawing was published in the *Tribune* ten months later showing a refined and taller version of the earlier design, this one to be forty-one stories.[77] Even though it was to be taller than originally proposed, the number of hotel sleeping rooms was cut from 600 to 538, the difference being the design of

Figure 5.24
Project, Medinah Club,
1925; Walter Ahlschlager,
architect. Reprinted from
the Chicago Tribune *(22*
November 1925).

larger rooms and the assignment of more space for club and athletic facilities.

Ground breaking for the new building occurred in December 1927, an event of great fanfare that was attended by Shriners and other prominent Chicagoans, along with Ahlschlager and Randall.[78] The caissons were in place by the end of January 1928, and the steel structure erected by June. The club was opened in August 1929.[79] Financing for the building's $8,000,000 cost was provided by mortgages and issues of common stock purchased by club members. Assyrian relief panels carved on the building's facade alone cost $50,000.[80]

As constructed, the building rises forty-two stories, about 480 feet. Its historicist imagery was somewhat reduced, a sense of modernism being suggested in its smooth-surfaced walls. The first eleven stories rise uninterrupted to the first setback, which occurs in the center of the facade, with two corner pavilions rising another seven stories to a second stepback that demarcates the building's base from its tower. The tower itself rises fifteen stories and is topped by a temple-like structure with a pear-shaped dome and a flanking slender tower.

A tapered entranceway rises through the first two stories and is flanked by two levels of shop windows. The fourth level is set off by three large windows recessed in niches and enclosed in elaborate frames with notched surrounds. The building's most distinguishing feature, three large Assyrian relief panels, are located at the eighth floor, on the main facade, and on the two side elevations. Executed by Chicago sculptor Leon Hermant, the south wall represents "Contribution," the north wall "Wisdom," and the west wall "Consecration," the carved figures being the physiognomies of the members of the committee as perpetual memorials to themselves.[81] Three sentinels in the form of Sumerian warriors cap off the central piers at the twelfth-floor setback (figure 5.25) of the facade's central bays. A final interesting sculptural feature appears in the presence of gargoyles projecting from the corners of the uppermost temple structure.

The interiors of the building were at once monumental and symbolic. While the structure is no longer used as a club, many of the features of the interior still remain. The entrance hall has a beamed ceiling, done in bold colors, with birds, animals, and geometric and decorative forms. Granite lions guard the double flight of stairs leading up to a restaurant. The space was expressive of legends such as:

Martial and austere to those who pass up this
staircase it would seem that a mere handful of
archers could withstand an army here. Flanking
balconies, rows of armored knights at each end
and a heavy barred-grille all in keeping with some
mighty fortress of a by-gone age.[82]

Other rooms in the building were equally impressive
and symbolic. The style of a meeting hall called the Celtic
Room referred back to the days of the Norsemen, cold
northern days, and Vikings. The main lounge had massive
engaged columns and large beams on which were portrayed
in highly colorful pictures the story of King Arthur, stories
from Parsifal, later Christian events, and scenes of daily
life in Gothic times. The tearoom had a fountain molded
after that of the Alhambra in Granada, Spain. The climax
of the main ceremonial rooms was the Grand Ballroom, an
elliptical room of 100 by 90 feet, rising two stories and surrounded by balconies. It was decorated by Assyrian and
Egyptian art combined with Greek elements.

As with its neighboring office buildings on North Michigan Avenue, the Medinah Club was advertised as "an address with distinction." Residence in the Medinah Athletic
Club was billed as a sign of social prestige and personal

taste suggesting character and culture.[83] One of the advertising slogans for the club read:

> Look me up at the Medinah Club. It is no wonder that men and women of discrimination, not in Chicago alone, but throughout the country, and even abroad, say these words with a pardonable touch of pride.
>
> For Medinah is the finest and richest expression of modern city club luxury and fine social life. Here is found every convenience, every necessity one could look for in a club, hotel, or even a home.[84]

As with the London Guarantee Building and others, the building's location outside the congested Loop was also stressed, free from the noise and smoke of trains and streetcars, yet convenient to transportation, with the added advantage of natural light and magnificent views on all sides.

It seems a mere coincidence that two of the tallest buildings on the avenue—the Medinah Club and the Tribune Tower—were built within one-half block of each other. The Tribune Tower and the Wrigley Building no longer stood alone as an isolated gateway to the north side of the river but, instead, became part of a larger ensemble of skyscraper buildings defining an evermore cavernous urban space. As one crossed the Michigan Avenue Bridge, one's view was now diverted from the Wrigley Building to the Tribune Tower and then beyond to the Medinah Club Building, the three becoming a tightly woven array of gridded and decorated high-rise facades.

THE LATER 1920s ARCHITECTURE OF HOLABIRD AND ROOT

Holabird and Root was the single most important architectural firm in the development of North Michigan Avenue in the last years of the 1920s. From 1926 to 1929 the firm designed in rapid succession the Tobey Building, 333 North Michigan, the Palmolive Building, Michigan-Chestnut Building, Michigan Square Building, and the Judah Building. All were rental office structures with commercial shopping space on the first two floors, the standard that had been set for buildings on the avenue at the beginning of the decade.[1]

The firm of Holabird and Root had itself become the standard of the time for the design of commercial office buildings. Established as Holabird and Roche in 1883, its distinguished original partners, William Holabird and Martin Roche had both gained their apprenticeship in the office of William LeBaron Jenney and had become adept at designing speculative office buildings in the Loop, a practice that flourished until Holabird's death in 1923 and that of Roche in 1927.[2] The buildings on North Michigan Avenue at the end of the decade came at a time when the leadership of the firm had passed into the capable hands of William Holabird's son, John A. Holabird, and John W. Root, son of the founding partner of Burnham and Root.[3] Both men had studied at the Ecole des Beaux-Arts, and both brought a distinctly new method of design into the firm, one that questioned the use of historical styles on new buildings.

Architectural historian Robert Bruegmann describes their buildings from this period as displaying an abstraction of traditional elements into a powerful, stripped style leaving behind almost entirely any reference to specific historical styles.[4] One important influence on the work of Holabird and Root in the late 1920s was the 1925 Paris Exposition Internationale des Arts Décoratifs. From this point on, Holabird and Root, and other American architects, began to show a considerable degree of interest in contemporary European work.[5] The exposition did not present a single coherent style of buildings but brought together many examples of nontraditional architecture. This international mixture of exhibition buildings generally shared three characteristics. First, forms were usually simple, with an emphasis on simple geometry, linearity, and verticality. Second, decoration was kept within the basic exterior shape of the forms and was kept close to the surface. Often, decorative interest was created from the use of textures and patterns. Last, many buildings used large areas of glass, both plain and colored.[6]

The most immediate influence on the designs of Holabird and Root was Eliel Saarinen's Tribune Tower proposal. Architectural critic Thomas Tallmadge wrote in 1927 that in Saarinen's design "lay the solution of the skyscraper, a veritable philosopher's stone that would transmute the drose of eclecticism into the gold of new architecture."[7] Saarinen himself stated in the *Western Architect* in 1923:

> One must consider the Gothic contribution as a
> transitory period. A new architecture must, in
> time, create a new form language of its own, and it
> is apparent that the American building art is
> headed toward this new architectural language
> (expression).[8]

Another project by Saarinen demonstrating his concept of a new architectural language, and one that influenced Holabird and Root, was his proposal in 1923 for the Chicago lakefront (figure 6.1).[9] A master plan that included a broad tree-lined boulevard traversing Grant Park from north to south, it had a skyscraper tower flanked by lower office blocks terminating one end. The architectural design of the buildings demonstrated his interest in the arrangement of vertical force against a contrasting and balancing horizontal volume. As with his Tribune Tower design, continuous vertical piers of the principal tower frame recessed

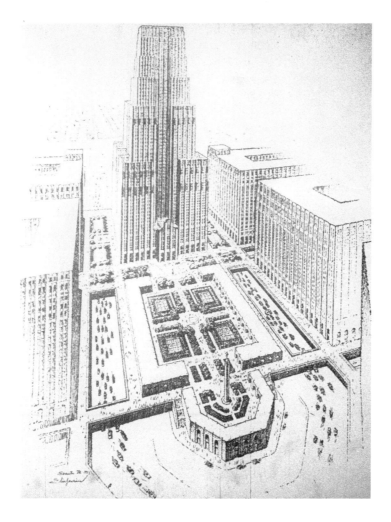

spandrels that approach the building's summit with agility and grace. Likewise, the use of small setbacks unified by continuous, deep channels of windows between plain wall surfaces, and the resulting elimination of all horizontal stops, became the hallmark of Holabird and Root's design from this period.[10]

TOBEY BUILDING

The first essay in their newly emerging style was the Tobey Building (figure 6.2), constructed at 200 North Michigan Avenue in 1925–26, while the firm was still known as Holabird and Roche. Though it is a relatively inauspicious design, the Tobey Building nevertheless introduced a number of elements that would become typical of the firm's succeed-

Figure 6.2
Tobey Building, 200 North
Michigan Avenue, 1925–26;
Holabird and Roche, ar-
chitects. Courtesy of the
Chicago Historical Society.

ing buildings.[11] It was described by *The Economist* magazine in 1925 as "simple and refined and thoughtfully ornamented . . . which has a modern tendency and indicates the
structural lines of the building."[12] There is a simplification
and reduction of Classical forms with a strong emphasis on
the structural frame underlying them. The abstract wall
surfaces are quite smooth, and the details are abstracted.

As was standard for new buildings on North Michigan
Avenue, Holabird and Roche placed repetitive shop fronts
on the first level, each with a large display window and a
glass entrance door, with an upper frieze for the store's
sign. Above was a second level of shops also with large rectangular display windows. The thought was that displays in
these windows would convince customers to enter the elaborately framed main entrance at the building's north end
and proceed up a flight of stairs to the second floor. The
third level, with its small windows and smooth-faced limestone surfaces, serves as a visual transition to the three up-

per office floors which have recessed spandrels framed by fluted pilasters. Foliated geometric reliefs are carved in the limestone surfaces between the third and fourth levels and in the upper cornice. While the building was an early step toward simplification, it still retained some traditional decorative elements. Most important of all, it marks the firm's transition between the historicism of the early years of the decade and the simplified style of its later years.

The building, constructed for the McCormick estate, fronts 166 feet on Michigan Avenue and 130 feet on Lake Street. The Holabird and Roche design was commissioned in 1925, with construction beginning in October of that year, and completed in the summer of 1926.[13] The Tobey Furniture Company, along with Ovington's, a world-famous gift shop of New York, and Kroch's International Bookstore signed leases before the building was opened.[14]

The Tobey Building was an effort by its architects to interpret the changing demands of economics and to characterize utility and structural form. The building was a response to business standards and business demands appropriate to North Michigan Avenue. Its design had to be of the highest quality, accenting the sound business principles of its tenants. Strength, honesty, and sincerity were features of design thought to be characteristic of high-grade commercial enterprise.[15]

333 NORTH MICHIGAN AVENUE

The second building on North Michigan Avenue by Holabird and Roche to express these principles was the 333 North Michigan Avenue Building, constructed in 1927–28 (figures 6.3 and 6.4).[16] It was also the first to be derived directly from Saarinen's designs for the Chicago Tribune Tower and his Grant Park skyscraper proposal. Located on the southeast corner of the Michigan Avenue Bridge Plaza, its construction effectively terminated the southern end of the Michigan Avenue axis from the Water Tower to the river. The axial relation of the site to the bridge and the avenue along with the building's narrow width gave it a sentinel-like quality (figure 6.5).[17]

The building was developed by a group of investors that included Holabird and Roche, soon to become Holabird and Root, along with a consulting engineer on the project, Martin C. Schwab, the contractor for the building, the Hegeman-Harris Company, and two additional owner-investors, Otto C. Doering and Jerome P. Bowes, Jr.[18] The

Figure 6.3
333 North Michigan Ave-
nue Building, 1927–28;
Holabird and Roche, ar-
chitects. Courtesy of the
Chicago Historical Society.

total investment in the land and building was estimated at
$9,000,000. Holabird and Roche was to occupy all of the
twenty-fourth and part of the twenty-fifth floors along with
two floors in the tower for a library and studio.[19]

The investor group, calling itself the 333 North Michigan Avenue Building Corporation, purchased the site at the
southeast corner of Michigan Avenue and Wacker Drive in
June 1927.[20] In addition, the company had to obtain rights
from the Illinois Central Railroad Company for caissons
along the site's eastern border.[21] Demolition of the existing
buildings, a group of three-story brick structures, was begun at the end of May, and construction of the new building
started shortly afterward.[22] The company obtained a mortgage from the Bank of America to finance the project. At
the time of the announcement of the building proposal, it
was reported that the Woman's Chicago Athletic Club
would occupy a large amount of space in the building; how-

ever, their lease was never signed, and they shortly there-
after decided to build their own structure at 626 North
Michigan Avenue.[23]

John Root acknowledged that it was Saarinen's design
for the Tribune Tower that strongly influenced the plans
for the 333 North Michigan Avenue Building.[24] The vertical
lines of the superstructure are simply carried up to the top
with small intermediate setbacks. There is no cornice, the
building ending with an abrupt finality. As with Saarinen's
design, this building is a unity in space with vertical lines
ascending with graceful power and simplicity.

Because of the relatively small area of the site, 62 by
200 feet, economy of space demanded that the entrance and
the elevator lobbies be placed in the center of the long axis
to permit the most flexible and economic subdivisions with
a minimal amount of corridor space (figure 6.6). The possibility of an eastern addition, though never built, was a

Figure 6.4
333 North Michigan Ave-
nue Building site plan.
Drawn by author.

Figure 6.5
333 North Michigan Ave-
nue Building, view from
the north. Courtesy of the
Chicago Historical Society.

151

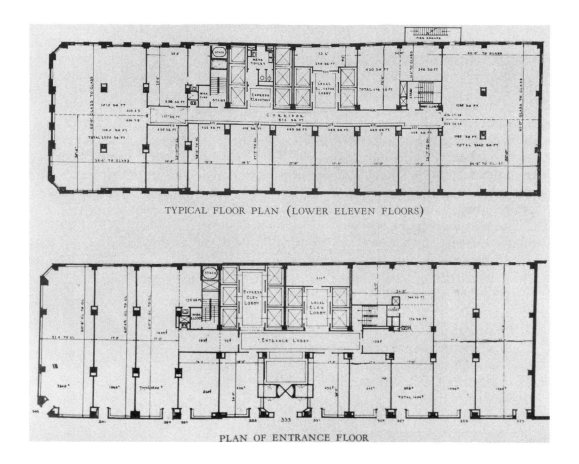

TYPICAL FLOOR PLAN (LOWER ELEVEN FLOORS)

PLAN OF ENTRANCE FLOOR

further consideration; thus the elevators were located along the east wall so that they could be continued in the new part.[25] The lot area is 12,300 square feet with the rentable area of a typical floor ranging from 9,400 to 9,700 square feet. The structure is a steel frame with column spacing set at seventeen feet, allowing individual offices of eight feet in width. The major block of the building rises twenty-four stories, with a tower at the north end extending eleven stories higher (figure 6.7), reaching a total of 426 feet.[26]

The first three floors of the building were designed to contain small shops, each of these with its own entrance on the ground floor. The narrow configuration of the plan provides an ideal layout for the offices on the upper floors, with a corridor down the center, offices on each side, all with their own windows facing either north, east, or west. The two corners of the north facade are beveled in plan, similar to the Tribune Tower, and providing a better view from the corner offices.

Figure 6.7
333 North Michigan Avenue Building, detail of tower. Courtesy of the Chicago Historical Society.

The tower-like facade is a little misleading, since the structure is really a long, narrow slab. When seen in its entirety from the west it actually looks like two buildings, with a Saarinen-like tower at the north and a lower office block at the south (figure 6.8). While the granite cladding of the lower floors is continuous across the length of the facade, the articulation of the upper floors is different in the two instances. A hierarchy of planes is established in the north portion with the two outer bays framing four recessed bays in the middle. The south portion is character-

Figure 6.8
333 North Michigan Ave-
nue Building, view from
the south. Courtesy of the
Chicago Historical Society.

ized simply by a repetition of double bays. While the tower
has no cornice, being terminated instead by a series of setbacks, the uppermost floors of the south portion are contained within a pair of cornices. The predominantly uniform rhythm of the south portion of the elevation reflects a
sober commercial spirit, while the balanced proportions
and graceful lines of the northern portion represent a light
and soaring design worthy of Saarinen's new style.

The granite cladding of the lower floors is oriental
granite from Rockville, Minnesota, with colors of black,
purple, mauve, gray, and pink. The display windows and
outer frames of the main entrance are constructed of cast
iron (figure 6.9). Buff-colored Bedford limestone is used for
the remainder of the exterior with the exception of terra
cotta spandrels in the recessed window bays.[27] Holabird
and Roche commissioned Chicago sculptor Fred M. Torrey, a member of the group around Lorado Taft, to pro-

Figure 6.9
333 North Michigan Ave-
nue Building, entrance de-
tail. Reprinted from Architectural Record *(February*
1929), copyright (1929) by
McGraw-Hill, Inc. All
rights reserved. Repro-
duced with the permission
of the publisher.

duce sculptural reliefs for a fifth-story frieze. Torrey carved a series of seven-foot-high figures in deep-cut outline that are simple and direct, suitable to the scale of the building. Since the building occupies a site with historic associations of Fort Dearborn, historic themes were chosen recalling the pioneer life of the earliest settlers: "The Pioneer Woman," "The Portage," "The Traders," "The Covered Wagon Era," "The Struggle," and "The Hunter."[28] Additional sculptural ornamentation is found on the upper levels of the building, particularly at the twenty-fourth level on the north and west sides.

155

The interiors of the building were handled in a way typical of rental office buildings of the period. The entrance, elevator lobby, and upper corridors were finely appointed while the office spaces were finished with a smooth plaster cement ready to receive covering materials chosen by the occupants. The floors of the entrance and elevator lobby were covered with patterned terrazzo, and the walls were faced with slabs of Greek Verde Antico. Window frames, elevator doors, grilles, and stair railings were all done in bronze. Typical corridors were given the same flooring as the main lobby, and the walls were wainscoted with Vermont marble. Their ceilings were plastered with carved cornices, and the office doors, transoms, and trim were of mahogany.[29]

Publicity for the building after its completion called attention to its convenient location, the availability of transportation, the flexibility and efficiency of space, and its desirable neighbors, namely, the Wrigley, Tribune, and London Guarantee buildings. Located at the gateway to Chicago's fastest growing commercial avenue, its visibility for nearly a mile down Michigan Avenue and its location within a five-minute walk of the Loop were emphasized. One newspaper advertisement stated, "333 is the ideal building for the exclusive store or shop, for the corporation seeking a central office location and for professional men."[30] Another asserted that the building "typifies everything that is ultra-modern in architectural design," and stressed the office views overlooking Wacker Drive, the bridge plaza, Michigan Avenue, and the lake.[31]

Occupying the twenty-fifth and twenty-sixth floors and adjoining roof terraces is the Tavern Club, a social organization of men from the arts, services, and business world (figure 6.10). Arranged in a series of small dining rooms and lounges, with a solar room and two open terraces, it originally featured simple modern furniture, bright colors with patterned tile floors, and murals by artists John Norton and Winold Reiss.[32] The Tavern Club was planned by Reiss, who is perhaps best known for his wall murals in Cincinnati's Union Terminal.[33] The club became in the 1920s a rendezvous for artists, writers, musicians, scholars, and other interesting people who came both to enjoy the company and the terrace views of the city.

In February 1929, the 333 North Michigan Avenue Building was awarded a gold medal for design by the Lake Shore Trust and Savings Bank.[34] In announcing their decision, the award committee stated:

SMOKING ROOM

CARD ROOM

Number 333 North Michigan has been called one of the finest examples of modernistic architecture in the country. It is characterized by sweeping vertical lines, which enhance the impression of height. A use is made of setbacks, though they are not particularly pronounced. The lines of the building, when observed in perspective, do not present a series of right angles as is often the case in New York structures employing setbacks. The result is softer lines which many admirers of sky-scraper architecture find more to their taste.[35]

The building was, therefore, successful in its visual imagery from the standpoint of architects and the public alike. The new simplified style of Holabird and Root was readily accepted as an economic and aesthetic entity expressive of the ideals of the developers of North Michigan Avenue.

Figure 6.10
333 North Michigan Ave-
nue Building, Tavern Club,
1928; Winold Reiss and
John Norton, designers
and muralists. Reprinted
from Architectural Record
(February 1929), copyright
(1929) by McGraw-Hill,
Inc. All rights reserved.
Reproduced with the per-
mission of the publisher.

PALMOLIVE BUILDING

Just two months after the announcement of the 333 North Michigan Avenue project, plans for Holabird and Root's next high-rise project were announced (figures 6.11 and 6.12).[36] Al Chase of the *Chicago Tribune* aptly reported:

157

*Figure 6.11
Palmolive Building, 925
North Michigan Avenue,
1927–28; Holabird and
Root, architects. Courtesy
of the Chicago Historical
Society.*

Upper Michigan Avenue is to have a 42 story monument to cleanliness—a soaring suds skyscraper, lathered into steel, stone and stability by the millions in all parts of the world who use the various bath and beauty products of the Palmolive Peet Company. In other words, the Palmolive interests, claimed to be the largest makers of toilet soap in the world, are going to erect a towering structure at the southeast corner of Michigan Avenue and Walton Place, directly across the street from the Drake.[37]

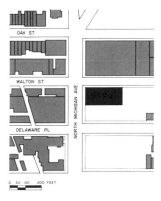

The building as constructed did not rise forty-two stories but rather thirty-seven, standing at a height of 468 feet.[38] Early in its planning stage, it was designed to be built in increments, adding additional floors when the need arose, but early in 1928, after construction had already started, the Palmolive Peet Company merged with the Colgate Corporation, and it was decided to build the entire structure at that time to house the newly expanded company.[39]

The building is located on a site fronting 172 feet on Michigan Avenue and 231 feet on Walton Place. The property was purchased from the Potter Palmer estate with an agreement that allowed the estate's trustees to approve the building plans before construction could start.[40] A mortgage to finance the $6,500,000 project was obtained from the First Trust and Savings Bank of Chicago.[41]

*Figure 6.12
Palmolive Building site
plan. Drawn by author.*

The Palmolive Peet Company had started in business in 1864 in Milwaukee as the G. J. Johnson Soap Company. It was incorporated as the Palmolive Company in 1916 and merged with the Peet Brothers Manufacturing Company of Kansas City early in 1927. The Palmolive general office was moved from Wisconsin to Chicago in 1923. It had manufacturing plants in Milwaukee, Kansas City, Berkeley, Mexico City, and Toronto as well as in several European, South American, and Australian cities. The company was said to be the largest user in the United States of olive oil for making bath soap and the largest user of cottonseed oil for making laundry soap. The officers of the company at the time of the construction of the Palmolive Building were A. W. Peet, chairman of the board and Charles S. Pearce, president.[42]

Holabird and Root strove to design for the company an edifice that would be monumental in character and at the same time simple and unassuming as a company advertisement (figure 6.13).[43] Following their simplified design motif

Figure 6.13
Palmolive Building, design
drawing. Courtesy of the
Chicago Historical Society.

established with 333 North Michigan Avenue, the architects designed a series of stepped-back volumes beginning with a two-story base that entirely fills the lot, then rising in six progressively smaller volumes, each related to the other by a continuity of vertical lines and recessed alternate bays in rectangular channels. These recessed bays are relatively shallow in the lower masses but are deeply indented in the tower rising above the seventeenth floor (figure 6.14).[44] The

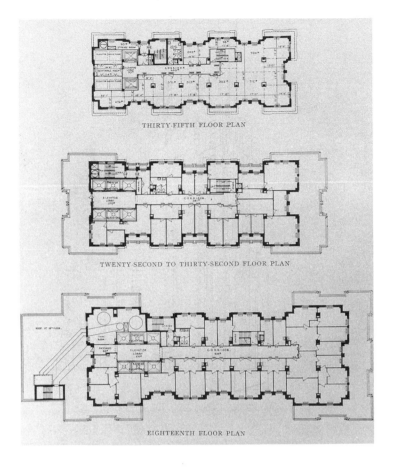

THIRTY-FIFTH FLOOR PLAN

TWENTY-SECOND TO THIRTY-SECOND FLOOR PLAN

EIGHTEENTH FLOOR PLAN

Figure 6.14
Palmolive Building, upper
level plans. Reprinted from
the Architectural Forum
(May 1930).

visual result of both the setbacks and the recessed bays is a rhythmic play of projecting and receding limestone surfaces that avoids the kind of boxy look in which one building seems to stand on top of another.

The two lower stories of the building, like 333 North Michigan Avenue, are lined with shop fronts (figure 6.15) set off from the rest of the building by the use of ornamental cast iron and metal with fluted colonettes forming vertical separations and framing the display window enclosures.[45] Above the second story, the building is clad with smooth-faced Bedford limestone. Corner and intermediate window bays have bronze spandrel panels ornamented with festoons.

Entrances to the building were originally located on both Michigan Avenue and Walton Place through vestibules to a central arcade lined with exclusive shops and restaurants (figure 6.16). Inside, the lobby floor was covered with patterned Tennessee marble, and the walls were

Figure 6.15
Palmolive Building, detail
of lower levels. Reprinted
from Architectural Forum
(May 1930).

covered with Circassian walnut in large flat panels vertically fluted over door openings. All of the door frames,
storefronts, and display cases were originally metal, contrasting sharply with the walnut woodwork.[46] The interior
design of the public spaces, with the rich materials arranged in simple forms of broad planes and long horizontal
bands, were meant to complement the building's exterior
simplified modernity.

An important feature of the Palmolive Building, as was
true with the Wrigley and Tribune buildings, is the use of
light to accent the building's various surfaces and levels.
Night illumination from floodlights placed on the setback
levels highlights the rhythmic play of projecting and receding surfaces. On a smaller scale, the colonettes separating
the shop windows around the building's perimeter each
have illuminated tops, thus marking the rhythm of the base
divisions. The lighting feature for which the building, and
the company, became famous, however, was the so-called
Lindbergh Beacon, a powerful revolving airplane beacon
supported on a 150-foot steel and aluminum mast. Until it
was removed, its two-billion candlepower beam was visible,
much to the chagrin of many nearby residents, at ground

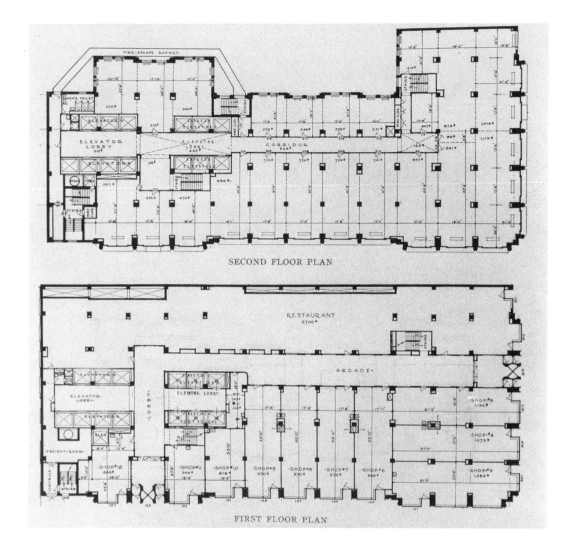

SECOND FLOOR PLAN

FIRST FLOOR PLAN

level throughout the city and suburbs and could be seen 500 miles away by airplane pilots.[47]

The building became an immediate success as a rental office structure despite its location nearly a mile outside the downtown area.[48] In fact, this worked to its advantage because it was located closer to its occupants' homes, as 35 percent of the executives with offices in the Palmolive Building lived within a radius of two miles. The tenants made up a sizable cross-section of Chicago businesses, including paper manufacturers, publishers, and advertising agencies as well as La Tour d'Argent restaurant located on the first floor. An article published in *Through the Ages* in 1931 stated:

Figure 6.16
Palmolive Building, first- and second-floor plans. Reprinted from Architectural Forum *(May 1930).*

While architectural tradition has been respectfully observed in designing this edifice, the practical necessities of modern commercial life and the advertising values of such an imposing structure, so conspicuously located in the public eye, have been shrewdly divined and provided for by the builders. The prominence of its site, close to the lake, at the dividing line between commercial and residential Chicago, as well as its commanding height and superb proportions—visible for miles in every direction—dominate the attention.[49]

One of the largest tenants in the building was the Celotex Corporation, which signed a long-term lease in 1929 for three floors, at an annual rental of $86,962.[50] Part of the quarters leased by the company were devoted to exhibition purposes to show how the products of the company could be used.[51] Other tenants included Household Finance, Kaiser Aluminum, Esquire Magazine, and many other major corporations. A Walden Bookshop, its interior designed by Harold Reynolds and Winold Reiss, was located on the first floor.[52] A choice location on the seventeenth and eighteenth floors was leased by the long-established Chicago advertising agency of Lord and Thomas, then headed by the dynamic Albert Lasker, who had personally tailored the Palmolive advertising campaign.[53]

MICHIGAN SQUARE BUILDING

Following in close succession to the 333 North Michigan Avenue Building and the Palmolive Building were three more Holabird and Root commissions, one for the Michigan Square Building at 540 North Michigan, the second for the Michigan-Chestnut Building at 842 North Michigan, and the third for the Judah Building at 700 North Michigan. All were built as low-rise structures, five to eight stories, though the Michigan Square Building was actually designed as a skyscraper. With the onset of the Depression, its construction stopped at the eighth floor. Intentionally or otherwise these buildings were more in the scale of the Burnham and North Central Business District Association plans in terms of their overall height and relation to the street and sidewalk, and all were designed in the simplified style which had now become characteristic of Holabird and Root.

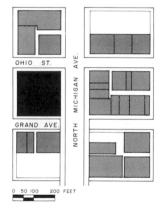

Figure 6.17
Michigan Square Building
site plan. Drawn by author.

The Michigan Square Building (figures 6.17 and 6.18) was designed for the real estate firm of McChesney, Rubens and Wolbach. The building was located on the block bounded by Michigan, Rush, Grand, and Ohio streets, the site of the present Marriott Hotel.[54] Murray Wolbach, in the real estate business since 1895 and a director of the North Central Association, purchased the various parcels of the block between the years 1919 and 1928.[55] There were nearly thirty structures on the property, most of them two- and three-story row houses, and they had many owners, including John Farwell and William Hoyt among others.[56] Financing for the new building in the amount of $3,200,000 was arranged with a loan made by the Northwestern Mutual Life Insurance Company.[57]

The original design for the Michigan Square Building (figure 6.19) called for a forty-story structure to be composed of a twenty-two story base filling the entire block and an eighteen story tower rising from the building's west half.

Figure 6.18
Michigan Square Building,
540 North Michigan Avenue, 1928–29; Holabird and Root, architects. Reprinted from Architectural Record *(October 1931), copyright (1931) by McGraw-Hill, Inc. All rights reserved. Reproduced with the permission of the publisher.*

Figure 6.19
Michigan Square Building,
design drawing, 1928; Hol-
abird and Root, architects.
Reprinted from Architectural Record *(May 1929),*
copyright (1929) by
McGraw-Hill, Inc. All
rights reserved. Repro-
duced with the permission
of the publisher.

The lower block itself was to be divided horizontally into
three stages, a single-story base, and seven intervening
floors separated from the remaining fourteen by a continuous cornice line. There was to be a strong emphasis on

verticality in both the base and the tower, with the window bays grouped in pairs with recessed spandrels. The design of the tower drew upon both 333 North Michigan and the Palmolive Building in projection and recession of vertical elements. The central bays of the east and west sides were to be recessed and framed by projecting outer bays, while the reverse was to occur on the north and south sides.

The first story was set off from the rest of the building with Belgian black marble framing large rectangular shop windows. The upper floors were faced with limestone with abstract carved reliefs in the spandrels above the third-floor windows and at the very top of each window bay as well as along the top of the parapets. A rhythm was established across the east facade with the alternating broad and narrow piers, a strong contrast to the static quality of the lower two floors whose large windows corresponded to two bays in the floors above. The entrance in the center of the Michigan Avenue facade rose through two stories, and the doorway itself was recessed several feet within the opening, giving it a three-dimensional appearance.

The most outstanding feature of the Michigan Square Building was the presence of a central court around which were located shops on two levels (figure 6.20). Called "Diana Court" for its fountain of Diana by sculptor Carl Milles, it was approached through lobby corridors from the Michigan, Grand, and Ohio street sides.[58] It was semicircular in shape, forty-two feet in diameter, with a sunken central area reached by a circuitous series of broad stairs, with the statue of Diana as a focal point. The shops around the perimeter of the building had entrances both on the exterior and the court itself (figure 6.21).[59] The layout was a model of intriguing shopping spaces designed to combine both the private economic activities of the individual shops with the social activities of the common public space. The presence of the interior court or mall was a big improvement over the small area for shops at 333 North Michigan Avenue or even the arcade of the Palmolive Building. This was the most immediate precursor of the much larger and more lavish Water Tower Place shopping mall of the 1970s.

The majority of the shop fronts and interiors for the Michigan Square Building, each in a different style, were designed by Holabird and Root. A small bakery, Socath's, for instance, had a facade of terrazzo in different shades of red and gray, while the Walden Bookshop next door was executed in white metal.[60] Individual shop bays were separated by wide marble frames. The design of the courtyard

167

Figure 6.20
Michigan Square Building,
Diana Court with statue of
Diana; Carl Milles, sculp-
tor. Reprinted from Architectural Record *(October*
1931), copyright (1931) by
McGraw-Hill, Inc. All
rights reserved. Repro-
duced with the permission
of the publisher.

suggests the influence of Swedish design. John Root and John Holabird had recently taken a trip to Sweden and had developed a great interest in Swedish architecture and crafts. In a letter to Walter Creese in 1949, John Root wrote that the Carl Milles fountain and the interior of the building were influenced by that trip.[61] Historian H. Stewart Leonard suggests that the specific influence was the Swedish Match Works in Stockholm.[62]

The true appeal of Diana Court was its dynamic tension: the sound of water, the multiple floor levels with balconies and open stairways, the richness of surfaces, and clarity of forms. The floors of the court were enriched with terrazzo designs, and the ceiling featured a large skylight and concealed indirect lighting along with gold leaf and symbols of Diana and the stars and the moon. Further com-

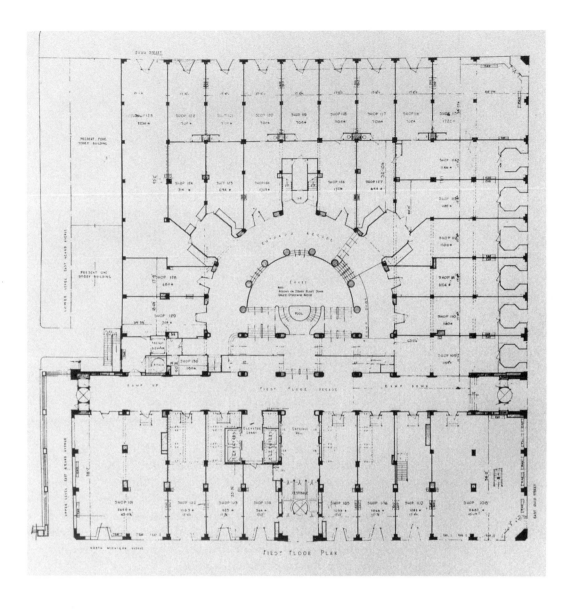

FIRST FLOOR PLAN

plementing the statue of Diana were nine large sandblasted panels representing attendants and aspects of the goddess. Executed by sculptor Edgar Miller, they were placed above the gallery level on the curved back wall and were lit from behind.[63]

MICHIGAN-CHESTNUT BUILDING

The Michigan-Chestnut Building, constructed in 1927–28 for the Michigan-Chestnut Building Corporation, is yet another speculative structure following the well-defined for-

Figure 6.21
Michigan Square Building plan. Reprinted from Architectural Record *(October 1931), copyright (1931) by McGraw-Hill, Inc. All rights reserved. Reproduced with the permission of the publisher.*

Figure 6.22
Michigan-Chestnut Build-
ing, 842 North Michigan
Avenue, 1927–28; Holabird
and Root, architects.
Photo by author.

mula established by Holabird and Root. Plans for the building, announced in November 1927 (figure 6.22), originally called for a six-story structure, the first two floors to be devoted to shops, the next two to offices, and those above to high-ceilinged studios suitable for interior decorators, painters, sculptors, and musicians.[64] When the building was finally constructed, however, a seventh floor was added for additional studios.

The need for such a building housing artist's studios had to do with its proximity to what was dubbed by the newspapers as "Towertown." The area west of Michigan Avenue, along Erie, Ohio, Huron, and Superior streets, the heart of old McCormickville, had become in the 1920s a considerable colony of artists, sculptors, and writers. They located there because old buildings could easily be converted into studios, and many of the old residences had stables. They also came there for the atmosphere of tearooms, art stores, antique shops, and bookstores.[65] By the time of the construction of the Michigan-Chestnut Building, however, as well as the Michigan-Superior Building which also housed artists' studios, the bohemian culture of Towertown was already beginning to disappear as rising land values and rents made the area too expensive for them to live and work there.[66] Fortunately, the high-ceilinged spaces of both buildings were adequately suited to more professional office uses as they made the transition without economic loss.

The building's client, W. B. Frankenstein, president of the Michigan-Chestnut Building Company, had purchased the site, located just south of the Fourth Presbyterian Church, from the Palmer estate in 1926.[67] Measuring 107 feet wide by 201 feet deep, the lot cost $725,000.[68] The cost of the building was $1,250,000.[69]

The building's facade is organized into three horizontal sections: a two-story base with cast-iron shop fronts and shallow second-floor bay windows, a three-story middle portion with smooth limestone wall surfaces framing single-window units, and two upper floors with fluted pilasters framing recessed windows the upper level of which is topped by segmented arches. As with the Michigan Square Building, there is no upper cornice but, instead, a low stepped-back parapet. Rhythm in the building's facades is created by the juxtaposition of the wide shop-level bays and the increasingly vertical emphasis at the top. In terms of height and proportion, the building was an appropriate complement to the Fourth Presbyterian Church and the 900 North Michigan Avenue Apartment Building.

JUDAH BUILDING

The last of Holabird and Root's structures on North Michigan Avenue from the 1920s was the Noble Judah Building at the northwest corner of Michigan and Huron Street (figure 6.23).[70] Its architectural elements were similar to those of the Michigan-Chestnut and Michigan Square buildings but arranged in a different manner. The building was owned by Dorothy Patterson Judah, the wife of Noble Judah, both of whom were prominent in Chicago social circles as well as national political affairs. Mr. Judah, an attorney, served from 1927 to 1929 as the United States ambassador to Cuba.[71] It was during this time that Mrs. Judah purchased the property from the estate of architect Charles Fox.[72] This had been the site of the Perry H. Smith House, already demolished for the widening of the avenue. Shortly after Mrs. Judah commissioned Holabird and Root to design the building, her husband died, but she carried out the

Figure 6.23
Judah Building, 700 North
Michigan Avenue, 1928–29;
Holabird and Root, archi-
tects. Reprinted from
American Architect *(20*
June 1929), copyright
(1929) by McGraw-Hill,
Inc. All rights reserved.
Reproduced with the per-
mission of the publisher.

project herself and managed the building until 1934. The construction cost was approximately $650,000.[73] There is no indication of a mortgage on the property, suggesting that the Judahs paid cash for the project.

Holabird and Root designed for Mrs. Judah a five-story building (figure 6.24) with a polished granite exterior on the first and second levels and Alabama limestone on the upper three levels. The building's structure was reinforced concrete with eleven-foot ceilings in the upper office floors.[74] As with the Michigan-Chestnut Building, the higher floor-to-floor dimension resulted in a more elegant proportion for the windows and spandrels. Also like the Michigan-Chestnut Building, rhythm was established by the play of wide ground-level bays with the narrow, vertical

bays of the upper floors. Subtle forms of ornamentation were used: rounding the corners of the polished granite base, inserting narrow engaged columns in the corners of the limestone walls above, placing segmental arches above the intermediate windows of the corner bays, and using a plain parapet set off by a decorative stringcourse in shallow relief.

Urbanistically, the building was an odd complement to the sixteen-story Central Life Insurance Company Building located just to the north. While the two buildings' intermediate shop-level cornices lined up, the discrepancy in their heights created a distinct mismatch that not only broke the harmony of the street frontage but left an unsightly bare wall looming above the Judah Building on the north. It was exactly this kind of contextual imbalance that Daniel Burnham and the architects for the North Central Business District Association had sought to avoid, but it was indeed this juxtaposition that became the norm for development on North Michigan Avenue as economic circumstances invariably became the key factor in determining building height.

TERMINAL PARK

At the very end of the decade, Holabird and Root, in association with three New York architectural firms, became involved in a project known as Terminal Park for the Illinois Central Railroad air rights east of Michigan Avenue between Randolph Street and the river.[75] Two schemes were proposed, each different in both form and content, yet sharing the concept of "a city within a city."[76] Like the proposal by Eliel Saarinen earlier in the decade, both relied on tall office slabs flanked by lower office blocks all organized within a harmonious and balanced plan.

The scheme proposed by Raymond Hood with Godley and Fouilhoux, and Voorhees, Gmelin and Walker featured a broad mall running east and west and intersected by a crossing street near the lakefront (figure 6.25). Four exceptionally tall towers flanked this intersection, and somewhat smaller slabs fronted on Michigan Avenue. Low-rise blocks framed the mall on the north and south and extended to the lakefront beyond the main towers. The

Figure 6.25
Project, Terminal Park, Illinois Central air rights, 1929; Raymond Hood and Ralph Walker, architects. Reprinted from Robert A. M. Stern, Raymond Hood *(New York, 1982).*

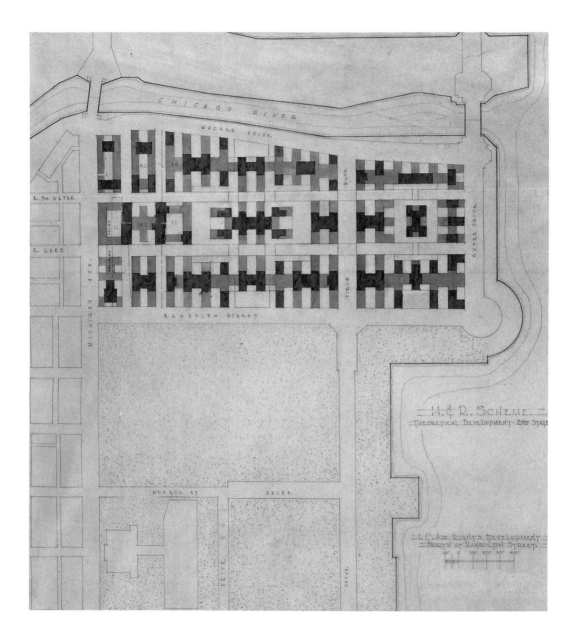

plan of Holabird and Root (figure 6.26) proposed more of a checkerboard plan without a central mall. In its place were to be a series of towers connected to lower wings forming H- and L-shaped configurations.

Had either of these plans been realized, in terms of size and sophistication of planning, it would have been the largest and most impressive building project in the city's history and would have had a major impact on North Michigan Avenue. Unfortunately, these plans were proposed just

Figure 6.26
Project, Terminal Park, Illinois Central air rights, Randolph Street between Michigan Avenue and North Lake Shore Drive, 1929; Holabird and Root, architects. Courtesy of the Art Institute of Chicago.

prior to the stock-market crash, which brought a halt to most building projects in the city. As it turned out, nothing would be built on the site until the late 1960s, some thirty years later.

COMMERCIAL ARCHITECTURE AT THE END OF THE DECADE

T he last years of the decade, leading up to the Depression of 1929, saw a continuing development of North Michigan Avenue, though the amount of construction in the rest of the city was steadily declining from the peak in 1926.[1] Four significant commercial buildings in addition to those of Holabird and Root were erected in 1928 and 1929, beginning with the Michigan-Superior Building and ending with the most outstanding work of architecture from the period, the Union Carbide and Carbon Building. Like the buildings of Holabird and Root, all of these shared the use of simplified forms and a general lack of traditional ornamentation.

MICHIGAN-SUPERIOR BUILDING

The Michigan-Superior Building (figure 7.1), at 737 North Michigan Avenue, now the site of the Nieman-Marcus department store, was planned to house a curious combination of shops and art studios as well as a penthouse apartment for one of its owners.[2] Similar to the uses of the Michigan-Chestnut Building, it played an important role for craftsmen, artists, and art and antique dealers who frequented and inhabited the North Michigan Avenue commercial district. It was erected by the estate of Charles Chapin, who had also owned the Fine Arts Building on South Michigan Avenue next to the Auditorium Theater. Chapin's three sons, who now controlled his estate, all had offices in the Fine Arts Building but lived on the Near North Side.[3] They purchased the site for the Michigan-Superior Building in 1928 and obtained financing for the

Figure 7.1
Michigan-Superior Build-
ing, 737 North Michigan
Avenue Building, 1928–29;
Andrew Rebori, architect.
Courtesy of the Chicago
Historical Society.

new building from the Northwestern Mutual Life Insurance Company.[4]

To design the building, the Chapins commissioned Andrew Rebori, who had been instrumental in producing the 1918 planning study for the North Central Business District Association. He was otherwise best known in the city for the Loyola University Library and the Loyola Della Strada Chapel.[5] Rebori's first proposal for the Chapin site called for a 268-foot-high building with a 158-foot tower.[6] However, it was far too ambitious for the Chapin heirs, who settled for something much smaller and more manageable for their purposes (figure 7.2).

The building that was finally constructed rose just five stories plus the penthouse, all on a reinforced concrete frame. The exterior was clad with Indiana limestone with fluted piers and ornamented spandrels, while the first two floors contained large rectangular shop windows, with bronze and silver-finished steel frames. The main entrance in the center of the west facade was a two-story round-arched opening leading to a central arcade that traversed the building from Michigan Avenue to a bank of elevators along the east wall. An added feature was a system of exte-

*Figure 7.2
Michigan-Superior Build-
ing, design drawing. Re-
printed from the* Chicago
Tribune *(27 May 1928).*

rior lighting with luminous bowls placed in the base of each
pier at the second floor to throw a vertical shaft of light at
night. The idea was to emphasize the perpendicular lines of
the exterior without interfering with the window lighting of
the shops.[7]

There were twenty shops in all on the ground floor,
each having an entrance both from the street and from the
central arcade. All of the shops were treated in a modern
design, expressive of the wares on sale, and each was different from the other. More shops were located on the second floor, along with a hall seating 350 for musicals, lec-
tures, and club meetings. The third and fourth floors were
specially designed with sound-deadening panels in the walls
and floors for use as practice rooms by musicians. The top
floor, planned for painters, jewel workers, interior decorators, fabric workers, and sculptors, had large windows
and skylights.[8] The most unusual feature of the building
was the penthouse apartment on the sixth level, its windows
overlooking the Michigan-Superior intersection, and its living room topped by a domed observatory built for a member of the Chapin family who was an amateur astronomer.[9]

McGRAW-HILL BUILDING

The McGraw-Hill Building (figures 7.3 and 7.4), at the
southwest corner of Michigan Avenue and Grand Avenue,
was built in 1928 by the Michigan-Grand Building Corporation, which was owned by the law firm of Winston,

*Figure 7.3
McGraw-Hill Building, 520
North Michigan Avenue,
1928–29; Thielbar and Fu-
gard, architects. Courtesy
of the Chicago Historical
Society.*

Strawn, and Shaw.[10] The company had a ninety-nine-year
lease on the site and obtained financing to build the new
structure from the Foreman State Bank.[11]

The building was designed by the firm of Thielbar and
Fugard, its first on North Michigan Avenue, although John
R. Fugard had worked as an associate architect on the Allerton Hotel. Frederick J. Thielbar had been a partner
with Holabird and Roche until 1918, and then had his own
practice before entering into partnership with John Fugard
in 1925. The firm specialized in Gold Coast apartment

Figure 7.4
View of the west side of
North Michigan Avenue
looking north from Tribune
Building; McGraw-Hill
Building is at left, 1957.
Courtesy of the Chicago
Historical Society.

buildings and was the supervising architect for the Jewelers Building at 35 East Wacker Drive.[12] Working with them on the McGraw-Hill Building was engineer James B. Black.[13]

When the building project was announced in June 1928 (figure 7.5), it was to be called 520 North Michigan Avenue. However, four months after construction was started, the mid-western general office of the McGraw-Hill Publishing Company of New York, one of the largest trade paper and book publishing concerns in the world, signed a twenty-five-year lease to occupy four floors of the structure with the stipulation that its name be changed to the McGraw-Hill Building. The company's Chicago offices had previously been housed in two buildings in the Loop. J. H. McGraw, the president of the company, stated that "the

Figure 7.5
McGraw-Hill Building, de-
sign drawing. Reprinted
from the Chicago Tribune
(10 June 1928).

decision to go to the new location was made not only on the northern trend in business offices in the city but on the growing concentration around the Tribune Square of publishing and advertising interests."[14] During this period, the company not only signed a lease for its new Chicago headquarters but also greatly expanded its operations by purchasing A. W. Shaw and Company, thus entering the field of business books.[15] By this time, it was the largest organization in the country specializing in the publication of magazines and books on engineering, industry, and business, controlling in all some twenty-four magazines.[16]

Also in 1928, yet another well-known corporate name became involved with the building when F. L. Maytag of Newton, Iowa, the world's largest manufacturer of washing machines, purchased control from the Michigan-Grand Building Corporation of the nearly completed $3,000,000 structure. Considered by real estate experts as one of the year's most significant real estate transactions, Maytag bought a majority interest in the company and became its president and director. The name of the building, McGraw-Hill, remained unchanged, however. Maytag saw this as an excellent investment, the building's location on North Michigan Avenue certain to insure large profits.[17]

As built, the structure rises sixteen stories with a granite base, limestone cladding on the walls above, and terra cotta spandrels and decorative panels at the top. The first floor has stores opening onto Michigan Avenue, with a two-story main entrance and lobby in the center. The second floor has large display windows in cast-iron frames topped by eagles. The fourth floor is highlighted by carved relief panels between the windows, and the fifth floor features standing mythological figures in a deeper sculpted relief. The upper corners of the building step back above the thirteenth floor, and a tall parapet with vertical openings rises above the sixteenth floor.

The building is rectangular in plan on the first two floors, measuring 100 feet on Michigan Avenue and 125 feet on Grand (figure 7.6).[18] Above the third floor, the southwest corner is cut away to form a light court measuring fifty-four by thirty-two feet. The basement level on the north, west, and south sides is exposed because of Michigan Avenue's elevated grade. A raised sidewalk with a concrete balustrade extends along the building's north side, and stairs at its west end descends to Grand Avenue. The building's structure is a reinforced concrete frame with experimental cast-iron cores.[19] Massive five- to eight-foot reinforced concrete girders support the offset floors at the upper levels.[20]

The McGraw-Hill Building unfortunately had a distinctly unattractive south elevation which directly faced the Wrigley Building two blocks away. The L-shaped plan configuration, combined with the transition at the second bay from limestone cladding to brick made it appear busy and unfinished. It was like the London Guarantee Building and the Central Life Insurance Company Building in that it relied on the construction of adjacent structures of similar height to complete its appearance. This facade aesthetic of

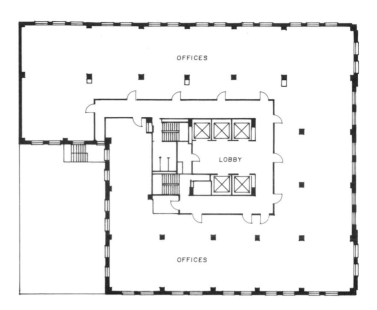

TYPICAL OFFICE FLOOR

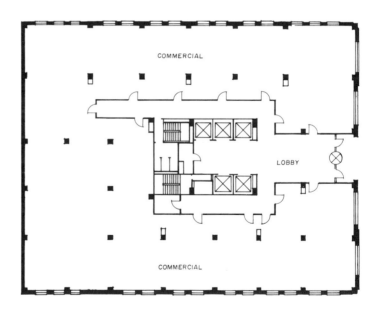

FIRST FLOOR PLAN

0 5 10   20 FEET

Figure 7.6
McGraw-Hill Building
plans. Redrawn by author
from Engineering News-
Record *(25 July 1929).*

only partially finished buildings represented a decidedly
different attitude toward the development of North Michigan Avenue than had been exhibited by the owners and
architects of such noble structures as the Wrigley, Tribune,

and Palmolive buildings. These were meant to be seen from all sides, from close up on the avenue itself or from several blocks away, from the Loop or the lakefront. The McGraw-Hill Building and others like it were meant to be seen only from the avenue and only in relation to other buildings erected around them. They were just one piece of a larger whole rather than a freestanding entity unto themselves. Such an aesthetic, of course, relied on the assumption that adjacent buildings would indeed be constructed, and the sooner the better. What no one had counted on was the stock market crash of 1929 and its resulting halt in building construction for more than two decades. This event did as much to play against the harmonious development of North Michigan Avenue as the lifting of the height restrictions in the building ordinance of 1923. Both worked to eliminate any hope of the kind of image proposed by Burnham and the architects of the North Central Business District Association.

MUSIC CORPORATION
OF AMERICA BUILDING

The Music Corporation of America Building at 430 North Michigan Avenue (figure 7.7), one block south of the McGraw-Hill Building, had a different sort of urbanistic problem. It had the dubious distinction of being the thinnest structure to be erected on the avenue, rising fourteen stories with a lot depth of only twenty-five feet. Seen from the front, it had the appearance of any modern skyscraper, having a frontage of 100 feet on Michigan Avenue, but as the *Chicago Tribune* stated at the time of its opening, "The boulevard motorists or pedestrian, however, will get a shock the first time he glimpses the new skyscraper from either the north or the south."[21] In comparison, the 333 North Michigan Avenue Building, which appears to be one of the city's narrowest skyscrapers, was nearly two-and-a-half times as wide.

Even with this narrow lot size and the resulting inefficiency in plan design, the building's owner, the 430 North Michigan Avenue Building Corporation, signed a property lease for a record high rate for the avenue of $25,000 yearly, its North Michigan Avenue address being the primary consideration.[22] The estimated cost of the building was $500,000, its construction financed by the Continental Illinois Bank.[23] The building's architect was Loebl, Schlossman and Demuth.[24] The building's design shared many of

Figure 7.7
Music Corporation of
America Building, 430
North Michigan Avenue,
1929; Loebl, Schlossman,
and Demuth, architects.
Courtesy of the Chicago
Historical Society. Photo
by J. Sherwin Murphy.

the same characteristics with Holabird and Root's North
Michigan Avenue buildings, a simplified style used to produce a sleek and dignified structure well suited to its location on a commercial avenue (figure 7.8). The first level and
the center three bays of the second and third floors were
clad with dark imported marble. Large plate-glass windows
with separate shop entrances filled out the bays of the first
floor. The upper floors were finished off with face brick,
with limestone trim on all sides. Verticality was emphasized
in the center bays with slender piers framing recessed spandrels. The uppermost floor was stepped back but continued
the recessed central bays and their framing piers. The lack

Figure 7.8
Music Corporation of
America Building, design
drawing. Reprinted from
the Chicago Tribune *(7*
April 1929).

of a cornice gave the building the same feeling of rising to infinity as found in the Saarinen Tribune Tower design and its imitators.

The Music Corporation of America Building was not tall enough to be a true skyscraper, yet its slender proportions and its stepped-back top gave it the character of a building taller than it really was, thus implying the same economic and symbolic connotations as 333 North Michigan or the Palmolive Building. Its great strengths as an integral element of North Michigan Avenue was its continuation of the lower shop levels with offices above, its emphasis on verticality, and its relative lack of ornamentation.

187

Figure 7.9
Union Carbide and Carbon
Building, 230 North Michi-
gan Avenue, 1928–29;
Burnham Brothers, Inc.,
architects. Reprinted from
Western Architect *(April*
1930).

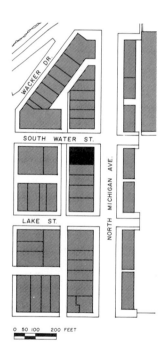

Figure 7.10
Union Carbide and Carbon
Building site plan. Drawn
by author.

UNION CARBIDE
AND CARBON BUILDING

The last high-rise office building to be erected on North Michigan Avenue in the 1920s was the Union Carbide and Carbon Building at 230 North Michigan (figures 7.9 and 7.10).[25] Designed by Burnham Brothers, Inc., formerly D. H. Burnham and Company, the project was announced in May 1928 by the 230 North Michigan Avenue Building Corporation, which already had the New York–based

Union Carbide and Carbon Corporation signed up as its major tenant.[26] The building was designed to house primarily subsidiaries of Carbide and Carbon, including the Oxweld Acetylene Company and the Presto-O-Lite Company, among others, with the ground floor to be used for display purposes.[27] The project cost was $4,700,000, with a mortgage bond issue underwritten by the Greenbaum Sons Investment Company and further financing provided by the Bank of America.[28]

With this building, North Michigan Avenue became the home of yet another nationally known company. The Union Carbide and Carbon Corporation was one of the country's largest industrial concerns in the 1920s. A conglomerate with twenty-four separate companies and ninety-eight plants and factories in the United States, Canada, and Norway, its products were sold through more than 15,000 service stations and 60,000 retail stores. Its primary source of income, however, came from its industrial production of calcium carbide, which produced acetylene gas, largely used in the steel industry.[29]

The Carbide and Carbon Building stands forty stories (figures 7.11 and 7.12), with a twenty-six-story main block, rectangular in plan, filling the property from lot line to lot line, and a fourteen-story tower rising on the Michigan Avenue side. This facade is flush the entire height with the piers thrusting through the main block to the top of the campanile. The north and south faces of the tower are set back two bays on either side (figure 7.13), thus making it a distinctly slender tower. The building's structure is a steel frame, designed by engineer Charles Harkins.[30]

Like Raymond Hood's American Radiator Building in New York, much of the design quality of the Carbide and Carbon Building is based on the use of color, in this case black, green, and gold. The first three floors are faced with black granite and gold terra cotta trim (figure 7.14); the fourth through twenty-sixth floors and the tower have dark green mottled terra cotta pilasters and piers with gold trim. The terra cotta spandrels are accented in a medium shade of green.[31] An article in the *Chicago Tribune* announcing the project related this unique use of exterior architectural polychromy to product design, stating:

> Although color is fast becoming an important factor in the sale of most American products, owners and architects have overlooked to a noticeable extent its use in buildings.[32]

Figure 7.11
Union Carbide and Carbon Building, design drawing. Reprinted from the Chicago Tribune *(13 May 1928).*

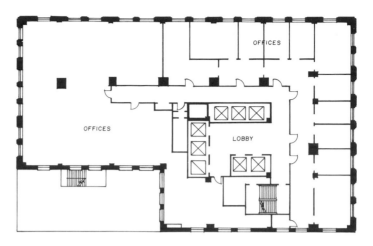

TYPICAL OFFICE FLOOR

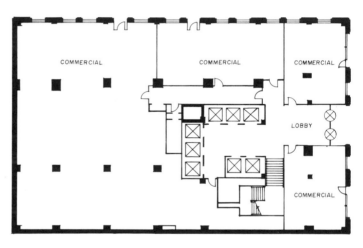

FIRST FLOOR PLAN

0 5 10   20 FEET

Figure 7.12
Union Carbide and Carbon
Building plans. Courtesy of
the Chicago Historical So-
ciety. Redrawn by author.

The Burnham Brothers design was characterized as a notable exception to this tendency. The use of color is carried through on the building's interior: a grand two-story lobby with a gray Tennessee marble floor with a Belgian black marble border (figure 7.15), and a ceiling of ornamental plaster in colors. All metalwork of the doors, elevators, and fixtures is bronze. Typical corridors have marble wainscoting, and the wood trim throughout is American walnut.[33]

A rental brochure published in the 1930s suggests the idea the developers had about the importance of good design and expensive materials in legitimizing the business in-

Figure 7.13
Union Carbide and Carbon
Building, detail of tower.
Photo by author.

terests housed in the structure. Pointing out the bronze ornament and black marble of the entrance (figure 7.16) and
the bronze-trimmed mezzanine floor in the lobby space, the
brochure states:

> The effect of such beauty in a building upon the
> morale of the people employed in it is unquestion-
> ably beneficial and inspiring: and to clients, busi-
> ness associates, and visitors, it is constant assur-
> ance that the organizations they are dealing with
> are of the highest calibre.[34]

191

Figure 7.14
Union Carbide and Carbon
Building, facade detail.
Photo by author.

Figure 7.15
Union Carbide and Carbon
Building, lobby detail. Re-
printed from Western Architect *(April 1930).*

Figure 7.16
Union Carbide and Carbon
Building, entrance detail.
Reprinted from Western
Architect *(April 1930).*

To this was added the idea of status and wealth with statements such as:

> Prestige. The desirability of any office building
> should be measured as much by the prestige the
> building can bestow upon its occupants as by its
> physical equipment, design, and service facilities.[35]

The final advertising pitch was made with the grand statement that the Carbide and Carbon Building "possesses prestige value unequalled in Chicago."[36]

CUNEO TOWER PROJECT

One building proposed in 1929, but never carried out, was
to be located at the northeast corner of Michigan Avenue
and Randolph Street, across from the Crerar Library.
John F. Cuneo, head of the Cuneo Press, announced that
he was having Graham, Anderson, Probst and White draw
up plans for a thirty-six-story tower for the site, which the
General Motors Corporation was contemplating leasing for
fifty years at an annual rent of nearly $700,000.[37] It was to
have the most spectacular open air advertising yet attempted for a skyscraper with electric flashing signs in
bright colors running from the sidewalk to the top, telling
the city of the automobile and refrigeration products of
General Motors.[38]

Just four months later, Cuneo announced yet another
project for the site, this one to be a sixty-story building
designed by Burnham Brothers, Inc., who had just designed the Carbide and Carbon Building. At 657 feet, it
would be the tallest building in Chicago (figure 7.17).[39]
While the existing zoning ordinance would have allowed the
main bulk of the building to be only 264 feet high, the City
Council passed an amendment in June 1929 raising the allowable main sections of buildings from 264 feet to 440 feet
if three sides of the building faced on streets, one of them
being more than 100 feet wide, and if one of the sides faced
a public park.[40] The Cuneo Tower met these conditions;
nevertheless, the building site was quite small, fronting just
ninety feet on Michigan Avenue and Beaubien Court, and
a mere seventy feet on Randolph.

Burnham Brothers, Inc., designed the building in the
prevailing style with an emphasis on vertical lines. It was
similar to a tower Andrew Rebori had proposed for another client for the same site in 1925 (figure 7.18), which
had a series of subtle setbacks leading to a pinnacle at the
top.[41] The Burnham Brothers design made a transition of
the structure's main shaft to the tower through a single
large setback, making it appear more like the Carbide and
Carbon Building with a main block and a tower. Also like
the Carbide and Carbon Building, the architects contemplated the use of colors, in this case to emphasize the impression of height. Dark hues at the base were to gradually
soften in tone as the structure climbed skyward until the
top was reached, where the lightest shades would be em-
ployed—with perhaps dark color used in spots to produce
an outline against the sky.[42] Because of the commanding

*Figure 7.17
Project, Cuneo Tower,
northeast corner of Michigan and Randolph, 1929;
Burnham Brothers, Inc.,
architects. Reprinted from
the* Chicago Tribune *(14
July 1929).*

position the structure would occupy, overlooking Grant
Park with a full view from South Michigan Avenue, the
matter of illuminating it at night was given careful attention.[43]

195

Figure 7.18
Project, northeast corner
of Michigan and Ran-
dolph, 1925; Andrew Re-
bori, architect. Courtesy of
the Chicago Historical So-
ciety.

The Cuneo Tower was planned at the very end of Chicago's 1920s building boom, at a time when optimism was still running high, when anticipated profits clouded any thoughts of caution, when an overextension in building development became as intensive as the overextended stock market. Cuneo was unable to obtain financing for his project, and what could have been North Michigan Avenue's most visible building, completing the gateway to its southern entrance, was never built. This was not necessarily an unfortunate conclusion. The building was, after all, grossly out of scale with its neighbors. It would have been 457 feet higher than the John Crerar Library and 207 feet higher than the Tribune Tower. It would have dwarfed everything around it and would have formed an awkward transition from Grant Park to North Michigan Avenue.

THE CORPORATE AND COMMERCIAL
AVENUE IN 1929

In the ten years since the widening of North Michigan Avenue and the construction of the Michigan Avenue Bridge, thirty-one major buildings had been constructed or remodeled along its path, ranging from low-rise commercial blocks, hotels, and apartments to high-rise clubhouses and corporate towers. While many of these buildings did not conform to the recommendations made in the previous decade by Daniel Burnham and the North Central Business District Association, the fact that they were built where they were attests to the importance of these early plans and to the level of interest they generated in the avenue. While the formal principles of urban design were not in every case followed, the idea of a significant new commercial avenue with the potential for a high return on investment was never lost among its developers. The plans succeeded in solidifying in investors' minds the idea that North Michigan Avenue was a location for the future, that anything they would build there would not only be profitable but would be an integral part of one of the city's most important new commercial areas.

The buildings that attracted the most attention and that represented the greatest concentration of capital and commercial activity were, of course, the skyscrapers. There were essentially three kinds of high-rise buildings constructed on the avenue: those that combined a low-rise mass with a tower, like the Wrigley building; those that rose straight up from the ground, like the Tribune Tower; and those that rose in stepped-back stages, like the Palmolive Building. Of these, five rose to over 400 feet, one was in the 300-foot range, six were in the 200-foot range, and nine were in the 100-foot range. Ten of the thirty-one major buildings constructed or remodeled on the avenue in the 1920s were under 100 feet (table 7.1). A number of styles

Table 7.1
Building heights on North Michigan Avenue in the 1920s

	Stories	Height in feet
Medinah Club	45	498
Tribune Tower	35	481
Union Carbide and Carbon Building	40	(470)
Palmolive Building	37	468
333 North Michigan Avenue	35	426
Wrigley Building	27	398
Allerton Hotel	25	253
National Life Insurance Company Project[a]	25	(250)
London Guarantee Building	21	(250)
Bell Building	23	(250)
Lake-Michigan Building	23	(250)
Illinois Women's Athletic Club	17	204
John Crerar Library	16	200
Central Life Insurance Company Building	16	197
McGraw-Hill Building	16	189
Music Corporation of America Building	14	(170)
Hibbard, Spencer, Bartlett and Company Building	14	(150)
Drake Hotel	14	144
Farwell Building	14	138
Woman's Chicago Athletic Club	9	129
900 North Michigan Avenue Apartment Building	10	114
Michigan Square Building	8	103
Michigan-Ohio Building	8	(90)
Judah Building	5	80
Michigan-Superior Building	6	(70)
Tobey Building	6	(70)
Erskine-Danforth Building	5	(70)
Michigan-Chestnut Building	7	66
Lake Shore Trust and Savings Bank	5	50
Italian Court Building	4	(50)
Palmer Shops Building	3	(35)
Malabry Court	3	(35)

Source: Paul Sprague, "Submission to Illinois Historic Sites Advisory Council—Magnificent Mile–Streeterville Historic District Nomination," August 1982.

Note: Numerals in parentheses = heights estimated to within ten feet.

[a]Project, not built.

were prevalent, ranging from the Spanish Renaissance style of the Wrigley Building and the Gothic style of the Tribune Tower to the Northern Italian style of the Allerton Hotel and the abstracted Classicism of Holabird and Root.

In virtually all of the buildings, whether low-rise or high-rise, the lower floors, at least the first two, were elaborately treated to set them off from the generally unadorned middle and upper floors. Here were located the shopfronts with their large display windows. They were ideal for the commercial activities of the street, while the office spaces above were ideal for the burgeoning corporations. Architecturally, the shops, restaurants, professional offices, hotels, and apartments were all of the highest quality and were available to the entire spectrum of society.

A check of the Chicago City Directory from 1928 to 1929 reveals the broad range of shops, stores, and restaurants found on the avenue at the end of the decade (table 7.2). The trend toward women's shopping clearly emerged: twelve women's clothing stores, ten fur dealers, nine dressmakers, and fourteen beauty parlors. This stood in sharp contrast to men's stores (table 7.3): only four men's furnishings stores and two men's tailors. There were, however, abundant barbershops.

In addition, there were thirteen restaurants and tearooms, five drugstores, two banks, two dry goods stores, and only one department store (table 7.4), a distinct contrast to State Street which had developed since the time of Potter Palmer as principally a department store district.

Furniture and antiques could be purchased on North Michigan Avenue in five antique stores, books in two bookstores, and art supplies in one art goods store. Selective social, political, and athletic activities occurred in the avenue's thirteen clubs, three of them in their own buildings, the rest in rented quarters high above the avenue. To these commercial and institutional spaces must be added, of course, the hundreds, if not thousands, of offices housed in the buildings: advertising agencies, architects, lawyers, insurance agencies, real estate offices, exporters, importers, entrepreneurs, doctors, dentists, and psychiatrists.

There had been a complex set of economic factors and personal and corporate motivations behind the development of North Michigan Avenue in the 1920s. Speculation that began in the Near North Side by the McCormicks, Palmers, and others was transformed into official city policy with the advent of the Burnham Plan and the formation of the Chicago Plan Commission. As Michigan Avenue was

Table 7.2
Women's shops and services on North Michigan Avenue, 1928–29

Address	Name
Women's clothing stores	
160	Joseph Abrams
160	Kernan's, Inc.
319	Rena Hartman, Inc.
328	Gertrude Kopelman
360	S. L. Hoffman and Company
650	Nelle Diamond, Inc.
669	C. Giddings
750	The Tailored Woman
820	Gordon's, Inc.
934	Castberg
936	Blenda J. Larson
946	Peck and Peck
Fur dealers	
163	Harry B. Melvoin
166	Rosenberg Bros.
168	Krotek and Pilney
169	David Adler
180	Jack Somers
180	Martin Tausz
180	Oswalk Karpf
301	L. Friedman, Inc.
333	Florence Seal Fur Co.
410	Stark-Wainwright, Inc.
Women's furnishings	
216	Harry M. Paradise
342	Mitzi Frocks
717	Czechoslovak Art Shop

identified as one of the city's major commercial avenues of the future, speculation in property and the development of buildings took on a whole new significance and intensity (figure 7.19). The marketplace ruled in this rapid urbanization of the area as competing alternate uses vied with each other for a limited amount of desirable real estate.[44] Real estate values were driven to unprecedented heights,

Table 7.2 (continued)

	Dressmakers
180	Bertha Grossman
180	Harold Spaulding
677	Robinson-Williams
820	Atelier Elegants
920	The Walton Shop
931	Martha Weathered
936	Madame Albert
936	Minnie Conroy
950	Misses' Weathered Shop

Source: *Polk's Directory of Chicago, 1928–29.*

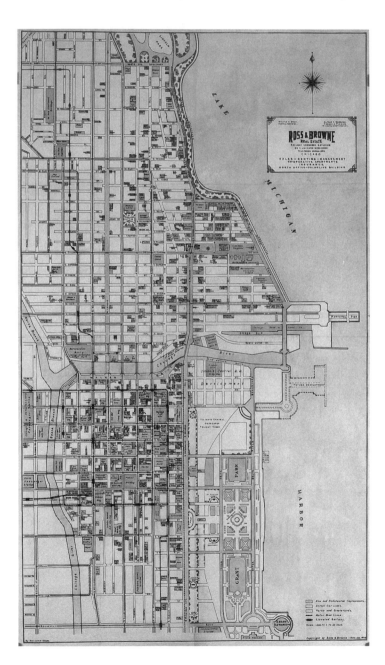

Figure 7.19
Map of Chicago showing the Loop and the Near North Side, 1928. Courtesy of the Chicago Historical Society.

and owners realized that a high standard of construction and design further enhanced the worth of their investment.[45]

According to statistics compiled by Homer Hoyt, the block on North Michigan Avenue between the river and South Water Street was valued at $3,500 per front foot in 1910, before the avenue was widened. In 1928, at the peak of the avenue's development, property in the same block, which now contained the London Guarantee Building, was valued at $20,000 per front foot. By comparison, property on State Street, between Washington and Madison Streets, was valued at $27,500 per front foot in 1910 and at $50,000 in 1928.[46] Though the value of land was not as high on North Michigan Avenue as it was on State Street, it did experience a much greater increase in value during the period from 1910 to 1928, nearly a sixfold increase as opposed to a twofold increase. This meant a higher rate of return for owners of Michigan Avenue property and an increased rate of development, all made possible by the widening of the avenue and the construction of the new bridge.

As building followed upon building, the development of the avenue took on a character that was both consistent and at variance with the ideals envisioned by Daniel Burnham and by the later planners for the North Central Business District Association. Contextual low-rise buildings, like the Drake Hotel or 900 North Michigan Avenue, were juxtaposed against high-rise structures, like the Palmolive Building, as technological and economic forces created a picturesque silhouette as varied as the extent of financial commitment for each individual building. These new buildings on North Michigan Avenue signified not only the success and power of their builders but also the beauty and grandeur of a young Chicago. While they integrated the past with the present stylistically, they acknowledged the progress of technology in their construction and economic need in their form.

Table 7.3
Men's shops and services on North Michigan Avenue, 1928–29

Address	Name
Men's furnishings	
150	John T. Shayne and Company
410	Fifield and Stevenson, Inc.
703	Allerton Men's Shop
900	Docktader and Sandberg
Men's tailors	
180	Joseph Frances
435	Clarence Gilmer
Barber shops	
168	James Barsano
180	George Andrews
307	Arthur Waddell
333	George Williams
410	George Andrews
435	Charles Jones
701	Allerton House Barbers
820	George Candoss
952	John Sherman

Source: *Polk's Directory of Chicago, 1928–29.*

Table 7.4

Restaurants, stores, and clubs on North Michigan Avenue, 1928–29

Address/Name		Address/Name	
Restaurants and tearooms		*Dry Goods*	
176	Fortune Tea Shop	314	Brant Linen Co.
206	Mullett's Candy and Tea Shop	307	Gabriel Plamondon
309	F. Couthoui, Inc.	*Druggists*	
310	Huylers Restaurant	180	Lake-Michigan Pharmacy
410	Charles B. Grayling		
506	Bide-A-Wee Sandwich Shop	307	George A. Hochhaus
520	Karola Tea Room	640	John F. Carnegie, Inc.
600	John R. Thompson	707	Allerton Pharmacy, Inc.
615	LePetit Gourmet Restaurant	943	John F. Carnegie, Inc.
631	Bright Shavel Tea Room		
661	Streeterville Tavern	*Department stores*	
725	Parkway Tea Room	605	F. W. Woolworth Co.
930	Wood Candy Company	*Art goods*	
Antiques		673	M. O'Brien and Son
541	Valentine's Antique Shop	*Clubs*	
673	M. O'Brien and Son	225	Matrix Club
910	Nachemsohn of London	307	Skyline Club
		333	Tavern Club
912	Syrie Maughan Inc.	360	Women's City Club of Chicago
932	Italian Antique Galleries	360	Illinois Republican Club
Bookstores		400	Acacia Athletic Club
206	Kroch's Bookstore	400	Chicago National League Ball Club
500	Phillip A. Stephens	410	The Arts Club
Banks		410	Caxton Club
		505	Medinah Club
400	Boulevard Bridge Bank	612	Wauconda Fields Country Club
605	Lake Shore Trust and Savings Bank	626	Woman's Chicago Athletic Club
		820	Illinois Women's Athletic Club

Source: *Polk's Directory of Chicago, 1928–29.*

I n the late 1920s, the possibility of any major financial crisis was to most people inconceivable. In the opinion of the experts, prices had reached new plateaus, new levels from which they could not and would not descend. By the end of 1929, however, it became apparent that the country was faced with an overproduction of capital, overambitious expansion of business, and an overproduction of commodities under the stimulus of installment buying.[1] On the memorable day of October 24, 1929, prices broke on the stock market and billions of dollars in paper profit were wiped out. The decline continued, and on Tuesday, October 28, more than sixteen billion shares were dumped in the most disastrous day in the history of the exchange.[2] From September to November of 1929 the value of stocks declined nearly 42 percent.[3] The stock market crash brought an end to the general prosperity that had sustained the extraordinary expansion of the city.

The crash proved that prosperity was more than just an economic condition: it was a state of mind. The bull market of 1929 was more than a climax of a business cycle in American mass thinking and mass emotion.[4] There was hardly a man or woman in Chicago, wealthy entrepreneur or blue-collar laborer, whose attitude toward life was not affected by the sudden and brutal shattering of hope. With the big bull market gone, and prosperity going, Chicagoans soon found themselves living in an altered world that called for new adjustments, new ideas, new habits of thought, and a new order of values. During the three years following the crash, stocks, bonds, and commodity prices continued to drop. Over 5000 banks across the nation failed during these three years.[5] The Depression hit Chicago hard as the city government went bankrupt, and banks refused to extend credit.[6] Construction was brought to a halt on North Michigan Avenue because of the lack of mortgage money and because there was no demand for new office or commercial space. Major concerns became unemployment, mortgage foreclosures, bank closings, and bread lines.

Architects began to feel the decline in business investment while the professional journals explained how to economize in the office, how to attract clients, and what to do when out of work. Walter Creese writes,

> The cessation of skyscraper building alone was enough to disturb the prevailing systems of thought, for the prestige of the leading architects as well as the richest corporations depended not a little on the fame conveyed by their tall buildings. A state of exhausted uncertainty known only to those who are no longer intoxicated by the fascination of action for its own sake fell over the whole architectural profession.[7]

The Depression was a moment of awakening of the architect's social conscience. Since much less money was spent on building so that there was less actual construction, most architectural activity was theoretical. Major new themes appeared in the journals: housing, prefabricated houses, and the use and effect of modern materials.

The damage wrought by the Depression was much deeper than most real estate analysts could have imagined. The number of property transactions in Cook County declined from 102,239 in 1927 to 67,770 in 1930. The value of new construction in Chicago fell off even more drastically, from $315,800,000 in 1928 to $79,613,400 in 1930.[8] By 1933 Chicago real estate reached its lowest ebb since the stock market crash. Average apartment rents had declined fully 50 percent from their 1928 level, while the reduction in store rents ranged from 40 to 90 percent. Vacant lots, even in a built-up area like North Michigan Avenue, were offered for sale at from 75 to 90 percent below 1928 prices. Many buildings could be bought at less than half of their original cost, but there were practically no buyers, the complications of unpaid creditors and taxes deterring purchasers.[9]

Besides the cessation of building activities on North Michigan Avenue, the most significant impact of the Depression was the eventual bankruptcy of many of the developers who had so lavishly invested their efforts in building up the avenue throughout the 1920s. The Music Corporation of America Building was one of the first, its mortgage foreclosed by the Continental Illinois Bank in 1930. The year 1932 saw the greatest number of building failures on North Michigan Avenue, including the Michigan-Ohio Building Corporation, the Central Life Insurance Company, and the Michigan-Grand Building Corporation. In addition, Straus and Company foreclosed on the 333 North Michigan Avenue Building and the Drake Hotel, while the Northwestern Mutual Life Insurance Company foreclosed on Charles and Raymond Cook's Malabry Court. Four years later, it foreclosed on their Italian Court Building.[10]

The year 1933 was nearly as disastrous for North Michigan Avenue. Eugene Lydon, the owner of the site of the Carbide and Carbon Building, went bankrupt, and there were foreclosures on the Bell Building, Murray Wolbach and the Michigan Square Building, Henry K. Chapin and the Michigan-Superior Building, and on the Illinois Women's Athletic Club. In 1934, the Lake-Michigan Building Corporation filed for bankruptcy, and the Erskine-Danforth Building, the Allerton Hotel, and the 900 North Michigan Avenue Apartment Building went into foreclosure.[11]

In many cases, arrangements for refinancing were made. The ownership of the Drake Hotel, for instance, was reorganized in 1932, the newly formed Whitestone Management Company taking over the property from the original company. A new loan was obtained from the Metropolitan Life Insurance Company, and even the building's furnishings were mortgaged.[12] In the same year, the 900 North Michigan Avenue Apartment Building was refinanced in a similar way.[13]

Possibly the most celebrated bankruptcy case of all was that of the Medinah Club, Walter Ahlschlager's grand vision of exoticism. Regarded as an economic white elephant from the moment of its construction—it initial occupancy being a mere 32 percent—it went into receivership early in 1932. In reorganizing, its restrictions on membership were lifted, and the rooms were altered to provide additional rental units. But after several more years of unpaid taxes and defaults on its mortgages and bond issues, foreclosure proceedings were taken up by the federal courts. A well-publicized trial was held in 1942 which brought to light its tangled financial problems: a $2,377,500 general mortgage, a $460,000 first mortgage, $412,877 in unpaid taxes, and several million dollars worth of common stock judged worthless.[14] Prosecutors of the case argued, "There are a great many millions of dollars spent over there that are strictly ornamental, that will never produce any revenue or add any value to the building."[15] Many of these expensive luxuries were enumerated: the swimming pool, Turkish bath, and the distinct design of the elevator cabs. But most ridiculed were the sculptural panels on the building's exterior, "attended by an expenditure estimated at $50,000, consisting of the carving of the physiognomies of the members of the committee as memorials to themselves."[16] It was suggested that the committee has "an unusually high mixture of incompetence, vanity, and liberality with other people's money."[17]

There were, to be sure, a number of building operations that survived the Depression, the Wrigley Building and Tribune Tower in particular. These buildings remained successful because their owners were not burdened by tremendous financial debt, the buildings having been paid for largely in cash. Oddly enough, the Palmolive Building, despite its location well outside the Loop, retained a strikingly high 88 percent occupancy rate throughout the Depression.[18]

A resumption of building activity on North Michigan Avenue did not occur until the late 1940s. With this resumption, however, the character of the avenue took on a dramatic new form as buildings climbed to unprecedented heights, buoyed by the enactment of more liberal zoning laws and ever escalating property values and rental demands. Much of the revived interest in North Michigan Avenue was initially due to the Magnificent Mile project of Chicago developer Arthur Rubloff in 1947. Rubloff projected upon North Michigan Avenue a plan for the construction of new buildings, the renovation of old ones, the addition of a park, and a more efficient traffic and parking system in an effort to revitalize what had been the city's fastest growing commercial area.

Rubloff had become interested in North Michigan Avenue in 1945 when he was asked to sell a foreclosed property at the corner of Michigan Avenue and Pearson Street.[19] The virtually complete lack of demand in the area led him to formulate a plan for the redevelopment of the entire length of the avenue from the river to Oak Street. To give physical form to his idea for the avenue, he commissioned Holabird and Root who produced a plan for new low-rise store and office buildings lining the avenue (figure E.1).[20] Behind them would be landscaped pedestrian promenades and then taller office and apartment buildings with shops on their ground floors. In addition, a plaza and ice-skating

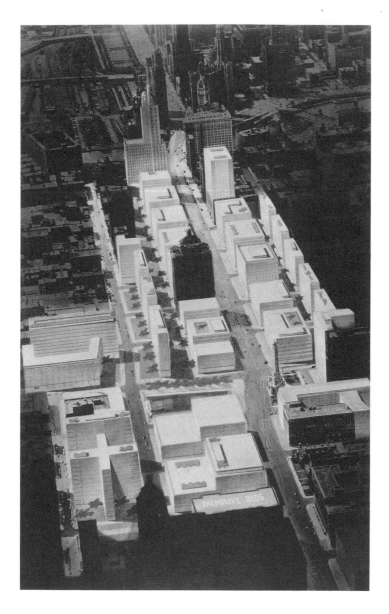

Figure E.1
Rubloff plan for the Mag-
nificent Mile, 1947; Hola-
bird and Root, architects.
Courtesy of the Chicago
Historical Society.

rink were planned for the site of the existing pumping station between Chicago Avenue and Pearson Street.

At the same time, Rubloff along with New York developer William Zeckendorf bought or gained management
control of a considerable amount of North Michigan Avenue property, still at Depression-level prices. Included
were the east side of Michigan Avenue between Delaware
and Pearson streets, the present sites of the John Hancock
Building and Water Tower Place, and the southeast corner

of Michigan and Chicago avenues, the present site of a high-rise apartment building. He also controlled the property on the west side of the avenue between Erie and Huron streets, and he controlled the Michigan Square Building, whose lower floors and shopfronts he remodeled. Independent of Rubloff and Zeckendorf was a plan by the Continental Hotel to build a twenty-two story, 500-room addition to the north side of the beleaguered Medinah Club Building.[21]

To carry out his redevelopment proposals for North Michigan Avenue, Rubloff launched an extensive promotional campaign in April 1947, sending publicity packages to major news media and trade journals, and unveiling Holabird and Root's plans and model at a well-advertised press conference.[22] He even went so far as to reactivate the former North Central Business District Association, now called the Greater North Michigan Avenue Association.[23] Modeling their promotional efforts after such organizations as the Fifth Avenue Association in New York and the Wilshire Boulevard Merchants Association in Los Angeles, they worked hard to attract business capital to the area and to make the Magnificent Mile, a term coined by Rubloff himself, a world-renowned center of shopping, culture, and good taste.

Rubloff's plans for the Magnificent Mile and his extensive promotional efforts indeed helped in bringing about a transformation of the avenue, although not exactly in the way he had envisioned. In fact, the physical form of the plan as prepared by Holabird and Root was hardly followed at all. In one sense, it was a misguided effort typical of the later 1950s and 1960s in the United States that called for wholesale clearance, even in this case, of such a notable landmark as the Chicago Pumping Station. In the end, the Chicago Pumping Station was not demolished, no skating rink was built, and no pedestrian promenades were built at mid-block.

Also, like Burnham before him, Rubloff failed to envision the extent to which North Michigan Avenue would continue to be developed with high-rise rather than low-rise buildings. While there may have been merit in Rubloff's desire for buildings of only six or seven stories for reasons of adequate light and human scale, the concept in the end would not allow for the kind of return on investment that developers and mortgage bankers carrying out the individual building projects wanted. This failure on the part of Rubloff, especially significant since he himself was a devel-

*Figure E.2
Prudential Building, Ran-
dolph Street north of
Grant Park, 1952–55;
Naess and Murphy, archi-
tects. Photo by author.*

oper, represents one of the persistent dilemmas of urban
design in the United States. There is essentially no control
where land value is high and is producing a good economic
return, as was the case with North Michigan Avenue in the
1920s and again in the late 1940s and beyond.

The first of the major high-rise buildings to begin the
transformation of North Michigan Avenue was the forty-
one story Prudential Building (figure E.2), constructed on
Randolph Street facing Grant Park.[24] It is located just east

209

Figure E.3
Equitable Building, northeast corner of the Michigan
Avenue Bridge Plaza,
1961–65; Skidmore, Ow-
ings and Merrill, archi-
tects. Courtesy of the Chicago Historical Society.
Photo by F. S. Dauwalger.

of the Michigan Avenue site of the proposed Cuneo Tower
and within the site of the proposed Terminal Park development. Built in the air rights over the Illinois Central
freight yards, its foundations are a series of caissons placed
between the tracks, a system used previously in the Mer-
chandise Mart.[25] Architecturally, its aluminum and glass
curtain wall construction is markedly different from the
Crerar Library, which it overshadowed at the entrance to
North Michigan Avenue.

The first significant structure to be constructed on North Michigan Avenue itself since the Depression was the Equitable Building (figure E.3). Standing thirty-five stories at the northeast corner of the Michigan Avenue Bridge Plaza, it added a fifth prominent building to this unique ensemble of Chicago urbanism.[26] Designed in 1961 by Skidmore, Owings and Merrill, its Miesian-inspired curtain wall construction and its 175-foot setback from the street makes it a prominent backdrop to the four principal limestone and terra cotta buildings from the 1920s. The 100,000-square-foot space in front, named Pioneer Plaza, and complete with a circular fountain commemorating twenty-five Chicagoans who made important contributions to the city's history, forms an effective forecourt to the Tribune Tower when seen from across the Michigan Avenue Bridge.[27]

Other buildings followed, including the Westin Hotel just south of the Palmolive Building, and the 777 North Michigan Avenue Apartment Building at the southeast corner of Michigan and Chicago avenues. The John Hancock Building, constructed in 1965–70 (figure E.4), was the structure from this time period that most radically altered the scale of construction on the avenue, tragically exceeding the limits of the 1920s urban context. Located on the east side of the avenue, halfway between the Palmolive Building and the historic Pumping Station, the site of the Hancock Building was the last on North Michigan Avenue to be developed, having remained largely vacant since the landfill project of the 1890s. The 100-story, 1107-foot building was designed by Bruce Graham and Fazlur Khan of Skidmore, Owings and Merrill.[28] The largest office/residential building in the world, its expressive sloping walls and diagonal bracing were designed with the aid of computers, and it was extensively studied for its aerodynamic effects through wind tunnel experiments. Half of the Hancock Building's site was left open, with the building itself being set back from the street with an intervening sunken garden/skating rink, a concept that further isolated the structure from the context of the avenue's 1920s buildings, all of which had fronted directly on the avenue.

The effect of the Hancock Building was to create a new focal point for North Michigan Avenue. It drew attention away from the avenue as a whole and became the new identifying feature of the North Side. Here it was not the building's image from the street that was important but rather how it was seen from several blocks away, or even a mile away. In fact, its image from the street was overwhelming,

Figure E.4
John Hancock Building,
North Michigan Avenue be-
tween Chestnut Street and
Delaware Place, 1965–70;
Skidmore, Owings and
Merrill, architects. Photo
by author.

staggering at the least. It was impossible to comprehend the building's true architectural form from close up. It demanded to be seen from a distance, a point tower rising above a mass of generic low-rise buildings, with no specific reference to North Michigan Avenue. Its spatial realm was that of the city, not of the avenue.

The impact of the Hancock Building on the avenue was only made worse with the construction in 1974–76 of Water Tower Place (figure E.5), an immense marble-clad commercial, hotel, and condominium building located on the lot directly south of the Hancock.[29] Its sixty-two-story tower is set at the back of a block-long twelve-story base which con-

Figure E.5
Water Tower Place, North
Michigan Avenue between
Chestnut and Pearson
streets, 1974–76; Loebl,
Schlossman, Bennett and
Dart, architects. Photo by
author.

tains an indoor vertical shopping mall centered around an open atrium with glass-enclosed elevators. Designed by the firm of Loebl, Schlossman, Bennett and Dart in association with C. F. Murphy and Associates, it was at the time of its construction the tallest reinforced concrete frame building in the world. While the building's cubical base is a noble concession to the context of the avenue's 1920s low-rise

213

structures, the tower is again a major intrusion onto the streetscape as well as a disconcerting neighbor for the Hancock Building, one that clashes with it not only in terms of form but in materials and color as well. Its squared-off static frame possesses nothing of the dynamic structural image of the Hancock Building, and its white-veined marble is a strong contrast to the blackish-brown metallic surface of the Hancock.

Similar urbanistic discrepancies are evident in Illinois Center, located just east of 333 North Michigan Avenue on a seventeen-acre tract that had been part of the Terminal Park project. It was finally developed by Metropolitan Structures, Inc., as a series of office and hotel towers standing on a raised open plaza with a series of interconnected commercial arcades below.[30] A site plan with a total of ten buildings was prepared by Mies van der Rohe in

Figure E.6
Illinois Center, 111 East
Wacker Drive, 1968–70;
Mies van der Rohe, archi-
tect. Photo by author.

1968, with the first building to be constructed being One Illinois Center at 111 East Wacker Drive (figure E.6). A thirty-story reinforced concrete frame building with a characteristic Miesian bronze-anodized aluminum and glass cladding, the building takes up less than half its site, the rest being given over to the plaza.[31] Though the building possesses Mies's typically refined sense of proportion and detail and its height is consistent with the nearby 333 North Michigan Avenue Building, it nevertheless looks awkward next to its 1920s neighbor. In comparison it is too short, too wide, and lacks a firm base. Its top is too abrupt, and its facade lacks scale. These problems, inherent in the International style, have further exacerbated the lack of cohesion and unity on North Michigan Avenue sought by its original planners.

Besides the urbanistic incongruities plaguing the avenue, the other major consequence of the present-day building boom has been the tragic demolition of significant 1920s landmark buildings. The John Crerar Library was demolished to make way for the Associates Building (figure E.7), a much taller structure with an overscaled diagonal glass roof. The London Guarantee and Accident Company Building was threatened with demolition in 1987, a move that was supported by the present North Michigan Avenue Business Association. The Central Life Insurance Company Building was demolished in 1980. The Hibbard, Spencer, Bartlett and Company Building was demolished in 1989. The 900 North Michigan Avenue Apartment Building was demolished to make way for a sixty-six story residential tower and department store. The Michigan Square Building with its famous Diana Court was demolished to make way for a Marriott Hotel. The Judah Building was demolished as was the Michigan-Superior Building and the Music Corporation of America Building.

The standard height for new buildings on the avenue of about sixty-five stories is quickly transforming what was once a pleasant shopping promenade into an incipient canyon-like corridor with little human appeal. What made North Michigan Avenue such an attractive focus of activity in the 1920s is being incrementally destroyed in the interest of maximizing return on investment. While many of the architects are making a noble attempt to respond to the street by placing towers at the back of lower block-like volumes, only so much can be done to try to retain a sense of human scale or maintain a minimal amount of natural sunlight. As the number of tall buildings on the avenue increases, the

Figure E.7
Associates Building, North
Michigan Avenue at Ran-
dolph Street, 1983; A. Ep-
stein and Sons, architects.
Photo by author.

closer it advances toward an urban wasteland of unprecedented dimension. The task undertaken by Daniel Burnham, the architects of the North Central Business District
Association, and again by Arthur Rubloff to maintain some
measure of control over the avenue's development is today
largely forgotten and its ideals certainly ignored. The future of the avenue hinges upon the achievement of a
balance between urban responsibility and the desire for
economic gain, and this can only occur when everyone involved—developers, architects, and lenders—come to
terms with the problems they are creating and search for
new solutions within an economic order tempered by a collective urban conscience.

THE PLANNERS OF NORTH MICHIGAN AVENUE

Edward H. Bennett   *Plan of Chicago*
           North Michigan Avenue Bridge

Edward Herbert Bennett was born in Bristol, England, in 1874. He moved to San Francisco in 1890, and in 1892 he went to work for the architect Robert White. In 1895, he enrolled at the Ecole des Beaux-Arts and received his diploma in 1902. Upon returning to the United States, he first entered the New York office of George B. Post, but the following year he moved to Chicago and went to work for Daniel Burnham, with whom he remained for nine years. Projects he worked on included the United States Military Academy at West Point and the Civic Center Scheme for San Francisco. From 1913 to 1930, he served as a consulting architect to the Chicago Plan Commission.

> Reference: Joan E. Draper, *Edward H. Bennett: Architect and City Planner, 1874–1954* (Chicago: Art Institute of Chicago, 1982), 7–30.

Daniel H. Burnham   *Plan of Chicago*

Daniel H. Burnham (1846–1912) was born in Henderson, New York, and moved with his parents to Chicago at the age of eight. He attended the public schools of Chicago, then studied in Bridgewater, Massachusetts, under a private tutor. Returning to Chicago in 1868, he entered the office of William LeBaron Jenney, and in 1872 he joined Carter, Drake and Wight. The following year, he formed a partnership with John Wellborn Root. Among their buildings were the Montauk Building, the Rookery, and the Masonic Temple Building.

When John Root died in 1891, the firm was engaged in preparing plans for the World's Columbian Exposition of 1893 as well as the Ashland Block and the Monadnock Building. The firm operated under the name D. H. Burnham from 1891 to 1896, then D. H.

Burnham and Company until Burnham's death in 1912. During the later years, the firm's major buildings included the Continental Bank Building, Flatiron Building in New York, the Plan for Washington, D.C., as well as numerous other city plans.

References: *Biographical Dictionary of American Architects*, ed. Henry F. and Elsie Rathburn Withey (Los Angeles: Hennessey and Ingalls, 1970), 96–99; Thomas S. Hines, *Burnham of Chicago: Architect and Planner* (New York: Oxford University Press, 1974).

Michael J. Faherty	*Michigan Avenue Improvement Project*

Faherty was president of the Chicago Board of Local Improvements during the time of the widening of North Michigan Avenue. He was instrumental in the accomplishment of the project. Born in Ireland in 1859, he immigrated to the United States in 1863, living first in East Windsor, Connecticut. He settled in Chicago in 1880 and entered the real estate business in 1885.

References: *Who's Who in Chicago* (Chicago: A. N. Marquis Co., 1926), 283; Chicago Board of Local Improvements, *A Sixteen-Year Record of Achievement 1915–1931*, comp. A. E. Burnett (Chicago, 1931).

Jules Guerin	*Plan of Chicago*

Jules Guerin was an American who had studied painting at the Ecole des Beaux-Arts and established a practice in New York in 1900 as an illustrator, renderer, painter, and set designer. He first worked with Burnham on the Plan for Washington, D.C.

Reference: Joan E. Draper, "Paris by the Lake: Sources of Burnham's Plan of Chicago," in *Chicago Architecture 1872–1922: Birth of a Metropolis* ed. John Zukowsky (Munich: Prestel-Verlag in association with the Art Institute of Chicago, 1987), 111.

Walter D. Moody	*Michigan Avenue Improvement Project*

Walter D. Moody was born in Detroit in 1874, the son of a Baptist clergyman. He began his active career in the dry goods trade at the age of fourteen, and from 1891 to 1898 he was a traveling salesman with the Detroit wholesale millinery firm of Macauley and Company. In 1898 he organized the wholesale millinery house of Mitchell-Moody-Garton and Company, of which he was vice-president and European buyer until 1904. For the next three years he served as sales manager of Gage Brothers and Company in Chicago until he became interested in the Chicago Commercial Association (later Chicago Association of Commerce). He became business manager of the association in 1907 and was elected general manager in 1909. He resigned to become managing director of the Chicago Plan Commission on January 15, 1911.

References: *The Book of Chicagoans* (Chicago: A. N. Marquis Co., 1911), 487; Michael Patrick McCarthy, "Businessmen and Professionals in Municipal Reform: The Chicago Experience, 1887–1920" (Ph.D. diss., Northwestern University, 1970), 254.

Thomas G. Pihlfeldt   *North Michigan Avenue Bridge*

Thomas G. Pihlfeldt was born in Vadso, Norway, October 11, 1858. He studied at the K-K Polytechnicum, Hanover, Germany, from 1875 to 1878, and the Polytechnicum in Dresden, Saxony, from 1878 to 1879. He came to the United States in 1879 and worked as a draftsman for various engineering firms in Chicago until 1889 when he went to work for the city's Engineering Department. He designed over thirty bridges for the City of Chicago.

Reference: *Who's Who in Chicago* (1911), 693.

Andrew Rebori   *North Central Business District Association Plan*

Andrew Rebori was born in New York, the son of an engineer. He attended M.I.T. and the Ecole des Beaux-Arts before coming to Chicago in 1909. He taught architecture for several years at the Armour Institute, and from 1914 to 1922 he worked in the office of Jarvis Hunt. In 1922 he founded his own firm of Rebori, Wentworth, Dewey and McCormick.

Reference: *Chicago Tribune* (1 June 1968): 1.

Charles Wacker   *Michigan Avenue Improvement Project*

Charles H. Wacker was born in Chicago in 1856. He was educated in the Chicago public schools and later attended college at Lake Forest, Illinois, and Stuttgart, and at the University of Geneva. He traveled in the United States, Europe, and Africa in 1876–79, and then joined his father in the malting business. Other business activities included serving as president of the Chicago Heights Land Association and the Chicago Heights Terminal Transfer Railway Company, and director of the Merchants Trust Company. He was also active in a number of charitable and social agencies.

References: *Who's Who in Chicago* (1926), 897; Michael P. McCarthy, "Chicago Businessmen and the Burnham Plan," *Journal of the Illinois State Historical Society* 63 (Autumn 1970): 248.

THE ARCHITECTS OF NORTH MICHIGAN AVENUE IN THE 1920s

Walter S. Ahlschlager   *Medinah Club*

Little biographical information is available on Ahlschlager except that he was the son and nephew of two Chicago architects, John and Frederick Ahlschlager. From 1905 to 1915 he was in partnership with his father, after which he started his own practice. Besides the Medinah Club and projects in New York and Cincinnati, Ahlschlager made design proposals for the High Noon Club, a forty-four-story apartment and theater building to be located at South Michigan Avenue and Eighth Street, and for the Crane Office Tower to be located over the Illinois Central Railroad tracks.

> References: *Chicago Tribune* (9 May 1920), sec. 10:28; ibid. (11 September 1927), sec. 3:1; ibid. (2 December 1928), sec. 3:1; Meredith Taussig, "North Michigan Avenue: A Story of a Street, 1918–1930" (unpublished class paper, University of Illinois at Chicago, March 1983), pt. 2:28.

Alfred S. Alschuler   *London Guarantee and Accident Building*
Michigan-Ohio Building
Lake-Michigan Building

Alschuler was born in Mattoon, Illinois, in 1876. He attended the Armour Institute of Technology and the Art Institute of Chicago before serving as an apprentice in the office of Dankmar Adler from 1900 to 1903. He then formed a partnership with Samuel A. Treat, which lasted until 1907 when he opened his own office where he specialized in commercial and industrial buildings.

> References: *Chicago Daily News* (23 January 1937), *Armour Engineer* (December 1940), *Chicago Tribune* (7 November 1940), in the Alfred Alschuler Pamphlet File, Chicago His-

torical Society Library; John Zukowsky, *Architecture in Context: 360 North Michigan Avenue* (Chicago: Art Institute of Chicago, 1981), 1; Donald Martin Reynolds, "Alschuler, Alfred S.," in *Macmillan Encyclopedia of Architects*, vol. 1, ed. Adolf K. Placzek (New York: Free Press, 1982), 72.

D. H. Burnham and Co. and Burnham Brothers, Inc.

Central Life Insurance Company Building
Union Carbide and Carbon Company Building
Cuneo Tower Project

Daniel Burnham, Sr., had operated under the name of D. H. Burnham and Company from 1896 until his death in 1912. After that, the company name was changed to Graham, Burnham and Company, with two of its partners being Burnham's sons, Daniel H. Burnham, Jr., and Hubert Burnham. In 1917, the brothers reestablished the original company, the name of which was changed in 1928 to Burnham Brothers, Inc.

Daniel Burnham, Jr., was born in Chicago in 1886 and attended the Lawrence Scientific Institute of Harvard University before joining his father's firm in 1908. He would serve in 1933 as vice-president and secretary of the Century of Progress Exposition and as president of the Chicago Regional Planning Association.

Hubert Burnham was born in Chicago in 1882. He attended the U.S. Naval Academy, graduating in 1905. He then attended the Ecole des Beaux-Arts before joining his father's firm in 1910.

References: Glenn A. Bishop and Paul T. Gilbert, *Chicago's Accomplishments and Leaders* (Chicago: Bishop Publishing Co., 1932), 89–91. *Who's Who in Chicago* (Chicago: A. N. Marquis Co., (1931), 153.

Robert DeGolyer

Italian Court Building

A native Chicagoan, Robert DeGolyer was born in 1876 and graduated in architecture from M.I.T. in 1898. He worked in Los Angeles for John Parkinson from 1902 to 1905, and then in Chicago for Marshall and Fox from 1905 to 1915. Besides the Italian Court Building, his works included the Ambassador East Hotel and numerous Gold Coast apartment buildings.

Reference: Taussig, "North Michigan Avenue," pt. 2:13.

Fugard and Knapp

Allerton Hotel (Associated Architects)

John Reed Fugard (1886–1968) was born in Newton, Iowa, and attended the University of Illinois from 1906 to 1910. In the 1930s he was an officer of the Illinois Society of Architects, the Chicago Housing Authority, and the American Institute of Architects. The firm specialized in residential architecture, designing numerous houses and Gold Coast apartment buildings.

References: *Chicago Architects Design: A Century of Architectural Drawings from the Art Institute of Chicago* (Chicago: Art Institute of Chicago and Rizzoli International Publications, 1982), 98; John Zukowsky, "The Capitals of American Architecture: Chicago and New York," in *Chicago and New York: Architectural Interactions* (Chicago: Art Institute of Chicago, 1984), 14–16.

| Graham, Anderson, Probst and White | *Wrigley Building* *Hibbard, Spencer and Bartlett Building* *National Life Insurance Company Project* |

The principal partner of Graham, Anderson, Probst and White was Ernest Graham (1868–1936), who was born in Lowell, Massachusetts, in 1868. He acquired a technical training at Coe College, Cedar Rapids, Iowa, and at the University of Notre Dame. Beginning his career at the age of twenty as a draftsman in the office of Daniel Burnham, he later became an important figure in the design of the World's Columbian Exposition and other Burnham city planning projects. Following Burnham's death in 1912, work in the office continued under the name of Graham, Burnham and Company until 1917, when Pierce Anderson, Edward Probst, and Howard J. White became partners.

Pierce Anderson was born in Oswego, New York, in 1870. After receiving his academic education at Harvard College, he went to Baltimore to enter Johns Hopkins for a postgraduate course in electrical engineering. Doubtful, however, that he wanted to make a career in that field, he traveled to Chicago to meet with Daniel Burnham, who advised him to take up architecture and study at the Ecole des Beaux-Arts. He passed the entrance exam in 1894 and became a member of the Atelier Paulin, where he remained for four years, receiving his diploma in 1899. He then proceeded on a tour of Europe, visiting Italy, France, and Spain. Returning to the United States the following year, he went directly to Chicago to enter the firm of D. H. Burnham and Company, where he was soon made chief designer.

Charles G. Beersman (1888–1946) attended the University of Pennsylvania, winning the Le Brun fellowship for a year in Europe. He joined the firm of Graham, Anderson, Probst and White in 1919.

References: *Biographical Dictionary of American Architects*, ed. Henry F. and Elsie Rathburn Withey (Los Angeles: Hennessey and Ingalls 1970), 245–46, 491, 651; *Chicago Architects Design* (1982), 81; Sally Chappell, "As If the Lights Were Always Shining: Graham, Anderson, Probst and White's Wrigley Building at the North Boulevard

Link," in *Chicago Architecture, 1872–1922: Birth of a Metropolis*, ed. John Zukowsky (Munich: Prestel-Verlag in association with the Art Institute of Chicago, 1987), 291–301.

Holabird and Roche	*John Crerar Library*
	Palmer Shops Building
	Tribune Tower Competition
	Tobey Building
	333 North Michigan Avenue

William Holabird (1854–1923) studied two years at the United States Military Academy at West Point before coming to Chicago in 1875. It was in the office of William LeBaron Jenney that he met Martin Roche (1853–1927), and the two formed their own practice in 1883. They became best known in Chicago for their designs of the Marquette Building, Old Colony Building, the Tribune Building of 1902, Cook County Courthouse and City Hall, and the Monroe Building.

References: Robert Bruegmann, *Holabird and Roche and Holabird and Root: A Catalogue of Works, 1880–1940*, 3 vols. (New York: Garland Publishing Co, 1989); Robert Bruegmann, "Holabird and Roche and Holabird and Root: The First Two Generations," *Chicago History* 9 (Fall 1980): 130–65; *Biographical Dictionary*, 293–94, 518–19.

Holabird and Root	*Palmolive Building*
	Michigan Square Building
	Michigan-Chestnut Building
	Judah Building
	Terminal Park Project

William Holabird died in 1923 and Martin Roche in 1927. John A. Holabird (1886–1945), son of William, was born in Evanston, Illinois, and was educated like his father at the U.S. Military Academy at West Point. He received his diploma from the Ecole des Beaux-Arts in 1923 and was made a partner in the firm.

John W. Root (1887–1963), son of the late John Wellborn Root, was born in Chicago and studied architecture at Cornell University before attending the Ecole des Beaux-Arts. He joined Holabird and Roche in 1914 and became a partner in 1920.

References: Bruegmann, *A Catalogue of Works*; Bruegmann, "The First Two Generations," 130–65; Earl H. Reed, Jr., "Some Recent Work of Holabird and Root, Architects," *Architecture* 61 (January 1930): 1–4; Robert F. Irving, "Holabird and Root: Still Going Strong after 95 Years," *Inland Architect* 20 (July 1976): 8–13; *Biographical Dictionary*, 292–93; *Who's Who in Chicago* (1950), 501.

John Mead Howells and   *Tribune Tower*
Raymond Hood

John Mead Howells was born in Cambridge, Massachusetts, in 1868.
He studied at M.I.T. and graduated from Harvard in 1891. He then
studied at the Ecole des Beaux-Arts where he received his diploma in
1896. From 1897 to 1917 he was a partner in the firm of Howells and
Stokes in New York and Seattle. He designed numerous buildings for
Harvard, Yale, Columbia, and for banks in New York, San Francisco, and Seattle.

Raymond M. Hood (1881–1934) was born in Pawtucket, Rhode Island, in 1881, and received his bachelor's degree in architecture
from M.I.T. in 1903. He worked in the offices of Cram, Goodhue and
Ferguson and for Palmer and Hornbostel before going to Paris to
study at the Ecole des Beaux-Arts. He opened his own office in New
York in 1914; at various times he worked in association with J. André
Fouilhoux. After the Chicago Tribune Tower project was completed,
Hood became a much sought-after architect for commercial high-rise
buildings, including the American Radiator Building and the Chicago
Daily News Building.

> References: *Biographical Dictionary*, 297–98; Robert A. M.
> Stern, *Raymond Hood* (New York: Rizzoli International
> Publications, 1982), 1; *Chicago Tribune* (2 December
> 1922): 1; Cynthia Field, "The Chicago Tribune Competition
> of 1922" (Master's thesis, Columbia University, 1968), 26;
> Holly Gerberding, "Tribune Tower" (unpublished paper
> for Northwestern University Department of Art History,
> 1983), 12–13; *Christian Science Monitor* (11 December
> 1922).

Jarvis Hunt   *Chicago Tribune Printing Plant*
                               900 North Michigan Avenue
                               Building

Jarvis Hunt (1859–1941), a nephew of New York architect Richard
Morris Hunt, was born in Wethersfield, Vermont. He was educated
at Harvard and M.I.T. and moved to Chicago in 1893 to work on the
Columbian Exposition. He remained in the city and established his
own practice, designing numerous train stations and commercial
buildings.

> Reference: *Biographical Dictionary*, 308.

Loebl, Schlossman and   *Music Corporation of America*
Demuth   *Building*

The firm of Loebl, Schlossman and Demuth established itself in the
1920s doing commercial buildings in Chicago. The firm was named
Loebl, Schlossman and Bennett from 1946 to 1965; Loebl, Schlossman, Bennett and Dart from 1965 to 1975; and finally Loebl,
Schlossman and Hackl.

Reference: Stuart E. Cohen, *Chicago Architects: Exhibition Catalogue* (Chicago: Swallow Press, 1976), 115.

Philip B. Maher   *Farwell Building*
Malabry Court Building
Erskine-Danforth Building
Woman's Chicago Athletic Club

Born in Kenilworth, Illinois, in 1894, Philip B. Maher was the son of the well-known Prairie School architect, George W. Maher. After studying at the University of Michigan, he traveled in England, France, and Italy before entering his father's firm in 1914. The firm was named George W. Maher and Son from 1921 to 1924, after which Philip established his own firm.

References: *Who's Who in Chicago* (1926), 556; Bishop and Gilbert, *Chicago's Accomplishments and Leaders*, 313.

Marshall and Fox   *Lake Shore Trust and Savings Bank*
Drake Hotel

Benjamin Marshall was born in Chicago and received his elementary and high school education at the Harvard School in Kenwood. He started to work for Oliver W. Marble and in 1893 entered the office of Henry R. Wilson. Two years later he became a junior partner under the firm name of Wilson and Marshall. From 1902 until forming his partnership with Charles Fox, he worked alone, designing the Illinois and Iroquois theaters.

Charles E. Fox was born in Reading, Pennsylvania, and studied architecture at "Boston Tech." He entered the office of Holabird and Roche at the age of twenty-one.

References: *Chicago Tribune* (20 June 1944): 12; *Biographical Dictionary*, 392–93; Commission on Chicago Historical and Architectural Landmarks, *East Lake Shore Drive District: Preliminary Summary of Information* (Chicago, 1984), 4; Carroll William Westfall, "Benjamin Henry Marshall of Chicago," *Chicago Architectural Journal* 2 (1982): 8–21.

Murgatroyd and Ogden   *Allerton Hotel*

Everett Murgatroyd (1881–1946), an architect and engineer, is identified with a number of public, commercial, and hotel buildings principally located in New York. These include the Governor Clinton Hotel, the Barbizon Hotel, and Grammercy Place.

Reference: *Biographical Dictionary*, 435.

Andrew Rebori   *Michigan-Superior Building*

(See Appendix 1.)

Eliel Saarinen   *Tribune Tower Competition*

Even though he did not build anything on North Michigan Avenue, Saarinen's presence is felt in the buildings designed late in the decade by Holabird and Root, especially 333 North Michigan Avenue. He was born in Finland in 1873 and was best known there for his design of the Helsinki Railroad Station. After winning second prize in the Tribune Tower competition, he moved to the United States, living first in Chicago, then in Bloomfield Hills, Michigan, where he designed the campus of Cranbrook Academy.

> References: Albert Christ-Janer, *Eliel Saarinen: Finnish-American Architect and Educator* (Chicago and London: University of Chicago Press, 1979); "Buildings by Eliel Saarinen," *American Architect* 124 (26 September 1923), plates.

Schmidt, Garden and Martin   *Illinois Women's Athletic Club*

Richard E. Schmidt (1865–1958) was born in Germany and came to the United States as a child. He was educated in Chicago's public schools and studied architecture at M.I.T. in 1883–85. Two years later he established his own practice in Chicago.

Schmidt often sought the services of Hugh M. G. Garden (1873–1961), who was born in Toronto and began his architectural career in Minneapolis. Upon moving to Chicago, Garden worked for several architects including Henry Ives Cobb, Shepley, Rutan and Coolidge, as well as Louis Sullivan, before going into partnership with Schmidt.

> References: H. Allen Brooks, *The Prairie School: Frank Lloyd Wright and His Midwest Contemporaries* (Toronto: University of Toronto Press, 1972), 48–52; *Chicago Architects Design*, 62–63.

Thielbar and Fugard   *McGraw-Hill Building*

The Thielbar and Fugard partnership was formed in 1925 from the original members of the firm Fugard and Knapp. Frederick J. Thielbar was born in Peoria and studied at the University of Illinois. He was a partner in the firm of Holabird and Roche before joining Fugard. They specialized in the 1920s and 1930s in commercial and institutional buildings.

> Reference: *Chicago Architects Design*, 98.

Karl Martin Vitzhum   *Bell Building*

Karl Martin Vitzhum was born in Tutzing, Germany, January 2, 1880, and studied architecture at the Royal College of Architecture in Munich. Upon coming to Chicago in the early 1900s, he joined the firm of D. H. Burnham and Company, and in 1919 he started his own firm. Besides the Bell Building, he designed the One LaSalle

Street Building, Steuben Building, and the Midland Club Building, all in Chicago.

Reference: *Who's Who in Chicago* (1931), 1003.

Frank Lloyd Wright   *National Life Insurance Company Project*

Frank Lloyd Wright was born in 1867 in Richland Center, Wisconsin. After attending the University of Wisconsin in 1886–87, he moved to Chicago and worked in the offices of Lyman Silsbee and, later, Adler and Sullivan. He began his own practice in 1893, designing such landmark buildings as the Unity Temple and the Robie House. He left his home and family in Oak Park to go to Germany in 1909 where he produced the Wasmuth portfolio of his work. When he returned to the United States a year later, he settled in Spring Green, Wisconsin, where he maintained an office and school until his death in 1959.

References: Harvey Einbinder, *An American Genius: Frank Lloyd Wright* (New York: Philosophical Library, 1986); Robert C. Twombly, *Frank Lloyd Wright: His Life and Architecture* (New York: John Wiley and Sons, 1979); Henry-Russell Hitchcock, *In the Nature of Materials: The Buildings of Frank Lloyd Wright* (New York: DaCapo Press, 1942); Olgivanna Lloyd Wright, *Frank Lloyd Wright: His Life, His Work, His Words* (New York: Horizon Press, 1966).

THE

DEVELOPERS OF

NORTH MICHIGAN

AVENUE

IN THE 1920s

Allerton House Company   *Allerton Hotel*

The Allerton House Company, based in New York City, was established to provide urban housing for young professionals in a club-like atmosphere. The company's president, James Stewart Cushman, was born in New York in 1871. He traveled widely in Europe as a young man, where he became interested in housing. One of the first of the many club-hotels his company built in New York was the Allerton House at 143 East 39th Street, with a gym, roof garden, reading room, shops, and restaurant, and with room rates from $7 to $16 per week.

References: *Who's Who in New York*, ed. Winfield Scot Downs
    (1929), 412; *New York Sun Herald* (18 April 1920).

Herbert E. Bell   *Bell Building*

Herbert E. Bell was born in Wisconsin in 1867. Upon moving to Chicago he joined Pease and Company, coal operators, in 1887. He later formed the Bell and Zollar Coal Company of which he was president until 1926 when he founded the Bell and Zollar Mining Company.

Reference: *Who's Who in Chicago* (Chicago: A. N. Marquis
    Co., 1931), 80.

Central Life Insurance   *Central Life Insurance Company*
Company   *Building*

The Central Life Insurance Company was organized in Ottawa, Illinois, in 1907. It specialized in twenty-year term life insurance. The company's organizers and directors were nearly all from Ottawa, mostly judges and businessmen. The president of the company was

H. W. Johnson, who died in 1925, shortly after the company's new building on North Michigan Avenue was completed.

> Reference: "Central Life Insurance Company of Illinois," *North Central Journal* (1929): 9.

Charles A. Chapin Estate   *Michigan-Superior Building*

The eldest Chapin son, Homer C. (b. 1875), attended the University of Michigan and was the president of several corporations. Henry K. Chapin (b. 1879), who attended M.I.T., was solely occupied with managing the estate. Lowell M. Chapin (b. 1885), a Yale graduate, was president of the Zauri Drawn Metals Company and treasurer of the Indiana and Michigan Electric Company.

> Reference: *Who's Who in Chicago* (1926), 171.

Chester A. and Raymond   *Italian Court Building*
C. Cook   *Malabry Court Building*

Chester A. Cook was born in Woonsocket, Rhode Island, in 1872. He graduated from Brown University in 1891 and received a law degree from Harvard in 1894. He and his brother, Raymond C. Cook, became trustees of their father's estate, Ira B. Cook Properties, in 1898. Chester Cook was also a director of E. C. McAvoy, Inc., Booth Fisheries Company, and Haas Brothers Company of Omaha, Nebraska.

> Reference: *Who's Who in Chicago* (1936), 215.

John Crerar Library   *John Crerar Library*

John Crerar (1827–89) was born and raised in New York and moved to Chicago in 1862. He established the firm of Crerar, Adams and Company, dealers in railroad supplies. He was also a director of the Pullman Palace Car Company, the Chicago and Alton Railroad Company, the Illinois Trust and Savings Bank, and the Chicago and Joliet Railroad Company. Directors of his estate, which oversaw the construction of the library, included Marshall Field, Robert T. Lincoln, and George A. Armour.

> References: J. Christian Bay, *The John Crerar Library, 1895–1944* (Chicago, 1945), 1–3; Bessie L. Pierce, *A History of Chicago* (Chicago: University of Chicago Press, 1957), 229; *The John Crerar Library Handbook* (Chicago: Crerar Library, 1929), 5–6.

John F. Cuneo   *Cuneo Tower Project*

John F. Cuneo was born in Chicago in 1885, the son of Frank and Amelia (Gondolfo) Cuneo. His father owned the firm of Garibaldi and Cuneo, wholesale fruit dealers. John F. was educated at the Chicago Latin School and the University of Chicago Laboratory School and attended Yale University from 1904 to 1906. He became president of the John F. Cuneo Company in 1907 and of the Cuneo Press in 1919.

References: *Who's Who in Chicago* (1931), 227–28; *Chicago Tribune* (3 March 1929), sec. 3:1.

Arthur L. Farwell   *Farwell Building*

Born in Chicago in 1863, Arthur L. Farwell graduated from Yale University in 1884. He then entered his father's business, John V. Farwell and Company, wholesale dry goods, becoming vice-chairman of the board. The company was purchased by Carson Pirie Scott and Company in 1925.

Reference: *Who's Who in Chicago* (1926), 287.

John V. Farwell   *Woman's Chicago Athletic Club*

The brother of Arthur L. Farwell, John Farwell was born in Chicago in 1858. He graduated from Yale in 1879. He was chairman of the board of John V. Farwell and Company and a director of the Bank of the Republic.

Reference: *Who's Who in Chicago* (1926), 287.

430 North Michigan Avenue   *Music Corporation of America*
Building Corporation   *Building*

An anonymous corporation represented by attorneys Sonnenschein, Berkson, Lautmann and Levinson, it leased the property for the Music Corporation of America Building from James S. Kirk and Company.

Reference: *Chicago Tribune* (7 April 1929), sec. 3:1.

Hibbard, Spencer,   *Hibbard, Spencer, Bartlett and*
Bartlett and Company   *Company Building*

In existence under various names in Chicago since 1855, this was one of the city's leading hardware businesses. In 1910, the company built a store at the southeast corner of State and South Water Streets.

Reference: *Chicago Tribune* (8 November 1946): 39.

Albert M. Johnson   *National Life Insurance Company Project*

Albert M. Johnson was born in Oberlin, Ohio, in 1872. He graduated from Cornell University in 1895, and then worked for a series of limestone supply and mining companies before becoming vice-president of the Arkansas Midland Railroad Company in 1901, then the president of the Oberlin Gas and Electric Company in 1902–3.

At the same time, he became treasurer, then vice-president, and finally, in 1906, president of the National Life Insurance Company.

Reference: *Who's Who in Chicago* (1926), 461.

Illinois Women's Athletic   *Illinois Women's Athletic Club*
Club

The Illinois Women's Athletic Club was founded in 1918 by Mrs. William Severin, who was prominent in business and political circles in Chicago. The club first met in the Century Building, moving later to the Stevens Building.

Reference: *Chicago Tribune* (11 June 1922), sec. 2:9.

Dorothy Patterson Judah   *Judah Building*

Dorothy Patterson Judah was the wife of Noble Judah, who at the time of the construction of the Judah Building was the United States Ambassador to Cuba. He had been a lieutenant colonel during World War I, a decorated war hero who was part of the march into Germany after the Armistice. While residing in Chicago, he was a member of the law firm of Judah, Willard, Wolf and Reichmann.

References: *Chicago Tribune* (26 August 1928), sec. 3:1; ibid. (27 February 1938), sec. 1:18.

Lake Shore Trust and   *Lake Shore Trust and Savings*
Savings Bank   *Bank*

The Lake Shore Trust and Savings Bank opened in 1920, occupying commercial space in a building on the west side of Michigan Avenue, across from the bank's present location. Its board of directors included—besides Colonel Robert McCormick, John Drake, Sheldon Clark, and Bertram Winston—Craig B. Hazelwood, vice-president of the Union Trust Company; Stanley H. Barrows, president of the Sierra Magnesite Company; William V. Kelley, chairman of the Miehle Printing Press and Manufacturing Company; Mellen C. Martin, of Kirkland, Patterson and Fleming; A. H. McConnell, president of the Central Scientific Company; R. H. Ripley, vice-president of the American Steel Foundries; Wheeler Sammons, president, A. W. Shaw Company; Edward F. Swift, vice-president, Swift and Company; and S. E. Thomason, publisher.

References: "The Lake Shore Trust and Savings Bank," *North Central Journal* 4 (December 1926), 50–51; Meredith Taussig, "North Michigan Avenue: A Story of a Chicago Street, 1918–1930" (unpublished class paper, University of Illinois at Chicago, March 1983), pt. 2:11.

Colonel Robert R. McCormick *Tribune Printing Plant*
Tribune Tower

Robert R. McCormick was born in Chicago in 1880, at 150 E. Ontario Street in McCormickville, just east of Pine Street. In his early childhood, the family moved three blocks west to the Ontario Apartments at the corner of State Street. McCormick graduated from Yale in 1903 and the following autumn enrolled in Northwestern University Law School. His education was interrupted when Republican boss Fred Busse persuaded him to run for alderman of his native Twenty-first Ward, which included the Near North Side and the Gold Coast. Winning in the 1904 election, McCormick served only one term, losing his reelection bid in 1906. In 1911, he assumed control of the *Tribune*.

References: Joseph Gies, *The Colonel of Chicago* (New York: E. P. Dutton, 1979), 11, 14, 20, 23, 101; Wayne Andrews, *Battle for Chicago* (New York: Harcourt, Brace and Co., 1946), 231–32; *Who's Who in Chicago* (1926), 578; Cynthia Field, "The Chicago Tribune Competition of 1922" (Master's thesis, Columbia University, 1968), 10–11; Holly Gerberding, "Tribune Tower" (unpublished paper for Northwestern University Department of Art History, 1983), 3, 7–9.

McCormick Estate   *Tobey Building*

The agent of the McCormick Estate was Judson P. Stone, born in Canton, Pennsylvania, in 1873. He studied two years at the University of Minnesota before joining the McCormick Harvesting Machine Company in 1892. He began to work for the McCormick Estate, which managed the fortune amassed by Cyrus McCormick, in 1905.

Reference: *Who's Who in Chicago* (1926), 839.

Medinah Club   *Medinah Club Building*

The Medinah Athletic Club was a Masonic organization composed of Shriners. Its president, Thomas J. Houston, was born in Chicago in 1877 and educated at the Morgan Park Military Academy and the Metropolitan Business College. Besides heading his own insurance business, he was a director of the Old Colony State Bank and the Patterson Pure Food Pie Company. He was the president of the Chicago Civil Service Commission from 1927 to 1929.

The head of the club's building committee, Urbine J. Hermann, was born in Chicago in 1872 and educated in public schools in Chicago and in Sac Bay, Wisconsin. He became vice-president, secretary, treasurer, and manager of the Cort Theatre Company in 1909, was vice-president of Seneca Securities, manager of the American Posting Service, and president of the Chicago Public Library.

Reference: *Who's Who in Chicago* (1931), 448, 477.

Michigan-Chestnut Building   *Michigan-Chestnut Building*
Corporation

The president of the company, W. B. Frankenstein, was born in Chicago in 1874. He was educated in the Chicago public schools, and in 1894 he and L. M. Willis formed the real estate partnership of Willis and Frank. From 1921 he operated his own real estate business.

Reference: *Who's Who in Chicago* (1926), 313.

Michigan-Grand Building   *McGraw-Hill Building*
Corporation

The Michigan-Grand Building Corporation was owned by the law firm of Winston, Strawn and Shaw, whose offices were located in the First National Bank Building. Partners in the firm were Silas H. Strawn, Ralph M. Shaw, John D. Black, Edward W. Everett, Frederick C. Hack, Walter H. Jacobs, J. Sidney Condit, James H. Winston, John C. Slade, and Harold Beacon.

Reference: *Chicago City Directory* (1928).

900 North Michigan Avenue   *900 North Michigan Avenue*
Building Corporation   *Apartment Building*

The 900 North Michigan Avenue Building Corporation was founded in 1925, its early co-owners including—besides Jarvis Hunt, Cyrus McCormick, Jr., and Cyrus Hall McCormick—Howard Elting, a builder and vice-president and treasurer of the J. B. French Company; Charles K. Knickerbacker, vice-president of the Griffin Wheel Company; Dr. George Paul Marquis, a noted surgeon at St. Luke's Hospital; and John Jay Bryant, Jr., an attorney and managing partner of James H. Oliphant and Company.

References: "Inlandscape: 900 North," *Inland Architect* 25 (March 1981): 47; *Who's Who in Chicago* (1931).

Palmolive Peet Company   *Palmolive Building*

The Palmolive Peet Company was founded in 1864 as the B. J. Johnson Soap Company. B. J. Johnson's son, Caleb, first conceived of the idea of Palmolive soap—a soap made entirely from vegetable oils. In 1909 Johnson saw an exhibit of French soap-making machinery for making hard-milled soaps. He bought the machinery and had it shipped to Milwaukee. The company merged with the Peet Brothers Manufacturing Company in 1927. Peet Brothers was founded in 1872 by William, Robert, and Jesse Peet of Kansas City.

References: William Lee Sims II, *150 Years . . . and the Future! Colgate-Palmolive (1806–1956)* (New York: Newcomer Society of America, 1956), 11–14; Meredith Taussig, "North Michigan Avenue," 39.

Potter Palmer Estate   *Palmer Shops Building*

Potter Palmer was born in Albany County, New York, the son of a Quaker farmer. Young Palmer began his career as a merchant when, at the age of eighteen, he worked as a clerk in the store of Platt Adams in Durham, New York. When he was twenty-one, he opened his own store in Oneida, New York, and three years later he moved to Chicago where he opened a dry goods store and made a fortune speculating in dry goods during the Civil War. In 1865, he sold his establishment to Field, Leiter and Company, and began investing in real estate.

After his death in 1902, his estate was managed by his two sons, Honoré and Potter, Jr. Honoré Palmer was born in Chicago in 1874 and graduated from Harvard in 1897. Potter Palmer, Jr., was born in Chicago in 1875 and graduated from Harvard in 1898. Besides managing the Palmer Estate, the two founded the East Chicago Company, which built up a large industrial center in East Chicago, Indiana.

> References: Joseph Siry, *Carson Pirie Scott: Louis Sullivan and the Chicago Department Store* (Chicago and London: University of Chicago Press, 1988), 15–20; Andrews, *Battle for Chicago*, 30–31; *Book of Chicagoans* (1906), 671.

Lake-Michigan Building   *Lake-Michigan Building*
Corporation

The Lake-Michigan Building Corporation was headed by Frederick T. Hoyt, president, and Charles L. Schwerin, vice-president. Hoyt had his real estate office at 160 North LaSalle Street. Schwerin, born in New York City in 1880, was president of the Linden Construction Company of New Jersey and the American Realty Company of New York from 1910 to 1917. In 1917–19, he was a project engineer for the U.S. Department of Housing. In 1919–21, he was president of the Industrial Housing Company. In Chicago he was also involved in the Reywall Building Corporation and the Astor Street Building Corporation.

> References: *Who's Who in Chicago* (1936), 899; *Chicago City Directory* (1928–29).

Site of Fort Dearborn   *London Guarantee and Accident*
Building Corporation   *Building*

This corporation was headed by Chicago attorney John S. Miller, who owned the site of the London Guarantee Building and who assembled the initial group of English investors to start the project.

> Reference: *The Economist* (2 July 1921): 35.

235

John R. Thompson, Jr. *Michigan-Ohio Building*

John R. Thompson, Jr., was born in Chicago in 1894. He attended the Taft School in Watertown, Connecticut, and then Yale University, where he graduated in 1917. He then returned to Chicago to work in his father's restaurant business which had been founded in 1891.

References: Glenn A. Bishop and Paul T. Gilbert, *Chicago's Accomplishments and Leaders* (Chicago: Bishop Publishing Co., 1932), 471; *Who's Who in Chicago* (1926), 868.

333 North Michigan Avenue *333 North Michigan Avenue*
Building Corporation *Building*

This corporation was headed by attorney John S. Miller, who was also the director of the Site of Fort Dearborn Building Corporation, and who had built the London Guarantee and Accident Building. Other members of the corporation were O. C. Doering, vice-president of Sears, Roebuck; John W. Root of Holabird and Roche; Martin C. Schwab, engineer; John W. Harris of Hegeman, Harris and Company; and Jerome P. Bowes, capitalist, as vice president; D. E. Sawyer, secretary; and Ralph A. Bard, treasurer.

Reference: *The Economist* (25 July 1927): 1690.

230 North Michigan Avenue *Union Carbide and Carbon*
Building Corporation *Building*

This corporation was headed by real estate operators Daniel A. Coffey and Alexander F. McKeown, Jr., of the realty firm of Coffey and McKeown.

Reference: *The Economist* (12 January 1929): 71.

Whitestone Hotel Company *Drake Hotel*

The principal officers of the Whitestone Hotel Company were Tracy C. and John B. Drake, the sons of John B. Drake, manager of the Grand Pacific Hotel. Tracy C. Drake was born in 1864 and John B. in 1872. Tracy Drake graduated from the Rensselaer Polytechnic Institute, while John B. went on an extended world tour after graduating from Phillips Academy in Andover, Massachusetts. The brothers built the Blackstone Hotel and the Blackstone Theatre in 1910.

References: Bishop and Gilbert, *Chicago's Accomplishments and Leaders*, 177–79; Commission on Chicago Historical and Architectural Landmarks, *East Lake Shore Drive District* (Chicago, 1984), 3.

William Wrigley, Jr.   *Wrigley Building and Annex*
                              North Bridge Houses of Michigan
                              Avenue Bridge

William Wrigley, Jr., was born in Philadelphia, September 30, 1864, the son of William and Mary (Ladley) Wrigley. He was educated in the Philadelphia public schools, and in 1885 he married Ada E. Foote of New York. He went into business with his father in 1882. He started the William Wrigley, Jr., Company in 1904. In addition, Wrigley was a director of the First National Bank, First Trust and Savings Bank, Boulevard Bridge Bank, Consumers Company, the Yellow Cab Company, and the Erie Railway. He was also chairman of the board of the Santa Catalina Island Company and the Chicago National League Baseball Club.

> References: William Zimmerman, Jr., *William Wrigley, Jr.: The Man and His Business* (Chicago: R. R. Donnelley and Sons, 1935); Bishop and Gilbert, *Chicago's Accomplishments and Leaders*, 533; *Who's Who in Chicago* (1926), 960.

Murray Wolbach   *Michigan Square Building*

Murray Wolbach was born in Chicago in 1876. He was educated in Chicago, Germany, and Switzerland, and entered the real estate business in Chicago in 1895. He served as president of the South Central Business District Association and as director of the North Central Association.

> Reference: *Who's Who in Chicago* (1926), 951.

Woman's Chicago Athletic   *Woman's Chicago Athletic Club*
Club

Established in 1898, this was the oldest women's club in the nation. It was founded by Mrs. Philip D. Armour both as a charitable organization and to provide a setting for balls and debuts. Mrs. Helen Pelouze, the club's president at the time of the construction of the new building, was married to William Pelouze, who had come to Chicago in 1882 and was with the Walter A. Wood Reaping Machine Company from 1882 to 1884 and the Tobey Furniture Company, from 1884 to 1892, before starting his own company.

> References: *Chicago Tribune* (25 September 1927), sec. 3:1; *Who's Who in Chicago* (1926), 681.

INTRODUCTION

1. For information on the Jean Baptiste Point DuSable house see Frank A. Randall, *History of the Development of Building Construction in Chicago* (Urbana: University of Illinois Press, 1949), 2; Commission on Chicago Historical and Architectural Landmarks, *Site of the DuSable/Kinzie House* (Chicago, 1977); Alfred T. Andreas, *History of Chicago: From the Earliest Period to the Present Time* (Chicago: A. T. Andreas, 1884), 1:72; *Prominent Citizens and Industries of Chicago* (Chicago: German Press Club of Chicago, 1901), 11; Paul E. Sprague, "The Origin of Balloon Framing," *Journal of the Society of Architectural Historians* 40 (December 1981): 311–14; Lois Wille, *Forever Open, Clear and Free: The Historic Struggle for Chicago's Lakefront* (Chicago: Regency, 1972), 9–12.

For information on Fort Dearborn see Randall, *History of the Development of Building Construction*, 2; Wille, *Forever Open, Clear and Free*, 13–14; Jane F. Babson, "The Architecture of Early Illinois Forts," *Journal of the Illinois State Historical Society* 41 (Spring 1968): 9–40; Harry A. Musham, *Report on the Location of the First Fort Dearborn* (Chicago: Fort Dearborn Memorial Commission, 1940); Paul Kunning, "Founding of Fort Dearborn" (paper for the Chicago Association of Commerce and Industry, 1953); Paul Angle, "Fort Dearborn, 1803–1812," *Chicago History* 2 (Summer 1949): 97–102; *Prominent Citizens and Industries of Chicago* (1901), 11.

2. Commission on Chicago Historical and Architectural Landmarks, *Site of the Beaubien Claim* (Chicago, 1975), 1–6; Andreas, *History of Chicago*, 1:72.

3. Beaubien had found an old law providing for the sale of unused public lands at the rate of $1.25 per acre, and he convinced the federal land agent for a time that this entitled him to buy all of the fort property. See Wille, *Forever Open, Clear and Free*, 21.

For biographical information on Beaubien see Commission on Chicago Historical and Architectural Landmarks, *Site of the Beaubien Claim*, 3–5.

4. Wille, *Forever Open, Clear and Free*, 2; and see ibid., *Site of the Beaubien Claim*, 6–7.

5. Homer Hoyt, *One Hundred Years of Land Values in Chicago* (Chicago: University of Chicago Press, 1933), 483.

6. Ibid., 95.

7. Wille, *Forever Open, Clear and Free*, 27–28.

8. George H. Douglas, *Rail City: Chicago U.S.A.* (San Diego, Calif.: Howell-North Books, 1981), 32–34.

9. Robert Kinzie and John Kinzie, Jr., were the sons of fur trader John Kinzie, who had purchased the property in 1803. Jean DuSable had sold the property in either 1800 or 1803 to John Laline, who in turn sold it to Kinzie. See Wille, *Forever Open, Clear and Free*, 8; Randall, *History of the Development of Building Construction*, 2; and Commission on Chicago Historical and Architectural Landmarks, *Site of the DuSable/Kinzie House*, 1–4.

10. The area subdivided by Robert and John Kinzie was originally surveyed in 1821 by a government surveyor, John Wall, as the north fractional section 10, township 39 North, of range 14 East. Along the east line of that section Wall indicated a meander line, that being the shore of Lake Michigan. The Wall survey had computed the contents of this section at 102 acres; however, natural accretions that extended the lakefront eastward between 1821 and 1831 had enlarged the tract by at least twenty acres. See Edward O. Brown, "The Shore of Lake Michigan" (paper read before the Law Club of the City of Chicago, 25 April 1902), 7–8.

11. The Canal Trustees subdivision, north of Kinzie's Addition, though platted in 1836, was not recorded until 2 May 1848. See Cook County Tract Records, Bk. 421:2B.

12. John Ashenhurst and Ruth L. Ashenhurst, *All about Chicago* (New York: Houghton Mifflin Co., 1933), 130.

13. For information on the Chicago Water Tower and Pumping Station see Guy Murchie, Jr., "The Drama of Chicago's Water System," *Chicago Tribune* (24 April 1938), Camera News Review section; Commission on Chicago Historical and Architectural Landmarks, *Old Chicago Water Tower District* (Chicago, 1984), 4; Department of Public Works, *Chicago Public Works: A History* (Chicago, 1973), 66; Carl Condit, *Chicago 1910–29: Building, Planning, and Urban Technology* (Chicago: University of Chicago Press, 1973), 248–49.

14. Commission on Chicago Historical and Architectural Landmarks, *Old Chicago Water Tower District*, 13–14.

15. There are numerous accounts of the Chicago Fire of 1871, including Mabel McIlvaine, *Chicago, Her History and Her Adornment* (Chicago: C. D. Peacock, 1927); Robert Cromie, *The Great Chicago Fire* (New York: McGraw-Hill Book Co., 1958).

16. Andreas, *History of Chicago*, 3:446.

17. Ibid.

18. Henry C. Johnson, *North Chicago: Its Advantages, Resources, and Probable Future* (Chicago, 1873), 6.

19. Ibid., 7.

20. For biographical information on Cyrus H. McCormick see William Thomas Hutchinson, *Cyrus Hall McCormick* (New York and London: Century Co., 1930); Joseph Gies, *The Colonel of Chicago* (New York: E. P. Dutton, 1979); Wayne Andrews, *Battle for Chi-*

cago (New York: Harcourt, Brace and Co., 1946); and see John Moses and Joseph Kirkland (eds.), *The History of Chicago, Illinois* (Chicago and New York: Munsell and Co., 1895), 1:130.

The McCormick House was designed by the firm of Cudell and Bluementhal. It was built in 1876–79 for a cost of $175,000. See John Drury, *Old Chicago Houses* (Chicago and London: University of Chicago Press, 1976), 97–98.

21. For information on the Perry H. Smith House see *Chicago Tribune* (30 July 1922): 11; Emmett Dedmon, *Fabulous Chicago: A Great City's History and People* (New York: Random House, 1953), 133; and John J. Flinn, *The Handbook of Chicago Biography* (Chicago: Standard Guide Co., 1893), 329.

22. For information on George Streeter and Streeterville see Edward O. Brown, "The Shore of Lake Michigan"; E. G. Ballard, *Captain Streeter Pioneer* (Chicago: Emery Publishing Service, 1914); John W. Stamper, "Shaping Chicago's Shoreline," *Chicago History* 14 (Winter 1985–86): 44–55.

23. The Palmer mansion was designed by the architectural office of Henry Ives Cobb and Charles S. Frost. It was a three-story limestone and granite house in the Gothic style with interiors by Silsbee and Kent. Its cost was estimated at $250,000. See Thomas Tallmadge, *Architecture in Old Chicago* (Chicago: University of Chicago Press, 1941), 184; Drury, *Old Chicago Houses*, 128–31.

24. Rand, McNally and Co., *One Hundred and Twenty-five Photographic Views of Chicago* (Chicago: Rand, McNally and Co., 1916), 182–83; Wille, *Forever Open, Clear and Free*, 58; *Chicago Times* (24 November 1893) (Chicago Historical Society Library); and Palmer Account Book, vol. 7, 1893–94 (Chicago Historical Society, Department of Archives and Manuscripts).

25. In 1894 Palmer purchased from the Chicago Title and Trust Company two lots on the north side of Chestnut Street where the Hancock Building now stands and, in the following year, he purchased three more lots in the same block from Tobias Allmendinger. The same year he purchased from Allmendinger four lots between Delaware and Walton where the Palmolive Building and the Westin Hotel now stand. This was followed by his purchase from the executors of the Sheldon Sturges estate of most of the corresponding block on the west side of Pine Street. In 1896 he purchased from Minna Allmendinger the northeast corner of Delaware and Pine. In May of 1898 he purchased from David B. Lyman eight lots on the east side of Pine Street between Walton and Oak streets, the present site of the Drake Hotel. In 1900 and 1901 he purchased from Louis Healy lots on Chestnut Street and Walton Place, and from Frederick Sherman lots on Oak Street and Walton Place. See Cook County Tract Records, Bks. 421–421C.

26. Potter Palmer Manuscript File (Chicago Historical Society, Department of Archives and Manuscripts).

27. For information about the building of the Fourth Presbyterian Church see Commission on Chicago Historical and Architectural

Landmarks, *Fourth Presbyterian Church* (Chicago, 1981); and W. A. Nichols, "Fourth Presbyterian Church of Chicago," *Architectural Record* 36 (September 1914): 177–97.

28. Sanborn Map Company, *Insurance Maps of Chicago, Illinois: North and West Division*, 2 vols. (New York, 1906), 1:49–50.

O N E

1. *Chicago Herald* (13 June 1888).

2. Ibid.

3. A group of businessmen opposed to the idea of a viaduct on North Michigan Avenue appeared before Alderman Dixon's committee in June of 1888. Represented by attorney John N. Jewett, they stated that the city had no legal right to change the street because it would damage the abutting properties. See the *Chicago Times* (16 June 1888).

4. The proposal for a subway under the river was made by a Mrs. Horatio May, the wife of city controller Horatio N. May. See the *Chicago Tribune* (14 May 1920): 2; and the *Chicago Post* (6 July 1892).

5. *Chicago Tribune* (11 October 1896): 4.

6. Burnham presented his plan for a lakefront park to members of the Commercial Club in October of 1896, at a dinner party held by James W. Ellsworth, president of the South Park Commission. He made a similar presentation to members of the Merchant's Club in 1897. See Wille, *Forever Open, Clear and Free*, 84–85.

The Commercial Club had been founded in 1877 to promote business interests of the city. Its early members included names like Field, Farwell, Pullman, Leiter, and Crerar. The club met approximately once a month for elaborate banquets and speeches by eminent figures on local and national topics. It had no formal clubhouse or meeting place, usually holding its banquets in the Chicago Auditorium. The Commercial Club committee on the Chicago Plan included Charles D. Norton, Charles H. Wacker, Frederick A. Delano, Walter W. Wilson, Edward B. Butler, John V. Farwell, Jr., Jay Morton, Charles G. Dawes, Harold F. McCormick, Victor F. Lawson, Charles H. McCormick II, and others. See Vilas Johnson, *A History of the Commercial Club of Chicago Including the First History of the Club by John J. Glessner* (Chicago, 1977), 9, 20, 92; and Thomas S. Hines, *Burnham of Chicago: Architect and Planner.* (New York: Oxford University Press, 1974), 247.

The Merchants Club was formed in 1896, with Dunlap Smith one of its founders and John Farwell its first president. The club consisted of young Chicago businessmen and became noted for its exposure of sloppy municipal auditing practices in Chicago. See R. P. Akeley, "Implementation of the 1909 Plan of Chicago: An Historical Account of Planning Salesmanship" (Master's thesis, University of Tennessee, 1973), 34; and see Johnson, *A History of the Commercial Club*, 22.

7. It was not until April 1902 that the Merchants Club endorsed the project of "The Lakefront Park," and in February 1903 it formed a committee to endorse the preparation of a bill to be submitted to the state legislature. The bill, drafted by John H. Hamline and supported by Graeme Stewart, was passed and Grant Park was officially created. See Johnson, *A History of the Commercial Club*, 199–200.

8. Charles Moore, *Daniel H. Burnham: Architect, Planner of Cities* (New York: Houghton Mifflin Co., 1921); Hines, *Burnham of Chicago*.

9. *Chicago Tribune* (14 May 1920): 2; Henry Justin Smith, *Chicago's Great Century: 1833–1933* (Chicago: Published for a Century of Progress by Consolidated Publishers, 1933), 149.

10. Mayor Carter Harrison II was born in Chicago on 23 April 1860. He graduated from St. Ignatius College in Chicago in 1881, after which he entered the Yale Law School, graduating in 1883. He practiced law in Chicago from 1883 to 1891, and was publisher and editor of the *Chicago Times* from 1891 to 1894. See F. Rex, *The Mayors of the City of Chicago* (Chicago: Chicago Public Library, 1933), 88–92; and Charles E. Merriam, *Chicago: A More Intimate View of Urban Politics* (New York: Macmillan Co., 1929), 190.

11. During the early 1900s, property on State Street was leasing for as much as $25,000 a front foot. See Hoyt, *One Hundred Years*, 211; and *Chicago: The Great Central Market* (Chicago: Marshall Field and Co., 1921), 30.

12. *Chicago Tribune* (2 May 1904): 3.

13. This Rush Street site had been the location of the city's first iron swing-type bridge built in 1859. Previous to this, Rush Street traffic had been served by a floating bridge, hinged to one bank and opened and closed by means of ropes. The iron swing bridge collapsed in 1863 and was replaced by another one, which eventually burned in the Fire of 1871. A new wrought-iron structure was built by the Detroit Bridge and Iron Works Company in 1872. It lasted until 1883 when it was struck by a barge and collapsed.

The 1884 structure was designed by DeWitt C. Creigier, commissioner of public works, and Samuel Artingstall, city engineer. The foundations were built by Fitz-Simons and Connell, and the bridge structure by Rust and Coolidge. The bridge's trusses were thirty feet high in the center and twenty feet high at the ends. The deck was made of four-inch white pine planks. The machinery for operating the bridge was located in a house over the roadway in the center of the bridge; the bridgeman operated from the floor of the bridge. See Department of Public Works, *Chicago Public Works*, 98–100; and see *New Rush Street Bridge, Chicago: A Brief Memoranda of its Construction*. (Chicago: Department of Public Works, 1884), 7–8.

14. *Chicago Tribune* (2 May 1904): 3.

15. *Chicago Tribune* (17 May 1904): 1.

16. The Chicago Real Estate Board appointed its own committee consisting of William A. Bond, Frank G. Hoyne, John B. Knight,

William D. Kerfoot, and Eugene H. Fishburn to cooperate in the matter with other public bodies. See *Chicago Tribune* (8 May 1904): 59.

17. Members of the joint committee included, in addition to McCormick, Graham, and Hunt, attorneys Alfred D. Williston and William J. Pringle from the City Council; realtors Henry G. Foreman and William Best and businessman Lyman A. Walton of the South Park Board; realtors William W. Tracey and Bryan Lathrop and businessman Francis T. Simmons of the Lincoln Park Board. In addition, there were six members from the Real Estate Board: John M. Ewen, William A. Bond, Eugene Fishburn, William D. Kerfoot, John B. Knight, and Frank Hoyne. See Commercial Club of Chicago, *Plan for a Boulevard to Connect the North and South Sides of the River on Michigan Avenue and Pine Street* (Chicago: R. R. Donnelley and Sons Co., 1908); and for members' addresses *The Lakeside Annual Directory*, 1904; see also *Chicago Tribune* (6 January 1905): 1.

18. *Chicago Tribune* (6 January 1905): 1.

19. Proceedings of the Chicago City Council (Municipal Reference Library) (16 February 1905), 2510; and *Chicago Tribune* (6 January 1905): 1.

20. For information on the merging of the Commercial and the Merchants clubs see Johnson, *A History of the Commercial Club*, 90–95; Cynthia Field, "The City Planning of Daniel Hudson Burnham" (Ph.D. diss., Columbia University, 1974), 307–18; Walter D. Moody, *What of the City? America's Greatest Issue: City Planning* (Chicago: A. C. McClurg and Co., 1919), 320–33.

21. *Chicago Tribune* (5 March 1907).

22. Ibid. (23 November 1907).

23. Ibid.

24. For information on the World's Columbian Exposition see Harold M. Mayer and Richard C. Wade, *Chicago: Growth of a Metropolis* (Chicago: University of Chicago Press, 1969), 142, 174–75; and Stanley Applebaum, *The Chicago World's Fair of 1893: A Photographic Record* (New York: Dover Publications, 1980).

25. Charles Mulford Robinson, "Improvement in City Life: Aesthetic Progress," *Atlantic Monthly* 83 (June 1899): 771.

26. John Burchard and Albert Bush-Brown, *The Architecture of America: A Social and Cultural History* (Boston and Toronto: Little, Brown and Co., 1961), 273–74.

27. William H. Wilson, "J. Horace McFarland and the City Beautiful Movement," *Journal of Urban History* 7 (May 1981): 315–34.

28. Daniel Burnham produced a plan for Cleveland in 1903 and participated in the McMillan Plan for Washington, D.C., in 1902.

29. Daniel H. Burnham and Edward H. Bennett, *The Plan of Chicago* (New York: DeCapo Press, [1909] 1970), 101.

30. Charles Moore, *Daniel H. Burnham*, 201; and see Field, "The City Planning of Daniel Hudson Burnham," 312. Frederick A.

Delano to Walter D. Moody, 7 July 1915, Moore papers, Library of
Congress, MSS division, p. 2, container 13.

31. Daniel Burnham made his first trip to Europe at the age of
forty-nine, in 1896. This trip included a tour of Spain, Egypt,
Greece, and Italy. His second trip was made during the course of
planning for the McMillan Commission, when Burnham arranged for
the team—consisting of himself, Frederick Law Olmsted, Jr.,
Charles McKim, and William E. Curtis—to go to Europe to see parks
in their relation to public buildings. The team traveled to Paris,
Rome, Venice, Vienna, Budapest, Frankfurt, Berlin, Holland, and
London. See Moore, *Daniel H. Burnham*, 142–56.

32. Burnham and Bennett, *Plan of Chicago*, 18.

33. Donald Drew Egbert, *The Beaux-Arts Tradition in French
Architecture*, ed. David Van Zanten (Princeton: Princeton University Press, 1980), 99–100; and Joseph Hudnut, *Architecture and the
Spirit of Man* (Cambridge, Mass.: Harvard University Press, 1949),
173.

34. Moody, *What of the City?* 132–34.

35. *Chicago Tribune* (3 June 1908); ibid. (4 June 1908).

36. George Packard was born in 1868, in Providence, Rhode
Island. He was a graduate of Brown University and Northwestern
University Law School. His firm served as the attorney for the park
board and had much to do in 1896–99 in establishing questions of
riparian rights in Illinois in connection with Lincoln Park. See *The
Book of Chicagoans* (1905), 444.

37. George Packard, *Argument on the Boulevard Link* (Chicago: Michigan Avenue Improvement Association, 14 May 1908), 2.

38. Ibid., 2.

39. Ibid., 3.

40. Ibid., 10.

41. Walter Moody, *Wacker's Manual for the Plan of Chicago*
(Chicago: 1912), 73.

42. Fred A. Busse was born in Chicago on 3 March 1866. He was
educated in Chicago's public schools. For a number of years he was
engaged in the hardware business with his father, then went into the
coal business as secretary-treasurer of the Northwestern Coal Company. He was later president of the Busse-Reynolds Coal Company
and the Busse Coal Company. Before becoming mayor of Chicago in
1907, he served as the city's postmaster. See Rex, *The Mayors of the
City of Chicago*, 98.

43. Johnson, *A History of the Commercial Club*, 203; Moody,
What of the City? 330–31; and Akeley, "Implementation of the 1909
Plan of Chicago," 54.

44. Among the most active members of the Chicago Plan Commission were David R. Forgan, Adolphus C. Bartlett, Clyde M. Carr,
John V. Farwell, Jay Morton, Charles H. Thorne, Charles L. Hutchinson, and Rollin S. Keyes. Attorney Frank I. Bennett was appointed
vice-chairman. See Moody, *What of the City?* 331; and *The Chi-*

cago Plan Commission: A Historical Sketch, 1909–1960 (Chicago, 1961), 6.

45. Moody, *What of the City?* 91.

46. Moody, *Wacker's Manuel for the Plan of Chicago*, 76.

47. *The Chicago Plan Commission, A Historical Sketch*, 7; Thomas Schlereth, "Burnham's *Plan* and Moody's *Manual*; City Planning as Progressive Reform." American Planner (1983): 75–99.

48. Chicago Plan Commission, *Chicago's Greatest Issue: An Official Plan Prepared under the Direction of the Chicago Plan Commission* (Chicago, 1911); Moody, *What of the City?* 94–95.

49. Chicago Plan Commission, *Chicago's Greatest Issue*, 25.

50. Ibid., 25–26.

51. Charles Wacker, *Argument in Favor of Michigan Avenue Boulevard Link* (Chicago, 1913), 3.

52. Ibid., 3.

53. Ibid., 3–4.

54. Ibid., 4.

55. Hoyt, *One Hundred Years*, 199, 205, 237, 485.

56. John Bell Rae, *The American Automobile* (Chicago: University of Chicago Press, 1965), 92–93.

57. Moody, *What of the City?* 144–46.

58. Ibid., 376.

59. Condemnation proceedings were carried out by the city between 1916 and 1918 for a number of public works projects in addition to the Michigan Avenue improvement. In all, court action was required for settlement with 8700 property owners, the trial being contested by 205 lawyers. A complete list of the parcels taken by the city, and the amounts paid, was published in *The Economist* (1 June 1918): 1009; see also Moody, *What of the City?* 379–80.

60. Moody, *What of the City?* 147–48.

61. Ibid., 139; and *Chicago Tribune* (14 April 1918): 11.

62. Moody, *What of the City?* 138–39.

63. *Chicago Tribune* (14 April 1918): 11.

64. William Hale Thompson was born in Boston, Massachusetts, in 1869, and moved to Chicago with his parents shortly afterward. He was educated in the public schools of Chicago, and as a young man he spent several years as a cattle ranchman in the west. Upon the death of his father, he returned to Chicago to look after his family's real estate holdings. See Rex, *The Mayors of the City of Chicago*, 103.

65. Charles H. Wacker, "The Michigan Avenue Extension: An Address in Commemoration of the Initial Work on the Extension of North Michigan Avenue (Chicago: Chicago Plan Commission, 13 April 1918), 3.

66. Ibid., 5.

67. *Chicago Tribune* (14 May 1920): 1–2; and ibid. (15 May 1920): 1.

68. Chicago Plan Commission, *Ten Years Work of the Chicago Plan Commission: 1909–1919* (Chicago: G. C. Burmeister Printing, 1920), 38.

69. See *Who's Who in Chicago* (Chicago: A. N. Marquis and Co., 1911), 693.

70. The bridge has two roadways, each twenty-seven feet wide with overhanging sidewalks on each side sixteen feet in width. The upper level south approach of the bridge is seventy-five feet wide with twenty-five foot sidewalks; the north approach as far as Ohio Street is eighty feet wide with thirty foot sidewalks. See Chicago Board of Local Improvements, *Chicago Board of Local Improvements* (Chicago, 1931), 14.

71. Stuart E. Cohen, "The Tall Building Urbanistically Reconsidered," *Threshold* 2 (1983): 11.

72. Chicago Board of Local Improvements, *Chicago Board*, 15–16.

73. Moody, *What of the City?* 14.

74. Carl Condit, *Chicago, 1910–29*, 250; and Andrew N. Rebori, "South Water Street Improvement—Chicago," *Architectural Record* 58 (September 1925): 222.

75. *Chicago Tribune* (14 January 1922): 3.

76. For further information on the Wacker Drive Improvement see Hugh E. Young, "New Wacker Drive Supplants 'Rundown' Water-Front Street," *American City Magazine* (April 1926): 3–7; and *Chicago Tribune* (13 March 1927), sec. 3:1; and ibid. (25 January 1928), sec. 3:1.

77. Chicago Board of Local Improvements, *A Sixteen Year Record of Achievement, 1915–1931*, comp. A. E. Burnett (Chicago, 1931), vi.

78. "Magnificent Mile—Streeterville Historic District," National Register Nomination (Chicago, 1982), 6; and *North Central Association Journal* (1918).

79. "The Chicago Improvement Scheme," *American Architect* 114 (11 December 1918): 701 ff.

80. Ibid., 697–98.

81. Ibid.

82. North Side property owners participating in the meetings to discuss land use along North Michigan Avenue included B. M. Winston, F. M. Bowes, Murray Wolbach, D. H. Perkins, Elmer C. Jensen, Eugene A. Bournique, Callistus S. Ennis, W. H. Bush, C. L. Strobel, A. N. Rebori, L. B. Walton, Charles Bohasseck, W. O. Melcher, J. P. Brady, Francis E. Manierre, S. C. Iversne, William H. Babcock, J. H. Van Vlissingen, Pierce Anderson, C. W. Hodgdon, Louis Nelson, P. F. Esser, Leo Heller, and O. P. Goudtner. See *The Economist* (16 March 1918): 484.

83. For the complete text of the North Central Business District Association agreement see ibid. (25 May 1918): 967.

84. Among those who signed the protective agreement were John and Charles Farwell, Mrs. Cyrus H. McCormick, James S. Kirk, and architects Benjamin Marshall and Charles S. Fox. See ibid. (6 December 1919): 1161.

85. For information on Chicago's early building height ordinances see Hoyt, *One Hundred Years*, 211, 224–25; and Graham Aldis, "History and Trend of Office Rentals," *Proceedings of the Annual Convention of the National Association of Building Owners and Managers* (Chicago, 1924), 61–62.

86. Hoyt, *One Hundred Years*, 224–25.

87. The actual ordinance for exceptions to the height limit in the Fifth Volume District reads:

> No building or part thereof shall be erected to a height at any street line or alley in excess of 264 feet, provided, however, that back from the street line or alley line such building or part thereof may be erected so as not to protrude above a plane sloping up an angle of 30 degrees with the horizontal from such street line or alley line at the height limit a distance from such street line or alley of 32 feet measured on the slope.
>
> If the area of a building is reduced so that above the street line height limit it covers in the aggregate not more than 25 percent of the area of the premises, the building above such height will be excepted from the volume and street line height limit regulations.

See *The Chicago Zoning Ordinance* (Chicago, 1923), 12.

T W O

1. *The Economist* (2 March 1918): 389.

2. *Chicago Tribune* (7 July 1918), sec. 2:5.

3. Building permits issued in Chicago the first seven months of 1922 totaled $127,712,000. See ibid. (6 August 1922): 1.

4. Ibid. (29 December 1922): 3; ibid. (6 August 1922): 1.

5. Bessie L. Pierce, *A History of Chicago* (Chicago: University of Chicago Press, 1957), 229.

6. The $2,500,000 endowment was given to the library in 1894, five years after Crerar died. See Walter D. Moody, *What of the City?* 283–84.

7. For information on the founding and early management of the Crerar Library see J. Christian Bay, *The John Crerar Library, 1895–1944* (Chicago, 1945).

8. Ibid., 28, 193–96; and see *The Economist* (8 February 1919): 256.

9. For information on other buildings by Holabird and Roche from the period see Robert F. Irving, "Holabird and Root, Still Going Strong after 95 Years," *Inland Architect* 20 (July 1976): 8–13;

and Robert Bruegmann, "Holabird and Roche and Holabird and Root: The First Two Generations," *Chicago History* 9 (Fall 1980): 133.

10. For a description and illustrations of the Crerar Library see "The Work of Holabird and Roche, Architects," *American Architect* 28 (25 August 1920): 231–34.

11. The building's original plans called for an additional thirty-five feet to be added to the west, a proposal that was never carried out. See illustration in ibid., 231–34.

12. The plans for the Crerar Library were released for bids in February 1919. Two alternate designs were bid, one as eventually built, the other calling for a five-story building and the remodeling of an adjoining five-story building. See *The Economist* (8 February 1919): 256; and see Bay, *The John Crerar Library*, 196.

13. For information on the Wrigley Building see Condit, *Chicago 1910–29*, 98; Sally Chappell, "As If the Lights Were Always Shining: Graham, Anderson, Probst and White's Wrigley Building at the North Boulevard Link," *Chicago Architecture, 1872–1922: Birth of a Metropolis,* ed. John Zukowsky (Munich: Prestel-Verlag in association with the Art Institute of Chicago, 1987), 291–301; Jill Oset, "Graham, Anderson, Probst and White: Architects of an Industrial Vision" (unpublished paper for Northwestern University Department of Art History, 1983); and Graham, Anderson, Probst and White, *The Architectural World of Graham, Anderson, Probst and White, Chicago: And Their Predecessors* (London: B. T. Batsford, 1933).

14. William Zimmerman, Jr., *William Wrigley, Jr.: The Man and His Business* (Chicago: R. R. Donnelley and Sons, 1935), 1, 28; Glenn A. Bishop and Paul T. Gilbert, *Chicago's Accomplishments and Leaders* (Chicago: Bishop Publishing Co., 1932), 533; and *Book of Chicagoans* (1926), 960.

15. Zimmerman, *William Wrigley, Jr.*, 23–28, 37–45.

16. Ibid., 141; Bishop and Gilbert, *Chicago's Accomplishments and Leaders*, 533.

17. Bertram Winston was born in Chicago, 9 April 1868, the son of Frederick H. Winston. He was educated in the Chicago public schools and entered the real estate and loan business at the age of twenty. Since 1906 he was a member of Winston and Company. He lived at 749 North Michigan Avenue. See *Book of Chicagoans* (1917), 738.

18. Zimmerman, *William Wrigley, Jr.*, 144.

19. *Chicago Tribune* (27 December 1958).

20. William Wrigley, Jr., was a friend of Mayor Thompson; the two often went sailing together on Lake Geneva. See F. K. Plous, Jr., "The Dowager of Michigan Avenue," *Midwest Magazine of the Chicago Sun-Times* (23 July 1972): 7.

21. Leo J. Sheridan, "Economic Factors of the Office Building Project," *Architectural Forum* 41 (September 1924): 121.

22. "The Wrigley Building," *Through the Ages* (October 1925): 34–38.

23. Ibid., 34; and see Cook County Tract Records, Bk. 459: 3–5.

24. *Biographical Dictionary of American Architects*, ed. Henry F. and Elsie Rathburn Withey (Los Angeles: Hennessey and Ingalls, 1970), 20, 245–46, 491, 651; and *Chicago Architects Design: A Century of Architectural Drawings from the Art Institute of Chicago* (Chicago: Art Institute of Chicago and Rizzoli International Publications, 1982), 81.

25. *Biographical Dictionary*, 20; and see obituary by Thomas Tallmadge in the *Architectural Record* 55 (May 1924).

26. Chappell, "As If the Lights Were Always Shining", 292.

27. The terra cotta for the Wrigley Building was supplied by the Northwestern Terra Cotta Company. See *Real Estate News* (1924): 5.

28. Chappell, "As If the Lights Were Always Shining," 298–99; Condit, *Chicago 1910–29*, 99; and Oset, "Graham, Anderson, Probst and White," 5–6.

29. Wrigley Building Pamphlet File (Chicago Historical Society); Chappell, "As If the Lights Were Always Shining," 298.

30. To produce the illumination of the Wrigley Building requires the use of 198 projectors with 500-watt lamps and 16 projectors with 250-watt lamps. The cost of installing the system was $30,000. See "Architecture and Illumination," *Architectural Forum* 35 (October 1921): 135; Chappell, "As If the Lights Were Always Shining," 301; and Condit, *Chicago 1910–29*, 99.

31. For detailed information about the plans of the Wrigley Building see *Real Estate News* (1924): 5; see also working drawings for the building in the Chicago Historical Society Architecture Department. None of the building's outer corners form a right angle. The northeast corner is 42°; the southeast 132°; the southwest 84°; the northwest 102°. Original sets of the Wrigley Building working drawings are located in the Wrigley office of Ragnar-Benson, contractors, and in the Chicago Historical Society Architecture Department.

32. The original plan of the first floor of the Wrigley Building was altered through the course of several renovations, the most recent being one by the interior design firm of Powell/Kleinschmidt in 1983–84. For a description of the plan layout see Chappell, "As If the Lights Were Always Shining," 294.

33. Condit, *Chicago 1910–29*, 99.

34. Ibid., 98–99; and Chappell, "As If the Lights Were Always Shining," 296.

35. Plous, "The Dowager of Michigan Avenue," 8.

36. Chappell, "As If the Lights Were Always Shining," 296; Leland M. Roth, *McKim, Mead & White; Architects* (New York: Harper and Row, 1983), 158–62.

37. William Wrigley, Jr., took out a permit for the construction of the building in November 1919. The cost was estimated at this time at $2,000,000. See *The Economist* (29 November 1919): 1108; *Real Estate News* (1924): 1.

38. For pictures of the Wrigley Building during construction and after see the Wrigley Photo Archives, Wrigley Building.

39. Wrigley Building Pamphlet File (Chicago Historical Society).

40. Earlier tenants in the Wrigley Building included Gaiver and Dinkelberg, architects and engineers; Vulcan Louisville Smelting Company; A. A. Boland, Jr., representing the Maine and New Hampshire Granite Company; J. A. Plowman, representing the Frinck Reflector Company; J. Williams Macy, representing *Field and Stream* and *Town and Country*; John Glass, publisher's representative; and A. D. Gleason, manager for a restaurant on the lower level with windows looking out over the river. See *The Economist* (29 January 1921): 255; and see Zimmerman, *William Wrigley, Jr.*, 153.

41. Wrigley was able to purchase for $350,000 the east half of the property, lots 2, 3, and 4 of Block 6 of Kinzie's Addition, from the William Hoyt estate in January 1923. He acquired title to the west half, lots 5 and 6, from Catherina Newman in 1927. See Tract Records, Bk. 459: 76–86; and see *Chicago Tribune* (16 January 1923): 27.

42. Zimmerman, *William Wrigley, Jr.*, 154.

43. Ibid., 154–55; and see letter from Gilbert H. Scribner (Winston and Co.) to Ernest Fuller (real estate editor of the *Chicago Tribune*), (22 December 1958), Wrigley Archives.

44. Condit, *Chicago 1910–29*, 99.

45. Smith, *Chicago's Great Century*, 168; and Scribner letter, 1958.

46. *The American Architect* 119 (11 May 1921): 553; and see *Guide to Monuments and Memorials* (Chicago, n.d.), 1–2. Benjamin F. Ferguson, a Chicago lumber merchant who died in 1905, left the bulk of his estate to the board of directors of the Chicago Art Institute for the erection and maintenance of statues and monuments in public places in Chicago.

47. *Guide to Monuments and Memorials*, 1–2.

48. For information and illustrations of the Italian Court see the *Chicago Tribune* (2 January 1921), sec. 10: 12.

49. Other tenants of the Italian Court were Mr. Pierre de Lanoux, a writer, and his wife, a portrait painter; Frederick Grant, artist; Mary H. Wicker, portrait artist; James H. Kehler, writer; Mrs. William Deane, sculptress; Alice Louise Karcher, interior decorator; Carolyn Hazard, social secretary; Neoma Nagel, interior decorator; Burleigh Withers Company, commercial studio; Oliver W. Snyder, designer; Evelyn Bridge, designer. See ibid.

50. Cook County Tract Records, Bk. 259A:242–44.

51. William Benke, *All about Land Investment* (New York: McGraw-Hill Book Co., 1976), 25.

52. C. Stanley Taylor, "Financing the Office Building, *Architectural Forum* 41 (September 1924): 137; Henry E. Hoagland and Leo D. Stone, *Real Estate Finance* (Homewood, Ill.: Richard D. Irwin, 1969), 259–65.

53. *Chicago Tribune* (20 June 1944): 12; *Biographical Dictionary*, 392–93; Commission on Chicago Historical and Architectural Landmarks, *East Lake Shore Drive District: Preliminary Summary of Information* (Chicago, 1984), 4; and Carroll William Westfall, "Benjamin Henry Marshall of Chicago," *Chicago Architectural Journal* 2 (1982): 8–21.

54. *Biographical Dictionary*, 217.

55. "The Lake Shore Trust and Savings Bank," *North Central Journal* 4 (December 1926), 50–51; and Meredith Taussig, North Michigan Avenue: A Story of a Chicago Street, 1918–1930 (unpublished class paper, University of Illinois at Chicago, March 1983), pt. 2:11.

56. "The Lake Shore Trust and Savings Bank," 50–51.

57. The working drawings of the Palmer Shops Building are located in the Chicago Historical Society Architecture Department. The building was constructed by the Dahl Stedman Company. A fifty-foot addition was built on the west side of the building in 1922–23, also designed by Holabird and Roche. See *The Economist* (15 April 1922): 860.

58. Taussig, "North Michigan Avenue," 14.

59. *The Economist* (20 December 1923): Special News Bulletin; and *The Economist* (4 February 1924): Special News Bulletin.

60. *The Economist* (28 July 1928): 220.

61. For information on the London Guarantee Building see John Zukowsky, *Architecture in Context: 360 North Michigan Avenue* (Chicago: Art Institute of Chicago, 1981); "London Guarantee and Accident Building, Chicago," *American Architect* 126 (27 August 1924): 191; and Condit, *Chicago 1910–29*, 100, 168, 176.

62. The London Guarantee Company announced in October 1923 that New York would be a more suitable place for its headquarters. It thus occupied only the second floor of the new building and moved about 100 employees to New York. See the *Chicago Tribune* (14 October 1923), sec. 2:13; ibid. (24 January 1959): 19; and London Guarantee Pamphlet File (Chicago Historical Society Library).

63. The London Guarantee site embraced 16,720 square feet, with the building covering 13,520 square feet. See *The Economist* (2 July 1921): 35; and see Cook County Tract Records, Bk. 460A: 44–46.

64. For a complete description of the London Guarantee Building bond issue see *The Economist* (11 May 1922): Special News Bulletin.

65. For detailed information on mortgage bond financing see Taylor, "Financing the Office Building," 138; Hoyt, *One Hundred Years*, 445; William T. Cross, *The Making of A Trust Company* (Chicago: Chicago Trust Co., 1923), 37–38; Robert A. M. Stern, Gregory

Gilmartin, and Thomas Mellins, *New York 1930: Architecture and Urbanism between the Two World Wars* (New York: Rizzoli International Publications, 1987), 514.

66. One disadvantage with real estate bonds was that the costs included that of selling the bonds and the overhead and profit of the mortgage company. There was no standard basis on which these costs could be estimated; however, a general figure was from 9 to 12 percent of the face value of the mortgage. See Taylor, "Financing the Office Building," 138.

67. Cross, *The Making of a Trust Company*, 37.

68. Ibid.

69. *The Economist* (11 May 1922): Special News Bulletin.

70. *Chicago Daily News* (23 January 1937): n.p.; *Armour Engineer* (December 1940): n.p.; and the *Chicago Tribune* (7 November 1940): n.p. These references can be found in the Alfred Ahlschuler Pamphlet File (Chicago Historical Society Library).

71. Condit, *Chicago 1910–29*, 100.

72. London Guarantee Pamphlet File (Chicago Historical Society Library).

73. In setting the building back six feet from the north lot line, the owners granted an easement to the city for the resulting plaza. See "London Guarantee and Accident Building, Chicago," 191.

74. Condit, *Chicago 1910–29*, 100.

75. *Chicago Tribune* (10 November 1946): 42; and Cook County Tract Records, Bk. 460A: 44–46.

76. "London Guarantee and Accident Building, Chicago," 191.

77. Ibid., 192.

78. Ibid., 191; *Chicago Tribune* (10 November 1946): 42.

79. The corridors above the first floor of the London Guarantee Building had Alabama marble wainscoting with floors of Carthage marble, with Westfield green marble borders. The wood trim throughout was Mexican mahogany. For a complete description of the London Guarantee Building interiors see London Guarantee Pamphlet File (Chicago Historical Society Library); and "London Guarantee and Accident Building, Chicago," 190–92.

80. Alfred Hoyt Granger, *Chicago Welcomes You* (Chicago: A. Kroch, 1933), 141.

81. Zukowsky, *Architecture in Context*, 3.

82. Ibid., 3.

83. Ibid., 15.

84. For lists of tenants in the London Guarantee Building see *The Economist* (1 September 1923): 472; and ibid. (1 March 1924): 519.

85. London Guarantee Pamphlet File (Chicago Historical Society Library).

86. Zukowsky, *Architecture in Context*, 19.

THREE

1. *To the Tower* (Chicago: *Chicago Tribune*, 1924), 5.

2. Ibid., 5.

3. For information on the history of the *Chicago Tribune* see Lloyd Wendt, *Chicago Tribune: The Rise of a Great American Newspaper* (Chicago: Rand McNally and Co., 1966); Frank C. Waldrop, *McCormick of Chicago: An Unconventional Portrait of a Controversial Figure* (Englewood Cliffs, N.J.: Prentice-Hall, 1966); Gies, *The Colonel of Chicago*; Cynthia Field, "The Chicago Tribune Competition of 1922" (Master's thesis, Columbia University, 1968); Holly Gerberding, "Tribune Tower" (unpublished paper for Northwestern University Department of Art History, 1983); and *Chicago Tribune* (10 June 1947): special section.

4. Joseph Medill, who had founded the Cleveland *Leader* in 1851, and Dr. Charles H. Ray, owner of the Galena *Jeffersonian*, acquired the *Chicago Tribune* in 1855. See Gies, *The Colonel of Chicago*, 8–9; Andrews, *Battle for Chicago*, 47; *Chicago Tribune* (10 June 1947), sec. C: 2.

5. Joseph Medill was born 6 April 1823 in New Brunswick, Canada. He studied and practiced law after his family moved to Ohio, but soon turned to newspaper work. Medill purchased the Coshocton *Whig* in Ohio in 1849 and renamed it the *Republican*. Soon he moved to larger and more influential circles in Cleveland and, as an editor, by 1855 he already was a dominant figure. He chose the name for the Republican party and presided at its first caucus in his own newspaper office. See the *Chicago Tribune* (10 June 1947) sec. C:2; Andrews, *Battle for Chicago*, 48–49; Gies, *The Colonel of Chicago*, 8–9.

6. Gies, *The Colonel of Chicago*, 9.

7. From its first home the *Tribune* moved in 1849 to an office space above Gray's Grocery at the northwest corner of Clark and Lake streets. The next move, a year later, was to the Masonic Building on Lake Street. In 1852 it moved to the Evans Block, a three-story building, where it occupied the second and third floors. Here it remained throughout the Civil War until it erected its own building in 1868. See *Chicago Tribune* (10 June 1947) sec. 2:1; and see H. Steward Leonard, "The History of Architecture in Chicago" (Master's thesis, University of Chicago, 1934), 104.

8. *Chicago Tribune* (10 June 1947) sec. C:3; Leonard, "The History of Architecture," 104; Field, "The Chicago Tribune Competition of 1922," 24.

9. With the *Tribune*'s real estate manager, Holmes Onderdonk, in charge, four locations for the new *Tribune* plant were considered: Market and Harrison streets, Market and Washington streets, Wells and North Water streets, and Michigan Avenue and Hubbard Street. See Holmes Onderdonk, "The Tribune Tower," *Journal of the Western Society of Engineers* 29 (December 1924): 443.

10. Andrews, *Battle for Chicago*, 231.

11. *Chicago Tribune* (19 May 1904): 4.

12. McCormick purchased a 100 by 100 foot lot at the northeast corner of Michigan Avenue and Hubbard Street from James S. Kirk and Company for $181,000; and a 150 by 100 foot lot lying 100 feet east of Michigan Avenue from William V. Kelly for $115,000; and a 50 by 100 foot lot at the northwest corner of Hubbard and St. Clair streets from George K. Schmidt for $181,000. See *The Economist* (4 October 1919): 688; and see Cook County Tract Records, Bk. 459:94B–105.

13. Letter from Robert R. McCormick to Arthur Rubloff, 7 December 1948, Rubloff Archives (Chicago Historical Society Library).

14. *The Economist* (4 October 1919): 688.

15. Ibid. Joseph B. Fleming was an attorney with the firm of McCormick, Kirkland, Patterson and Fleming. See *Who's Who in Chicago*, 301.

16. The contractor for the *Tribune* printing plant was R. C. Wiebolt. See *The Economist* (4 October 1919): 688.

17. Wendt, *Chicago Tribune*, 469.

18. Holmes Onderdonk credits the idea of a competition to Colonel Patterson. See Onderdonk, "The Tribune Tower," 444; Condit, *Chicago 1910–29*, 108–14; *The International Competition for a New Administration Building for the Chicago Tribune 1922* (Chicago: Tribune Company, 1923); Field, "The Chicago Tribune Competition of 1922;" Gerberding, "Tribune Tower," 2–6, 9–12; David Van Zanten, "Twenties Gothic," *New Mexico Studies in the Fine Arts* 7 (1982): 19–24; *Chicago Tribune* (10 June 1922): 1.

19. *Chicago Tribune* (10 June 1922): 1.

20. Ibid.

21. Ibid., 2.

22. Ibid.

23. The competition prize money was to be distributed on the following basis: $50,000 first prize award, $20,000 for second place, $10,000 for third place, and ten prizes of $2,000 each for the ten architects specially invited to enter the competition. See ibid.; and *The International Competition;* Gerberding, "Tribune Tower," 5; Field, "The Chicago Tribune Competition of 1922," 14–15; Condit, *Chicago 1910–29*, 109; *Chicago Tribune* (10 June 1922): 1; and ibid. (1 August 1922): 1–5.

24. *Chicago Tribune* (10 June 1922): 1; and ibid. (1 August 1922): 1, 5; see also *The International Competition*, 10–12; and Field, "The Chicago Tribune Competition of 1922," 20.

25. *Chicago Tribune* (6 July 1922): 21; and Field, "The Chicago Tribune Competition of 1922," 23.

26. *The International Competition*, 12; Gerberding, "Tribune Tower," 9.

27. The complete list of the ten specially invited participants included, besides Holabird and Roche, D. H. Burnham and Company, and John Mead Howells, the offices of Jarvis Hunt; Andrew Rebori; Schmidt, Garden and Martin; Bertram Goodhue; Benjamin

Wistar Morris, who designed the Aetna-Phoenix Life Insurance Company Building in Hartford, Connecticut; James Gamble Rogers; and Bliss and Faville, of San Francisco, who had designed several buildings for the Panama-Pacific Exposition. See *Chicago Tribune* (1 August 1922): 5; Condit, *Chicago 1910–29*, 168; Gerberding, "Tribune Tower," 9; and Field, "The Chicago Tribune Tower Competition of 1922," 23.

28. *Chicago Tribune* (10 June 1922): 1; Walter L. Creese, "American Architecture from 1918 to 1933 with a Special Emphasis on European Influence" (Ph.D. diss., Harvard University, 1949), pt. 1:4.

29. *The International Competition*, 35; Field, "The Chicago Tribune Competition of 1922," 26.

30. Irving K. Pond, "High Buildings and Beauty," *Architectural Forum* 38 (February 1923): 41–44; Gerberding, "Tribune Tower," 6–7; Van Zanten, "Twenties Gothic," 22; Field, "The Tribune Tower Competition of 1922," 13–14.

31. *Chicago Tribune* (18 June 1922), rotogravure section: 13.

32. Field, "The Chicago Tribune Competition of 1922," 8; Gerberding, "Tribune Tower," 6; and *Chicago Tribune* (12 June 1922): 1.

33. Field, "The Chicago Tribune Competition of 1922," 16, 27; Gerberding, "Tribune Tower," 6; *Chicago Tribune* (18 June 1922), rotogravure section: 13; and ibid. (9 July 1922), rotogravure section: 13.

34. *Chicago Tribune* (20 August 1922), rotogravure section: 14.

35. *Chicago Tribune* (19 November 1922), rotogravure section: 30.

36. Condit, *Chicago 1910–29*, 108–110; Onderdonk, "The Tribune Tower," 444; *The International Competition*, 40–42; Creese, *American Architecture from 1918 to 1933*, pt. 1:4–6; *Chicago Tribune* (2 November 1922): 11; ibid. (23 November 1922): 7.

37. The six appointees of this committee were Jay Morton and Harry A. Wheller from the Chicago Plan Commission, E. I. Frankhauser and Dorsey Crowe from the City Council, and Bertram M. Winston and Sheldon Clark from the North Central Improvement Association. See *Chicago Tribune* (16 July 1922): 1; and Gerberding, "Tribune Tower," 10; Field, "The Chicago Tribune Competition of 1922," 17, 20.

38. Alfred Hoyt Granger (1867–1939) was educated at Kenyon College in Ohio and later graduated in architecture from M.I.T. In 1887 he studied at the Ecole des Beaux-Arts. Upon returning to the United States he joined the firm of Shepley, Rutan and Coolidge, which in 1891 sent him to Chicago to supervise the construction of the Art Institute and the Public Library. He later formed a partnership with Charles S. Frost, with whom he designed the Chicago and Northwestern train station and the LaSalle Street station. At the time of his involvement with the *Tribune* building competition, Granger

was the president of the Chicago chapter of the A.I.A. See *Biographical Dictionary*, 247; and Field, "The Chicago Tribune Competition of 1922," 19.

39. Creese, "American Architecture from 1918 to 1933," pt. 1: 5; Condit, *Chicago 1910–29*, 109; Field, "The Chicago Tribune Competition of 1922," 17.

40. Granger, *Chicago Welcomes You*, 142.

41. *Chicago Tribune* (6 June 1925): 6. See also Condit, *Chicago 1910–29*, 111; and *The Story of the Tower*. (Chicago: Tribune Company, 1968), 3.

42. The quotation is from an unpublished letter by Raymond Hood, a copy of which is filed under "Tribune Tower," in the library of the *Tribune*. See Leonard, "The History of Architecture in Chicago," 105–6.

43. Raymond M. Hood, "Exterior Architecture of Office Buildings," *Architectural Forum* 41 (September 1924): 97.

44. Ibid.

45. *Chicago Tribune* (2 December 1922): 1.

46. Ibid.; this quote was recounted in "The Tribune Tower, Chicago," *Architectural Forum* 43 (October 1925): 187.

47. The *Tribune*'s headline of the announcement of the winner stated, "Novelist's Son Gains Architect Prize." See *Chicago Tribune* (2 December 1922): 1.

48. Ibid.

49. *Biographical Dictionary*, 297–98; Gerberding, "Tribune Tower," 12–13.

50. Robert A. M. Stern, *Raymond Hood* (New York: Rizzoli International Publications, 1982), 1; Leon V. Solon, "The Evolution of an Architectural Design: The Tribune Building Tower, Chicago," *Architectural Record* 59 (March 1926): 215–22; Field, "The Chicago Tribune Competition of 1922," 25.

51. *Chicago Tribune* (2 December 1922): 1.

52. Thomas Tallmadge, "A Critic of the Chicago Tribune Building Competition," *Western Architect* 32 (January 1923): 7.

53. Ibid., 8.

54. Irving K. Pond, "High Buildings and Beauty," *Architectural Forum* 38 (February 1923): 43.

55. Louis H. Sullivan, "The Chicago Tribune Competition," *Architectural Record* 53 (February 1923): 156.

56. Ibid.

57. Tallmadge, "A Critic of the Chicago Tribune Building Competition," 7; Pond, "High Buildings and Beauty," 42; and Field, "The Chicago Tribune Competition of 1922," 48.

58. Sullivan, "The Chicago Tribune Competition," 153.

59. Ibid., 153–56.

257

60. Leonard, "The History of Architecture in Chicago," 109; Robert Bruegmann, "The Tribune Competition: The Metropolis," *Inland Architect* 24 (June 1980): 20; Robert Bruegmann, "When Worlds Collided: European and American Entries to the Chicago Tribune Competition of 1922," in John Zukowsky, ed., *Chicago Architecture, 1872–1922: Birth of a Metropolis* (Munich: Prestel-Verlag in association with the Art Institute of Chicago, 1987), 303–17; Condit, *Chicago 1910–29*, 110.

61. Condit, *Chicago 1910–29*, 110; Bruegmann, "Holabird and Roche and Holabird and Root," 153–160.

62. Tallmadge, "A Critic of the Chicago Tribune Building Competition," 8.

63. Raymond M. Hood, "The Tribune Tower—the Architect's Problem," *Western Architect* 34 (November 1925): 114.

64. Condit, *Chicago 1910–29*, 108, 169.

65. Hood, "The Tribune Tower," 99.

66. The Methodists planned to erect their building at the southeast corner of Clark and Washington Streets according to plans by Holabird and Roche. For information on this building see *Chicago Tribune* (28 December 1922): 1.

67. Ibid. (29 December 1922): 9.

68. Ibid. (28 December 1922): 5.

69. Ibid. (27 December 1922): 3.

70. Ibid. (20 January 1924): 5.

71. The Tribune Tower has two floors and six basements below the grade of North Michigan Avenue, extending forty-one feet below mean water level in the river. See Condit, *Chicago 1910–29*, 112.

72. Cook County Tract Records, Bk. 459:98B–99, 101–2.

73. *Chicago Tribune* (6 June 1925): 1.

74. Condit, *Chicago 1910–29*, 112–13.

75. Condit, *Chicago 1910–29*, 113.

76. Ibid.

77. John Mead Howells, "The Production of High Class Office Space as Affected by Architectural Design," *Proceedings of the Sixteenth Annual Convention of the National Association of Building Owners and Managers* (Chicago, 1923), 260.

78. "Tribune Plans to Expand in Rear of Tower," *Chicago Tribune* (9 December 1961): 6.

FOUR

1. Hoyt, *One Hundred Years*, 475.

2. Ibid., 238–39.

3. Harvey Warren Zorbaugh, *Gold Coast and Slum: A Sociological Study of Chicago's Near North Side* (Chicago: University of Chicago Press, 1929), 4–20.

4. For information on the Central Life Insurance Company Building see "Central Life Insurance Company of Illinois," *North Central Journal* (1929): 9–10; *Chicago Tribune* (5 November 1922), sec. 2:5; and ibid. (17 December 1922), sec. 2:2.

5. *Chicago Tribune* (5 November 1922), sec. 2:5; Cook County Tract Records, Bk. 460:3–8.

6. Bishop and Gilbert, *Chicago's Accomplishments and Leaders*, 89–91; *Who's Who in Chicago* (1931), 153.

7. "Central Life Insurance Company of Illinois," 9.

8. Ibid., 10.

9. *Chicago Tribune* (17 December 1922), sec. 2:2.

10. Zukowsky, *Chicago Architecture 1872–1922*, 464.

11. For information on the second proposed National Life Insurance Company Building see the *Chicago Tribune* (5 January 1922): 1.

12. Ibid.

13. Ibid.

14. Finis Farr, *Frank Lloyd Wright* (London: Jonathan Cape, 1962), 177.

15. For information on Frank Lloyd Wright's proposal for the National Life Insurance Company Building see Frank Lloyd Wright, *An American Architecture*, ed. Edgar Kaufmann (New York: Horizon Press, 1955), 115–19; Frank Lloyd Wright, *The Future of Architecture* (New York: Horizon Press, 1953), 148–71; Arthur Drexler, ed., *The Drawings of Frank Lloyd Wright* (New York: Horizon Press, 1962); Robert C. Twombly, *Frank Lloyd Wright: An Interpretive Biography* (New York: Harper and Row, 1973), 200–201; and Frank Lloyd Wright, "In the Cause of Architecture," *Architectural Record* 64 (October 1928): 334–42.

16. Twombly, *Frank Lloyd Wright*, 138.

17. Ibid., 161.

18. Ibid., 158–59.

19. Between 1924 and 1932 Wright erected only five buildings. See ibid., 154.

20. Ibid., 143; *Chicago Tribune* (26 November 1924): 5.

21. To escape Miriam Noel, Wright fled Taliesin in 1925 and went into hiding in Minnetonka, Minnesota. See Twombly, *Frank Lloyd Wright*, 150.

22. In Wright's words: "I began work upon this study in Los Angeles in the winter of 1923 having had the main features of it in mind for many years. I had the good fortune to explain it in detail to 'liebermeister' Louis Sullivan, some months before he died." See Wright, "In the Cause of Architecture," 342.

23. Twombly, *Frank Lloyd Wright*, 230.

24. Wright, "In the Cause of Architecture," 334–35.

25. Ibid., 338.

26. Ibid., 340.

27. Ibid., 342.

28. Ibid.

29. Wright, *The Future of Architecture*, 163.

30. Farr, *Frank Lloyd Wright*, 180.

31. Twombly, *Frank Lloyd Wright*, 162.

32. For information on the Bell Building see *Chicago Daily News* (10 May 1924): 17; and *Chicago Tribune* (20 January 1924), sec. 9:22.

33. *Who's Who in Chicago* (1931), 80.

34. *The Economist* (19 May 1917): 1078; *Chicago Daily News* (10 May 1924).

35. Ibid.

36. *Who's Who in Chicago* (1931), 1003.

37. Thompson's Restaurant was established by John R. Thompson, Sr., in 1891, at 397 State Street. Four years later he began branching out in Chicago and opened restaurants in the principal cities of the United States and Canada. In 1925 the company was incorporated with a capital of $6,000,000. See *Who's Who in Chicago* (1926), 868.

38. The first design proposal for the Michigan-Ohio Building was published in the *Chicago Tribune* (6 January 1924), sec. 2:8; the final design of the Michigan-Ohio Building was published in the *Chicago Tribune* (28 September 1924), sec. 10:28.

39. *Chicago Tribune* (20 January 1924), sec. 9:22.

40. For information on the property transactions for the Michigan-Ohio Building see *The Economist* (12 January 1924): 99; *Chicago Tribune* (6 January 1924), sec. 2:8; and Cook County Tract Records, Bk. 459B:120–22.

41. For information about the Hibbard, Spencer, Bartlett and Company Building see Frank A. Randall, *History of the Development of Building Construction in Chicago* (Urbana: University of Illinois Press, 1949), 269; Lewis Mumford, "New York vs. Chicago in Architecture," *Architecture* 56 (November 1927): 241–43; see the *Chicago Tribune* (8 November 1946): 39. The contractor for the building was the Henry Ericsson Company.

42. The Hibbard, Spencer, Bartlett and Company Building was sold to a group of New York investors in 1946. The Mandel Brothers Department Store, for which the building was later named, was one of the first lessees from the new owner. See the *Chicago Tribune* (8 November 1946): 39.

43. For information on the Lake-Michigan Building see *North Central Journal* (1929): 14; and *The Economist* (30 May 1925): 1414; ibid. (9 January 1926): 113; and ibid. (20 February 1926): 519.

44. *Chicago Tribune*, (25 January 1927): 22 (advertisement).

45. The engineer for the Lake-Michigan Building was Lieber-

mann and Hein. See Randall, *A History of the Development of Building Construction in Chicago,* 273.

46. For an illustration of the Lake-Michigan Building see *North Central Journal* (1929): 14.

47. *Who's Who in Chicago* (1936), 899.

48. *The Economist* (9 January 1926): 113.

49. For information on the mortgage bond issue for the Lake-Michigan Building see ibid. (20 February 1926): 519.

50. Management companies for the building included Robert White and Company, then John R. Magill and Company. See ibid; *Chicago Tribune* (1 February 1928): 20 (advertisement).

51. For information on the Farwell Building see *Chicago Tribune* (5 September 1926), sec. 3:1.

52. Wendt, *Chicago Tribune,* 126.

53. The original John V. Farwell House had been sold in 1905 and now served as a restaurant. See Drury, *Old Chicago Houses,* 110–12; and see Cook County Tract Records, Bk. 421C:35–37.

54. *Who's Who in Chicago* (1926), 287.

55. Cook County Tract Records, Bk. 459B:140–42; and ibid. Bk. 460:116–19.

56. *Chicago Tribune* (5 September 1926), sec. 3:1.

57. Bishop and Gilbert, *Chicago's Accomplishments and Leaders,* 313.

58. *The Economist* (10 March 1928): 617.

59. *Chicago Tribune* (19 February 1928), sec. 3:1.

60. For information and illustrations of the Malabry Court Building see ibid. (12 September 1926), sec. 3:1; and Anne Lee, "Malabry Court, Chicago—a Remodeled Building," *Architectural Record* 63 (February 1928): 97–104.

61. "Malabry Court, Chicago," 97, 104.

62. Ibid.

63. *Chicago Tribune* (12 September 1926), sec. 3:1.

64. The Erskine-Danforth Corporation leased the existing building measuring 100 by 75 feet in January 1928. The lease called for rental terms of $20,000 for the first year, $25,000 for the second, $30,000 for the third, $35,000 for the fourth, and $40,000 for each remaining year. See *The Economist* (14 January 1928): 81. Louis Nelson had owned the property since 1901. See Cook County Tract Records, Bk. 459A:207–9.

65. The Erskine-Danforth Building was commonly known as the Decorative Arts Building and later as the Breskin Building. See *North Central Journal* (December 1928), n.p.

66. For information and illustrations of remodeled buildings on the Near North Side during the 1920s see the *Chicago Tribune* (4 December 1927), sec. 3:1–5.

FIVE

1. The Chicago Association of Commerce, *Chicago: The Great Central Market* (Chicago: R. L. Polk and Co., 1923), 148.

2. For information on other North Side hotels see Granger, *Chicago Welcomes You*, 162–63.

3. Commission on Chicago Historical and Architectural Landmarks, "East Lake Shore Drive District," Historic District Nomination (1981): 6.

4. The first example of a cooperative apartment building in New York was the Randolph, erected on West Eighteenth Street in the 1880s, designed by Hubert and Pierson, followed closely by several others designed by the same firm. See Frederic Culver, "Cooperative Apartments," *Proceedings of the Sixth Annual Convention of the National Association of Building Owners and Managers* (Chicago, 1923): 145–46.

5. Taussig, "North Michigan Avenue," 23; Carroll William Westfall, "From Homes to Towers: A Century of Chicago's Best Hotels and Tall Apartment Buildings," in *Chicago Architecture 1872–1922*, ed. John Zukowsky, 278.

6. Dedmon, *Fabulous Chicago*, 302; Condit, *Chicago 1910–29*, 161–62; Finis Farr, *Chicago: A Personal History of America's Most American City* (New Rochelle, N.Y.: Arlington House, 1973), 343.

7. Farr, *Chicago*, 343–44; and Condit, *Chicago 1910–29*, 163.

8. *North Central Journal* (December 1927), n.p.

9. Granger, *Chicago Welcomes You*, 179; and William Hudson Harper, ed., *Chicago: A History and Forecast* (Chicago: Chicago Association of Commerce, 1921), 64.

10. For information on the Drake Hotel see Commission on Chicago Historical and Architectural Landmarks, *East Lake Shore Drive District*, 3–6; Condit, *Chicago 1910–29*, 119, 155; Westfall, "From Homes to Towers," 279–82; David Norris, "Drake Hotel National Register Nomination," unpublished paper, Landmarks Preservation Council of Illinois, Chicago, 1977; and Westfall, "Benjamin Henry Marshall of Chicago," 17–18.

11. Bishop and Gilbert, *Chicago's Accomplishments and Leaders*, 177–79; and Commission on Chicago Historical and Architectural Landmarks, *East Lake Shore Drive District*, 3.

12. The original owner of the Drake Hotel property, lots 15–28 of the Fitz-Simons Addition to Chicago, was Tobias Allmendinger, who obtained title in 1868, when it was still largely under water. He sold it to Malcolm McNeill and David Lyman in 1886, who in turn sold it to Potter Palmer in 1898 and 1901. See Cook County Tract Records, Bk. 421A:201–5.

13. The Gazley proposal for a hotel was to be financed with $1,000,000 preferred stock, $700,000 common stock, $1,100,000 first mortgage bonds, and $500,000 second mortgage bonds. The purchase price of the land was set at $550,000, with the cost of the build-

ing to be $1,400,000. See *The Economist* (26 October 1912): 706; and *The Book of Chicagoans* (1917), 250.

14. *The Economist* (25 November 1916), 1061.

15. S. W. Straus and Company provided for an issue of $2,500,000 worth of preferred stock, along with $100,000 worth of common stock, and $2,000,000 worth of first mortgage bonds. See *The Economist* (22 March 1919): 525; ibid. (10 May 1919): 836–37; and ibid. (28 July 1928): 220.

16. Ibid. (22 March 1919): 525; and ibid. (10 May 1919): 860.

17. Ibid. (10 May 1919): 860.

18. Commission on Chicago Historical and Architectural Landmarks, *East Lake Shore Drive District*, 4.

19. For information on the first design for the Drake Hotel by Marshall and Fox see *Chicago Tribune* (27 April 1919), sec. 2:11.

20. Westfall, "From Homes to Towers," 280–82.

21. Henry W. Frohne, "A New Idea in Hotel Decoration: The Drake Hotel," *Good Furniture* 16 (May 1921).

22. Robert F. Irving, "Benny Marshall: The Dreams That Money Could Buy," *Inland Architect* (January 1978): 14–17.

23. For information on the Allerton Hotel see Palmer H. Ogden, "The Chicago Allerton House," *Architectural Forum* 42 (May 1925): 313–16. For information on "club hotels" see "The Fraternity Clubs Building, New York," *Architectural Forum* 41 (July 1924): 9; and Stern, Gilmartin, and Mellins, *New York 1930: Architecture and Urbanism between the Two World Wars*, 207–8.

24. Letter from William H. Silk to Charles Dickenson (10 October 1923), Allerton Hotel Pamphlet File (Chicago Historical Society Library).

25. For information on the Allerton Houses designed by Arthur Loomis Harmon see *New York Sun Herald* (21 September 1919): n.p. (New York Historical Society Clipping File); and illustration in the *Architectural Forum* 48 (January 1928): 67.

26. For information on the Fraternity Clubs Building see the *Architectural Forum*, (July 1924): 9–16, pl. 1. For information on the Barbizon Hotel see the *New York Times* (18 April 1931): n.p.; "Barbizon Hotel" (New York Historical Society Clipping File); and illustration in the *Architectural Forum* 48 (May 1928): pl. 121.

27. *Biographical Dictionary*, 435. Ogden is not listed in the *Biographical Dictionary* nor in *Who's Who in New York*.

28. The Allerton Hotel lot, the southeast quarter of Block 45 of Kinzie's Addition, measured 150 by 109 feet. The broker for the transaction was Frederick S. Oliver of Oliver and Company. The purchase price was not disclosed. See *The Economist* (7 June 1922): cover; and ibid. (10 June 1922): 1332. See also Cook County Tract Records, Bk. 460:3–8.

29. The mortgage note for the Allerton Hotel was in the name of Melvin L. Straus, a vice-president of S. W. Straus and Company.

See Cook County Tract Records, Bk. 460:3–8. For information on the Straus Company financing of the New York Allerton House see the *New York Evening Mail* (23 March 1922) (New York Historical Society Clipping File).

30. Condit, *Chicago 1910–29*, 155; Ogden, "The Chicago Allerton House," 313.

31. Randall, *History of the Development of Building Construction in Chicago*, 264; Ogden, "The Chicago Allerton House," 313–16.

32. Ogden, "The Chicago Allerton House," 313–16; Paul Thomas Gilbert and Charles Lee Bryson, *Chicago and Its Makers* (Chicago: F. Mendelsohn, 1929), 318.

33. Ogden, "The Chicago Allerton House," 316.

34. Ibid.

35. Stern, Gilmartin, and Mellins, *New York 1930*, 195, 207.

36. John Ashenhurst and Ruth L. Ashenhurst, *All about Chicago* (New York: Houghton Mifflin Co., 1933), 69.

37. For information on the 900 North Michigan Avenue Apartment Building see Commission on Chicago Historical and Architectural Landmarks, *900 North Michigan Avenue: A Preliminary Survey of Information* (Chicago, 1982); "Inlandscape," *Inland Architect* 25 (March 1981): 2, 46–48; *A Portfolio of Fine Apartment Houses* (Chicago: Baird and Warner, 1928), 40; and Carroll William Westfall, "900 Michigan Avenue North, Illinois Register of Historic Places Application" (Chicago, 1981).

38. Taussig, "North Michigan Avenue," 23.

39. *Biographical Dictionary*, 308.

40. Commission on Chicago Historical and Architectural Landmarks, *900 North Michigan Avenue*, n.p.

41. *North Central Journal* (December 1926): 11.

42. A list of the original co-owners of 900 North Michigan Avenue is given in "Inlandscape," 47.

43. *Who's Who in Chicago*, (1931), 646.

44. Potter Palmer had purchased three of the site's four parcels from trustees of the Sheldon Sturgis estate in 1895. He purchased the fourth the following year from Tobias Allmendinger. See Cook County Tract Records, Bk. 421:40–41.

45. Randall, *History of the Development of Building Construction*, 273.

46. "Inlandscape," 47; *A Portfolio of Fine Apartment Houses*, 40.

47. For information on the Illinois Women's Athletic Club see *Chicago Tribune* (27 March 1919): 1; ibid. (11 June 1922), sec. 2:19; and *North Central Journal* (December 1929), n.p.

48. *Chicago Tribune* (11 June 1922), sec. 2:19.

49. L. M. Corrigan, "My Felicitations," *Woman Athlete* (March 1927): 18–19.

50. Ibid.

51. Wendt, *Chicago Tribune*, 333.

52. Cook County Tract Records, Bk. 421C:195–99; *The Economist* (10 June 1922): 1334.

53. *North Central Journal* (December 1929): n.p.

54. Brooks, *The Prairie School*, 48–52; *Chicago Architects Design*, 62–63; *Chicago Tribune* (11 June 1922), sec. 2:19.

55. Brooks, *The Prairie School*, 48–52.

56. *North Central Journal* (December 1929): n.p.

57. *Chicago Tribune* (11 June 1922), sec. 2:19.

58. Ibid.

59. For information on the Woman's Chicago Athletic Club see "History of the Woman's Athletic Club," *Townsfolk* 25 (April 1955): 19; and *Chicago Tribune* (25 September 1927) sec. 3:1.

60. Ibid.

61. William N. and Helen (Thompson) Pelouze were married in Chicago and lived at 3400 Sheridan Road. William Pelouze had come to Chicago in 1882 and was with the Walter A. Wood Reaping Machine Company from 1882 to 1884, and the Tobey Furniture Company from 1884 to 1892, before starting his own company. See *Who's Who in Chicago* (1926), 681.

62. The ninety-nine year lease between John V. Farwell and the Woman's Athletic Club was negotiated by Frederick Bowes of the Bowes Realty Corporation. The graduated rental agreement called for a payment of only $1 for the first year, $32,500 annually for the second, third, and fourth years, $27,500 for the fifth year, $30,000 annually for the sixth to tenth years, $32,500 for the eleventh through fifteenth years, and $37,500 for the remaining eighty-four years. The club had the option to buy the site between the twentieth and twenty-fifth years for $900,000, and for $975,000 between the twenty-fifth and thirtieth years. See the *Chicago Tribune* (25 September 1927), sec. 3:1; and *The Economist* (30 July 1927): 282. After leasing the building to the Woman's Club, Farwell obtained a series of mortgages from the Northwestern Mutual Life Insurance Company in 1927, the National Republic Bank in 1928, and the Northern Trust Company in 1930. He used this money to finance other building projects. See Cook County Tract Records, Bk. 459B:140–42.

63. Letter from Franklin D. Bowes, son of Frederick M. Bowes, to Meredith Taussig, dated 15 April 1982. See Taussig, "North Michigan Avenue," 34.

64. Leonard, *The History of Architecture in Chicago*, 110.

65. For information on the Medinah Club Building see Condit, *Chicago 1910–29*, 129, 157, 172; *The Scimitar* and *Pictorial Views of the Medinah Club* (Chicago Historical Society Pamphlet File); H. G. Phillips, *America's Most Distinctive Club: Medinah Athletic Club* (Chicago, c. 1929); and *Chicago Tribune* (22 November 1925), sec. 3:1; and ibid. (26 September 1926), sec. 3:1.

66. By the time of the announcement of the plan for the Medinah Club, 1000 of its 3500 members had already taken out founder memberships. See the *Chicago Tribune* (22 November 1925), sec. 3:1.

67. *The Scmitar*, n.p.

68. *The Economist* (28 November 1925): 1428; and Cook County Tract Records, Bk. 459:243–44.

69. *Chicago Tribune* (22 November 1925), sec. 3:1.

70. Ibid.

71. *Pictorial Views of the Medinah Club*, n.p.

72. The author has been unable to determine who the other invited architects might have been for the Medinah Club competition. Walter Ahlschlager's design was first published in the *Chicago Tribune* on 22 November 1925, sec. 3:1. He was announced as the winner of the architectural competition on 19 September 1926 in the *Chicago Tribune*, sec. 3:2.

73. *Pictorial Views of the Medinah Club*, n.p.

74. Frederick Ahlschlager (1858–1905) was born in Modena, Illinois, and studied at the University of Illinois. Among his important church commissions were Holy Cross Lutheran Church (1886), First Immanuel Lutheran Church (1888), Concordia Evangelical Lutheran Church (1892–93), and Pillar's Rock Baptist Church, 1893. See *Biographical Dictionary*, 11; Taussig, "North Michigan Avenue," 28; George Lane, *Chicago Churches and Synagogues: An Architectural Pilgrimage* (Chicago: Loyola University Press, 1981), 228.

75. *Chicago Tribune* (9 May 1920), sec. 10:28; ibid. (11 September 1927), sec. 3:1; and ibid. (2 December 1928), sec. 3:1.

76. Ibid. (22 November 1925), pt. 3:1.

77. Ibid. (26 September 1926), pt. 3:1.

78. Randall, *A History of the Development of Building Construction*, 285.

79. *The Scmitar*, 136.

80. *Chicago Sun* (31 May 1942): n.p. (Chicago Historical Society Pamphlet File).

81. Leon Hermant, an architect and sculptor, was born in France. Most of his active career was spent in Chicago, with works for Grant Park, the Illinois Athletic Club, and the LaSalle Hotel. See Esther Sparks, "A Biographical Dictionary of Painters and Sculptors in Illinois, 1808–1945" (Ph.D. diss., Northwestern University, 1971), 640.

82. For illustrations and descriptions of the interiors of the Medinah Club see *Pictorial Views* and *The Scmitar*, n.p. All interior decorating, painting, and murals were designed and executed by Walter Ingstrup and Company of Chicago.

83. Phillips, *America's Most Distinctive Club*, 1.

84. Ibid.

1. For information on the firm of Holabird and Root at the end of the 1920s see Robert Bruegmann, *Holabird and Roche and Holabird and Root: A Catalogue of Works, 1880–1940,* 3 vols. (New York: Garland Publishing Co., 1989); Robert Bruegmann, "Holabird and Roche and Holabird and Root," 130–65; Earl H. Reed, Jr., "Some Recent Work of Holabird and Root, Architects," *Architecture* 61 (January 1930): 1–4; and Irving, "Holabird and Root, Still Going Strong after 95 Years," 8–13.

2. *Biographical Dictionary,* 292–93.

3. *Who's Who in Chicago* (1950), 501.

4. Bruegmann, "Holabird and Roche and Holabird and Root," 163.

5. Parker Morse Hooper, "Modern Architectural Decoration," *Architectural Forum* 48 (February 1928): 153–60.

6. Cervin Robinson and Rosemarie Haag Bletter, *Skyscraper Style: Art Deco, New York* (New York: Oxford University Press, 1975), 44–48.

7. Thomas E. Tallmadge, *The Story of Architecture in America* (New York: W. W. Norton, 1927), 290–91.

8. Eliel Saarinen, "A New Architectural Language for America," *Western Architect* 32 (February 1923): 13.

9. Eliel Saarinen left Finland for Chicago in 1923, staying for a time in the Blackstone Hotel on South Michigan Avenue. It was here, with a panoramic view of the lakefront, that he developed his plan. It was published in *American Architect* in 1923. See Albert Christ-Janer, *Eliel Saarinen* (Chicago: Helsingissa: Kustannusosakeyhtio Otava, 1951), 58–59; and Eliel Saarinen, "Project for Lake Front Development of the City of Chicago," *American Architect* 124 (December 1923): 487–514.

10. Bruegmann, "Holabird and Roche and Holabird and Root," 163.

11. For information on the Tobey Building see Carl Condit, *Chicago 1910–29,* 118; and *Chicago Tribune* (20 September 1925), sec. 2:15.

12. *The Economist* (19 September 1925), special news bulletin.

13. The site was originally occupied by John A. Tolman and Company, wholesale coffee dealers. See the *Chicago Tribune* (3 June 1923), sec. 9:27. The drawings for the Tobey Building are dated 2 October 1925 and labeled as a Mercantile Building for Judson F. Stone and W. O. Melcher. The drawings are located in the Chicago Historical Society Department of Architecture.

14. Albert H. Wetten and Company were brokers for the Tobey Furniture Company while Winston and Company represented Ovington's. See *The Economist* (19 September 1925), Special News Bulletin; and ibid. (19 January 1925), Special News Bulletin; *Chicago Tribune* (20 September 1925), sec. 2:15; and *The Economist* (6 August 1927), Special News Bulletin.

15. R. W. Sexton, *American Commercial Buildings of Today* (New York: Architectural Book Publishing Co., 1928), 5.

16. For information on 333 North Michigan Avenue see Condit, *Chicago 1910–29*, 119–20; "333 North Michigan Avenue, Chicago: Holabird and Root, Architects," *Architectural Record* 65 (February 1929): 157–66; *Chicago Tribune* (1 May 1927), sec. 3:1, and *The Economist* (25 July 1927): 1690.

17. "333 North Michigan Avenue," 157.

18. *Chicago Tribune* (1 May 1927), sec. 3:1.

19. Condit, *Chicago 1910–29*, 118.

20. The property was known as the old United States Marine Hospital site. McLaughlin purchased it in 1900. See *The Economist* (6 January 1900): 16.

21. Cook County Tract Records, Bk. 460A:99–102.

22. *Chicago Tribune* (1 May 1927), sec. 3:1.

23. Ibid. Holabird and Root produced a complete set of floor plans for the proposed club. See drawings in the Chicago Historical Society Department of Architecture.

24. Leonard, "The History of Architecture in Chicago," 109–10; and Bruegmann, "Holabird and Roche and Holabird and Root," 163.

25. "333 North Michigan Avenue, Chicago," 158; and author's interview with Ambrose Richardson, 21 February 1984.

26. The height of the first story of 333 North Michigan Avenue is thirteen feet six inches, and the third is eleven feet two inches. Typical stories are ten feet ten inches floor to floor. See "333 North Michigan Avenue," 158.

27. Ibid.

28. "Fred M. Torrey's Decorative Panels for a Chicago Skyscraper," *American Magazine of Art* 19 (September 1928): 483–88.

29. "333 North Michigan Avenue," 158.

30. *Chicago Tribune* (31 January 1928): 5.

31. Ibid. (1 May 1928): 6.

32. Artist John Warner Norton (1876–1934) was born in Lockport, Illinois, and attended Harvard University for two years beginning in 1894. He entered the Art Institute School in 1899 and later taught mural painting there. His works include a thirty-one-foot painting for the Chicago Board of Trade of the Roman goddess of grain, Ceres; murals for the Logan Museum in Beloit, Wisconsin; the Chicago Daily News Building concourse ceiling; murals in the courthouses of Birmingham, Alabama, and St. Paul, Minnesota; and murals for the Science Building of the 1933 Chicago World's Fair. He was president of the Tavern Club in 1931–34. He received for his Tavern Club murals the Gold Medal in Painting from the Architectural League of New York. See Henry J. B. Hoskins, "John Norton," *Illinois Society of Architects* (1934): monthly bulletin 6 (Ryerson Library Pamphlet File); and Thomas E. Tallmadge, "John Warner Norton" (1935) (Ryerson Library Pamphlet File).

33. Winold Reiss (1886–1953) was born in Karlsruhe, Germany, the son of a noted portrait and landscape painter, Fritz Reiss. He studied at the Munich Academy and at the Kunstgewerbeschule where he was influenced by the Blaue Reiter and Die Brücke movements. He moved to New York in 1913 where he became a successful commercial artist and painter. He taught mural painting and design for over a decade at New York University. In 1928 he had an exhibition of his works at the Chicago Art Institute. His project for the Tavern Club was his first publicized commission. He produced the glass mosaic murals for the Cincinnati Union Terminal in 1933, consisting of scenes of the city of Cincinnati, the history of transportation, and industries of Cincinnati. A major exhibition of his portraits of American Indians toured Europe in 1936 and the United States in 1947. See letter from Dr. Fred Brauen to the Art Institute of Chicago, 23 October 1980 (Ryerson Library Pamphlet File); Paul Raczka, *Winold Reiss: Portrait of the Races Exhibition Catalog* (Great Falls, Mont.: C. M. Russell Museum (1986); Adolph C. Glassgold, "The Decorative Arts," *The Arts* 15 (March 1929): 194–201, 218.

34. The jury which selected the winners of the annual award given by the Lake Shore Trust and Savings Bank was composed of C. Herrick Hammond, president of the A.I.A.; Howard White, president of the Illinois Society of Architects; and John C. Bollenbacher, president of the Chicago Chapter of the A.I.A. See *Chicago Tribune* (3 February 1929), sec. 3:1.

35. Ibid.

36. For information on the Palmolive Building see Condit, *Chicago 1910–29*, 119–20; Henry J. B. Hoskins, "The Palmolive Building, Chicago: Holabird and Root, Architects," *Architectural Forum* 52 (May 1930): 655–66; Henry J. B. Hoskins, "Structure and Equipment of the Palmolive Building, Holabird and Root, Architects," *Architectural Forum* 52 (May 1930): 730–36; William Marlin, "That Palmolive Look," *Inland Architect* 26 (May/June 1982): 8–17.

37. *Chicago Tribune* (24 July 1927), sec. 3:1.

38. Ibid. (15 July 1928), sec. 3:1; Hoskins, "The Palmolive Building, Chicago," 655.

39. *Chicago Tribune* (15 July 1928), sec. 3:1.

40. Ibid. (15 July 1928), sec. 3:1.

41. Cook County Tract Records, Bk. 421B:107–8; and see Marlin, "That Palmolive Look," 8.

42. *Chicago Tribune* (24 July 1927), sec. 3:1.

43. Hoskins, "The Palmolive Building, Chicago," 655.

44. Condit, *Chicago 1910–29*, 120.

45. The facades of the building's first two stories were restored by Skidmore, Owings and Merrill in 1979–80.

46. Hoskins, "The Palmolive Building, Chicago," 657.

47. The beacon, intended to aid pilots in the days before radar, was the idea of Edward N. Hurley, chairman of the organizing committee for the 1933 Chicago World's Fair. In 1927, the same year the

Palmolive Company bought the land for its new building, Hurley suggested the construction of a giant "Lindbergh Tower" complete with aerial beacon. Hurley wished to honor Charles A. Lindbergh, whose trans-Atlantic flight a few weeks earlier had made him an international hero. In the end, the thirty-seven-story Palmolive Building was picked because of its location and height. The beacon itself was given to the city by inventor and former Chicagoan Elmer A. Sperry, head of the Sperry Gyroscope Company of Brooklyn, New York. It was lighted for the first time on 27 August 1930 by President Herbert Hoover, who pressed a button in the White House. The light was named the Lindbergh Beacon though the famous pilot did not want his name connected with it. Thus it was renamed the following year to the Palmolive Beacon. See the *Chicago Tribune* (20 November 1983): 10; *Chicago Tribune* (21 February 1959), sec. 2:5; and Condit, *Chicago 1910–29*, 120.

48. Marlin, "That Palmolive Look," 7–17.

49. *Through the Ages* (1931), Palmolive Building Pamphlet File (Chicago Historical Society Library).

50. The three floors of the Palmolive Building occupied by the Celotex Corporation were the sixth, seventh, and eighth. See the *Chicago Tribune* (27 January 1929), sec. 3:7.

51. Subsidiaries of the Celotex Company which also had their offices in the Palmolive Building were the Southern Sugar Company, the South Coast Company, Dahlberg and Company, Inc., the Clewiston Company, and the Dahlberg-American Corporation. See *Chicago Tribune* (27 January 1929), sec. 3:7.

52. Harold Reynolds was an interior designer who worked for Holabird and Root through the 1920s.

53. Farr, *Chicago*, 372.

54. For information on the Michigan Square Building see "Michigan Square Building, Chicago, Illinois; Holabird and Root, Architects," *Architectural Record* 70 (October 1931): 257–62; and *Chicago Tribune* (30 December 1928), sec. 2:5.

55. *Chicago Tribune* (22 December 1928): 26.

56. Cook County Tract Records, Bk. 459A:119–20.

57. *Chicago Tribune* (22 December 1928): 26.

58. Carl Milles (1875–1955) was born near Stockholm, Sweden. He was apprenticed to a cabinetmaker at the age of thirteen. He studied at the Technical College and the Naas Sloyd School, then moved to Paris where he worked under Rodin. He won a competition for a sculptural monument in Sweden in 1900. Later in his life he moved to the United States and taught at Cranbrook Academy. The Diana fountain was the first of three commissions he did for Holabird and Root, who brought him on his first visit to the United States. See Arvid Baeskstrom, *Carl Milles: The Swedish Sculptor* (Stockholm: C. E. Fritze, 1935); *Artist in Bronze, Water, Space: Carl Milles and His Sculpture* (St. Louis: Laumeier Sculpture Park and Gallery, 1985); and "The Unveiling of the Fountain of Diana, Carl Milles,

Sculptor, Diana Court, Michigan Square Building" (Chicago, 6 November 1930).

59. *Chicago Tribune* (30 December 1928), 2:5.

60. Leonard, "The History of Architecture in Chicago," 113.

61. Creese, "American Architecture from 1918 to 1933," pt. 2, p. 7 of notes.

62. Leonard, "The History of Architecture in Chicago," 113.

63. *Chicago Daily News* (9–10 June 1973) (Chicago Historical Society Pamphlet File).

64. For information and an illustration of the Michigan-Chestnut Building see *Chicago Tribune* (6 November 1927), sec. 3:1.

65. Harvey N. Zorbaugh, *Gold Coast and the Slum*, 12, 87.

66. Ibid.

67. *The Economist* (26 June 1926): 1809.

68. At the time of the Chicago Fire of 1871, the site of the Judah Building was owned by Leander McCormick. He sold it to Perry H. Smith in 1873, who immediately built his lavish house. Architect Benjamin Marshall purchased the house in 1915, and it was demolished in 1918 for the widening of the avenue. Marshall sold the property to his partner Charles Fox in 1925, and it was purchased after his death in 1927 by Mrs. Judah. After constructing her new building, she sold it in 1934 to William A. Mulligan, who in turn sold it to Marshall Field in whose name it remained until 1957. See Cook County Tract Records, Bk. 460:9–12.

69. *Chicago Tribune* (6 November 1927), sec. 3:1.

70. For information on the Judah Building see ibid. (26 August 1928), sec. 3:1.

71. Ibid. (26 August, 1928), sec. 3:1; ibid. (27 February 1928): 18.

72. Ibid. (26 August 1928), sec. 3:1.

73. Ibid.

74. Ibid.

75. For information and illustrations of the Hood/Holabird and Root design for Terminal Park see Stern, *Raymond Hood*, 13; and *Chicago Architects Design*, 95–96.

76. Stern, *Raymond Hood*, 13.

SEVEN

1. Hoyt, *One Hundred Years*, 258.

2. For information on the Michigan-Superior Building see *Chicago Tribune* (27 May 1928), sec. 3:3; and Meredith Taussig, "North Michigan Avenue," 24–25.

3. *Who's Who in Chicago* (1926), 171.

4. Homer Chapin purchased the site from Frank B. Klock, president of the Murray and Nickell Manufacturing Company. See *The*

Lakeside Annual Directory of the City of Chicago (Chicago, 1928–29), 1732; and Cook County Tract Records, Bk. 460:161–64.

5. *Chicago Tribune* (1 June 1968): 1.

6. Rebori's design for a 421-foot building for the Chapin estate at 737 North Michigan Avenue was dated 31 January 1928. It is in the Chicago Historical Society Department of Architecture.

7. *Chicago Tribune* (27 May 1928), sec. 3:3.

8. Ibid.

9. *Chicago Today* (16 May 1969): n.p.

10. For information on the McGraw-Hill Building see "Cast-Iron Cores Used in Columns of 16-story Concrete Building," *Engineering Record* (23 July 1929): 129–31; *Chicago Tribune* (10 June 1928), sec. 3:1; and ibid. (21 October 1928), sec. 3:1.

11. The rental for the McGraw-Hill Building site was to be paid in increasing increments of $31,250 per year for the first ten years; $37,500 for the next ten; $43,750 for the next ten; then $50,000 yearly for the balance of the term. See the *Chicago Tribune* (10 June 1928), sec. 3:1; and Cook County Tract Records, Bk. 459:218–20.

12. The Thielbar and Fugard partnership was formed in 1925. See *Chicago Architects Design*, 98.

13. Randall, *History of the Development of Building Construction*, 281.

14. The total rental of McGraw-Hill's lease for the new building was $1,250,000. See *Chicago Tribune* (21 October 1928), sec. 3:1.

15. For information on the McGraw-Hill Company see *McGraw-Hill: The Story of Forty Years of Growth, 1909–1949.* (New York: McGraw-Hill Book Co., 1950), 3–6.

16. Some of the magazines owned by McGraw-Hill included *The Magazine of Business, System, Factory and Industrial Management, Harvard Business Review, and Industrial Engineering.* See *The Economist* (20 October 1928): Special News Bulletin.

17. Ibid. (20 April 1929): 938; *Chicago Tribune* (7 April 1929), sec. 3:1.

18. *Chicago Tribune* (10 June 1928), sec. 3:1.

19. For information on the structural system of the McGraw-Hill Building see "Cast Iron Cores Used in Columns of 16-Story Concrete Building," 129–31.

20. Ibid., 129–30.

21. For information on the Music Corporation of America Building see the *Chicago Tribune* (7 April 1929), sec. 3:1.

22. The 430 North Michigan Avenue Building Corporation had a fifteen-year option to purchase the property within the first five years for $555,000, for $625,000 within the second five years, and for $741,250 during the last five years. See the *Chicago Tribune* (7 April 1929), sec. 3:1; and *The Economist* (13 April 1929): 879.

23. *The Economist* (13 April 1929): 879.

24. *Chicago Tribune* (7 April 1929), sec. 3:1.

25. For information on the Union Carbide and Carbon Building see Condit, *Chicago 1910–29*, 121; "The Plate Section," *Western Architect* 39 (April 1930): 60–61; *Chicago Tribune* (13 May 1928), sec. 3:1; and *Carbide and Carbon Building, Chicago* (Chicago: Union Carbide and Carbon Corporation, 1932).

26. *Chicago Tribune* (13 May 1928), sec. 3:1.

27. The subsidiaries of the Union Carbide and Carbon Corporation housed at 230 North Michigan Avenue were Carbide and Carbon Chemicals Corporation, Electro Metallurgical Sales Corporation, Haynes Stellite Company, the Linde Air Products Company, the National Carbon Company, the Oxweld Company, Oxweld Railroad Service Company, Presto-O-Lite Company, and Union Carbide Sales Company. See Union Carbide and Carbon Pamphlet File (Chicago Historical Society Library).

28. *Chicago Tribune* (13 May 1928), sec. 3:1; and Cook County Tract Records, Bk. 460A:159–61.

29. *Chicago Tribune* (6 July 1924), sec. 2:10.

30. Condit, *Chicago 1910–29*, 121.

31. "The Plate Section," 60.

32. *Chicago Tribune* (13 May 1928), sec. 3:1.

33. "The Plate Section," 60; ibid.

34. *Carbide and Carbon Building, Chicago*, n.p.

35. Ibid.

36. Ibid.

37. Chicago Tribune (3 March 1929), sec. 3:1.

38. Ibid.

39. Ibid., (14 July 1929), sec. 3:1.

40. Ibid.

41. Plans for Andrew Rebori's proposed high-rise for North Michigan Avenue and Randolph Street are in the Chicago Historical Society Department of Architecture.

42. *Chicago Tribune* (14 July 1929), sec. 3:1.

43. Ibid.

44. Robert M. Haig, "Toward an Understanding of the Metropolis," *Quarterly Journal of Economics* 40 (1926): 433.

45. Robert A. M. Stern, Gregory Gilmartin, and John M. Massengale, *New York 1900: Metropolitan Architecture and Urbanism 1890–1915* (New York: Rizzoli International Publications, 1983), 20–21.

46. Hoyt, *One Hundred Years*, 345.

EPILOGUE

1. Frederick Lewis Allen, *Only Yesterday: An Informal History of the 1920's* (New York: Harper and Bros., 1931), 337–38.

2. Earl C. May and Will Ourseler, *A Story of Human Security; the Prudential* (Garden City, New Jersey: Doubleday 1950), 207.

3. Irving Fisher, *The Stock Market Crash—and After* (New York: Macmillan Co., 1930), xviii.

4. Allen, *Only Yesterday*, 338.

5. Chester Whitney Wright, *Economic History of the United States* (New York and London: McGraw-Hill Co., 1941), 847.

6. Wille, *Forever Open, Clear and Free*, 95.

7. Creese, "American Architecture from 1918 to 1933," pt. 2:32.

8. Hoyt, *One Hundred Years*, 266.

9. Ibid., 270–72.

10. For details of building foreclosures see Cook County Tract Records.

11. Ibid.

12. *The Economist* (29 August 1932): 172.

13. Ibid. (16 April 1932): 374.

14. For information on the 1942 court case against the Medinah Club see the *Chicago Sun* (31 May 1942), n.p. (Art Institute of Chicago Scrapbook).

15. Ibid.

16. Ibid.

17. Ibid.

18. *Chicago Tribune* (21 February 1959), sec. 2:5.

19. George Roeder interview with Arthur Rubloff, 20 October 1981 (Northwestern University Archives); Betsy Pegg, *Dreams, Money, and Ambition: A History of Real Estate in Chicago* (Chicago: Chicago Real Estate Board, 1983), 144.

20. For information on the Holabird and Root proposal for Rubloff see *Chicago Tribune* (10 April 1947): 5; "Magnificent Mile for Windy City: City Plan Proposal for Upper Michigan Avenue, Chicago," *Architectural Record* 101 (June 1947):96–99.

21. Rubloff address, 9 April 1947 (Rubloff papers, Chicago Historical Society).

22. Rubloff Papers (Chicago Historical Society, Department of Archives and Manuscripts).

23. Letter from Joseph R. Frey to Arthur Rubloff, 17 April 1947 Rubloff Papers (Chicago Historical Society, Department of Archives and Manuscripts).

24. For information on the Prudential Building see "Chicago's Prudential Building," *Architectural Forum* 97 (August 1952): 91–97; and Prudential Building Pamphlet File (Chicago Historical Society Library).

25. "Chicago's Prudential Building," 95.

26. For information on the Equitable Building see *Chicago Tribune* (9 December 1961): 1; and *Chicago Daily News* (22 June 1965): 38.

27. For information on Pioneer Court see *Chicago Tribune* (10 November 1964): 1; ibid. (21 June 1965), sec. 3:11.

28. For information on the John Hancock Building see Condit, *Chicago 1930–70*, 102; John Morris Dixon, "The Tall One," *Architectural Forum* 133 (July/August 1970): 37–44; *Chicago Daily News* (25 March 1965): 64; ibid. (4 September 1965), sec. 2:9; and Arthur Drexler and Axel Menges, *Architecture of Skidmore, Owings & Merrill, 1963–1973* (New York: Architectural Book Publishing Co., 1974), 162–69.

29. For information on Water Tower Place see "The Malls at Water Tower Place," *Architectural Record* 162 (October 1977): 99–104; and "The Seven Level Shopping Mall at Water Tower Place: a Try for a Revolution in Retailing," *Architectural Record* 159 (April 1976): 136–40.

30. For information on Illinois Center see *Chicago Sun Times* (24 May 1968): 1; ibid. (9 July 1969): 3; *Chicago Daily News* (30 September 1966): 46; and John W. Stamper, "Patronage and the City Grid: The High-Rise Architecture of Mies van der Rohe in Chicago," *Inland Architect* 30 (March/April 1986): 40.

31. Stamper, "Patronage and the City Grid," 40.

BOOKS

Abbey, Ferry. *Reminiscences of John V. Farwell*. Vols. 1 and 2. Chicago: Ralph Fletcher Seymour, 1928.

Abbot, Willis John. *Carter Henry Harrison: A Memoir*. New York: Dodd, Mead and Co., 1895.

Ade, George. *The Chicago Record's Stories of the Streets and of the Town*. 8 vols. Chicago: Reprinted from the *Chicago Record*, 1894–1900.

Allen, Frederick Lewis. *The Big Change: America Transforms Itself 1900–1950*. New York: Harper and Bros., 1952.

———. *Only Yesterday: An Informal History of the 1920's*. New York: Harper and Bros., 1931.

Andreas, Alfred T. *History of Chicago: From the Earliest Period to the Present Time*. Chicago: A. T. Andreas, 1884.

Andrews, Wayne. *Architecture, Ambition and Americans: A Social History of American Architecture*. New York: Macmillan Publishing Co., 1978.

———. *Architecture in Chicago and Mid-America: A Photographic History*. New York: Atheneum, 1968.

———. *Battle for Chicago*. New York: Harcourt, Brace and Co., 1946.

Appelbaum, Stanley. *The Chicago World's Fair of 1893: A Photographic Record*. New York: Dover Publications, 1980.

Artist in Bronze, Water, Space: Carl Milles and His Sculpture. St. Louis: Laumeier Sculpture Park and Gallery, 1985.

Ashenhurst, John and Ruth L. *All about Chicago*. New York: Houghton Mifflin Co., 1933.

Bach, Ira J. *Chicago's Famous Buildings: A Photographic Guide to the City's Architectural Landmarks and Other Notable Buildings*. Chicago: University of Chicago Press, 1980.

———. *Chicago on Foot: Walking Tours of Chicago's Architecture*. 3d ed. Chicago: Rand McNally and Co., 1979.

Badger, Reid. *The Great American Fair: The World's Columbian Exposition and American Culture*. Chicago: N. Hall, 1979.

Baekstrom, Arvid. *Carl Milles: The Swedish Sculptor*. Stockholm: C. E. Fritze, 1935.

Ballard, E. G. *Captain Streeter Pioneer*. Chicago: Emery Publishing Service, 1914.

Baston, E. E. *A Business Tour of Chicago Depicting Fifty Years Progress.* Chicago, 1887.

Bay, J. Christian. *The John Crerar Library, 1895–1944.* Chicago, 1945.

Benke, William. *All about Land Investment.* New York: McGraw-Hill Book Co., 1976.

Bergen, Marie. *See Chicago on Your Own: An Illustrated Guide to Chicago.* Chicago: 1959.

Biographical Dictionary of American Architects, ed. Henry F. and Elsie Rathburn Withey. Los Angeles: Hennesey and Ingalls, 1970.

Biographical Sketches of the Leading Men of Chicago. Chicago: Wilson and St. Clair, 1868.

Bishop, Glenn A., and Paul T. Gilbert. *Chicago's Accomplishments and Leaders.* Chicago: Bishop Publishing Co., 1932.

Board of Local Improvements. *Chicago Board of Local Improvements.* Chicago, 1931.

Book of Chicagoans. Chicago: A. N. Marquis Co., various years.

Boorstin, Daniel. *The Americans: The National Experience.* New York: Random House, 1966.

Boyer, N. Christine. *Manhattan Manners: Architecture and Style 1850–1900.* New York: Rizzoli International Publications, 1985.

Brittain, Joseph K. *Public Improvements and Permanent Real Estate Values.* Chicago: Chicago Real Estate Board, 1926.

Brooklyn Institute of Arts and Sciences. *The American Renaissance: 1876–1917.* New York, 1979.

Brooks, H. Allen. *The Prairie School: Frank Lloyd Wright and His Midwest Contemporaries.* Toronto: University of Toronto Press, 1972.

Brown, George P. *Drainage—Canal and Waterway.* Chicago: R. R. Donnelley and Sons Co., 1894.

Bruegmann, Robert. *Holabird and Roche and Holabird and Root: A Catalogue of Works, 1880–1940.* 3 vols. New York: Garland Publishing Co., 1989.

Buley, R. Carlyle. *The Equitable Life Assurance Society of the United States, 1859–1959.* New York: Appleton-Century-Crofts, 1959.

Burchard, John, and Albert Bush-Brown. *The Architecture of America: A Social and Cultural History.* Boston and Toronto: Little, Brown and Co., 1961.

Burgess, Ernest W., and Charles Newcomb. *Census Data of the City of Chicago, 1920, 1930.* Chicago: University of Chicago Press, 1933.

Burlingame, Roger. *Endless Frontiers: The Story of McGraw-Hill.* New York: McGraw-Hill Book Co., 1959.

Burnham, Daniel H., and Edward H. Bennett. *The Plan of Chicago.* New York: DeCapo Press, [1909] 1970.

————. *Planning the Region of Chicago*. Chicago: Chicago Regional Planning Assoc., 1956.

Bush-Brown, Harold. *Beaux-Arts to Bauhaus and Beyond: An Architect's Perspective*. New York: Watson-Guptell Publications, 1976.

Butler, Rush Clark, Jr. *Chicago: The World's Youngest Great City*. Chicago: Chicago American Publishers Corp., c. 1929.

Butt, Ernest. *Chicago Then and Now: A Pictorial History of the City's Development and a Reprint of the First City Directory Published in Chicago in 1844*. Chicago: Aurora, Finch and McCullouck, 1933.

Casari, Maurizio, and Vincenzo Pavan, eds. *Beyond the International Style: New Chicago Architecture*. Chicago: Rizzoli Press International, 1981.

Centennial History of the City of Chicago: Its Men and Institutions. Chicago: Inter Ocean, 1905.

Chapman, J. M. and Brian. *The Life and Times of Baron Haussmann: Paris in the Second Empire*. London: Weidenfeld and Nicolson, 1957.

Chicago and Its Makers. Chicago, 1930.

Chicago Architects Design: A Century of Architectural Drawings from the Art Institute of Chicago. Chicago: Art Institute of Chicago and Rizzoli International Publications, 1982.

Chicago Architectural Exhibition Yearbook 1923. Chicago: Chicago Architectural Club, 1923.

Chicago Association of Commerce. *Chicago: The Great Central Market*. Chicago: R. L. Polk and Co., 1923.

————. *Survey of Local and Retail Conditions*. Chicago, 1925.

Chicago Board of Local Improvements. *A Sixteen Year Record of Achievement 1915–1931*, comp. A. E. Burnett. Chicago, 1931.

The Chicago Book/Photographs by Korth. Chicago: F. G. Korth, 1949.

Chicago Central Business and Office Building Directory. Chicago: Winters Publishing Co. (Chicago Public Library).

Chicago Department of Development and Planning. *Historic City: The Settlement of Chicago*. Chicago, 1976.

Chicago: Eight Years of Progress. Chicago, 1923.

Chicago Land Use Atlas 1970. Chicago: Chicago Department of Development and Planning, 1974.

Chicago in the Nineties: 23 Photographs. Portland, Maine: Chisholm Bros., 1893.

Chicago Plan Commission. *The Chicago Plan in 1933*. Chicago, 1933.

————. *Ten Years Work of the Chicago Plan Commission, 1909–1919*. Chicago: G. C. Burmeister Printing, 1920.

The Chicago Story 1904–1954. Chicago: Chicago Association of Commerce and Industry, 1954.

279

Chicago Tribune. *The WGN*. Chicago: Chicago Tribune, 1922.

Christ-Janer, Albert. *Eliel Saarinen*. Helsingissa: Kustannusosake-yhtio Otava, 1951.

———. *Eliel Saarinen: Finnish-American Architect and Educator*. Chicago and London: University of Chicago Press, 1979.

Claar, Elmer A., and Co. *The Epic of Lake Shore Drive*. Chicago [c. 1950].

Cohen, Stuart E. *Chicago Architects: Exhibition Catalogue*. Chicago: Swallow Press, 1976.

Colbert, Elias, and Everett Chamberlin. *Chicago and the Great Conflagration*. Chicago: J. S. Goodman and Co., 1871.

Coles, William A., and Henry Hope Reed, Jr., eds. *Architecture in America: A Battle of Styles*. New York: Appleton-Century-Crofts, 1961.

Commercial Club of Chicago. *Plan for a Boulevard to Connect the North and South Sides of the River on Michigan Avenue and Pine Street*. Chicago: R. R. Donnelley and Sons Co., 1908.

Condit, Carl W. *Chicago 1910–29: Building, Planning, and Urban Technology*. Chicago: University of Chicago Press, 1973.

———. *Chicago 1930–70: Building, Planning, and Urban Technology*. Chicago: University of Chicago Press, 1974.

———. *The Chicago School of Architecture: A History of Commercial and Public Building in the Chicago Area 1875–1925*. Chicago and London: University of Chicago Press, 1964.

———. *The Rise of the Skyscraper*. Chicago: University of Chicago Press, 1952.

Contemporary American Architects: Ralph Adams Cram, Firm of Cram and Ferguson. New York: McGraw-Hill Book Co., 1931.

Cover, John Higson. *Business and Personal Failure and Readjustment in Chicago*. Chicago: University of Chicago Press, 1933.

Cox, Wilson H. *The Greatest Conspiracy Ever Conceived: Chicago Lake Front Lands*. Chicago, 1908.

Cram, Ralph Adams. *My Life in Architecture*. Boston: Little Brown and Co., 1936.

Cromie, Robert. *The Great Chicago Fire*. New York: McGraw-Hill Book Co., 1958.

Cromie, Robert, and Arthur Haug. *Chicago*. Chicago: Ziff-Davis Publishing Co., 1948.

Cross, William Thomas. *The Making of a Trust Company*. Chicago: Chicago Trust Co., 1923.

Cummins, J. David, ed. *Investment Activities of Life Insurance Companies*. Homewood, Ill.: R. D. Irwin, published for the S. S. Huebner Foundation for Insurance Education, University of Pennsylvania, 1977.

Currey, J. Seymour. *Chicago: Its History and Its Builders*. Vols. 1–3. Chicago: S. J. Clarke Publishing Co., 1912.

Cutler, Irving. *Chicago: Metropolis of the Mid-Continent*. Chicago: Geographic Society of Chicago, c. 1976.

Dedmon, Emmett. *Fabulous Chicago: A Great City's History and People*. New York: Random House, 1953.

Douglas, George H. *Rail City: Chicago U.S.A*. San Diego, Calif.: Howell-North Books, 1981.

Downie, Leonard, Jr. *Mortgage on America*. New York and Washington: Praeger Publishers, 1974.

Draper, Joan E. *Edward II. Bennett: Architect and City Planner, 1874–1954*. Chicago: Art Institute of Chicago, 1982.

Drexler, Arthur, and Axel Menges. *Architecture of Skidmore, Owings and Merrill, 1963–1973*. New York: Architectural Book Publishing Co., 1974.

Drury, John. *Chicago in Seven Days*. New York: R. M. McBride and Co., 1930.

———. *Old Chicago Houses*. Chicago and London: University of Chicago Press, 1976.

Duncan, Hugh Dalziel. *Culture and Democracy: The Struggle for Form in Society and Architecture in Chicago and the Middle West during the Life and Times of Louis Sullivan*. Totowa, N.J.: Bedminster Press, 1965.

Eaton, Leonard K. *Two Chicago Architects and Their Clients: Frank Lloyd Wright and Howard Van Doren Shaw*. Cambridge, Mass.: M.I.T. Press, 1969.

Edgell, G. H. *The American Architecture of Today*. New York and London: Charles Scribner's Sons, 1928.

Egbert, Donald Drew. *The Beaux-Arts Tradition in French Architecture*, ed. David Van Zanten. Princeton: Princeton University Press, 1980.

———. *Social Radicalism and the Arts*. New York: Alfred A. Knopf, 1970.

Eisenstadt, S. N. *Tradition, Change and Modernity*. New York: John Wiley and Sons, 1973.

Ely, Richard Theodore, and Edward W. Morehouse. *Elements of Land Economics*. New York: Macmillan Co., 1924.

———. *Elementary Principles of Economics*. New York: Macmillan Co., 1905.

———. *Property and Contract in Their Relations to the Distribution of Wealth*. New York: Macmillan Co., 1914.

Engelhardt, George W. *Chicago: The Book of Its Board of Trade and Other Public Bodies*. Chicago, 1900.

English, Maurice. *The Testament of Stone: Themes of Idealism and Indignation from the Writings of Louis Sullivan*. Evanston: Northwestern University Press, 1963.

Ericsson, Henry, with Lewis E. Myers. *Sixty Years a Builder: The Autobiography of Henry Ericsson*. Chicago: A. Kroch and Son, 1942.

Ettleson, Samuel A. *The Chicago Municipal Code of 1922*. Chicago: T. H. Flood & Co., 1922.

Fairchild, Fred R., Edgar S. Furniss, and Norman S. Buck. *Elementary Economics*. New York: Macmillan Co., 1928.

Farr, Finis. *Chicago: A Personal History of America's Most American City*. New Rochelle, N.Y.: Arlington House, 1973.

———. *Frank Lloyd Wright*. London: Jonathan Cape, 1962.

Federal Writers Program (WPA). *Up from the Mud: An Account of How Chicago's Streets and Buildings Were Raised*. Chicago, 1941.

Fein, Albert. "The American City: The Ideal and the Real." In *The Rise of an American Architecture*, ed. Edgar Kaufmann Jr., 51–111. New York: 1970.

Fernandez, Jose A. *The Speciality Shop (A Guide)*. New York: Architectural Book Publishing Co., 1950.

Ferriss, Hugh. *The Metropolis of Tomorrow*. New York: Ives Washburn, 1929.

Fisher, Irving. *The Stock Market Crash—and After*. New York: Macmillan Co., 1930.

Fiske, Horace Spencer. *Chicago in Picture and Poetry*. Chicago: Ralph Fletcher Seymour for the Industrial Art League, 1903.

Fitch, James Marston. *American Building 1: The Historical Forces That Shaped It*. Boston: Houghton Mifflin Co., 1966.

Flinn, John J. *The Handbook of Chicago Biography*. Chicago: Standard Guide Co., 1893.

Foglesong, Richard E. *Planning the Capitalist City: The Colonial Era to the 1920s*. Princeton: Princeton University Press, 1986.

Furen, Howard B. *Chicago: A Chronological and Documentary History 1784–1970*. Dobbs Ferry, N.Y.: Oceana Publications, 1974.

Gebhard, David, and Tom Martinson. *A Guide to the Architecture of Minnesota*. Minneapolis: University of Minnesota Press, 1977.

Giedion, Sigfried. *Space, Time and Architecture*. 5th ed. Cambridge, Mass.: Harvard University Press, 1967.

Gies, Joseph. *The Colonel of Chicago*. New York: E. P. Dutton, 1979.

Gilbert, Paul Thomas, and Charles Lee Bryson. *Chicago and Its Makers*. Chicago: F. Mendelsohn, 1929.

Goldberger, Paul. *The Skyscraper*. New York: Alfred A. Knopf, 1982.

Gosnell, Harold. *Machine Politics: Chicago Model*. Chicago: University of Chicago Press, 1937.

Gottfried, Alex. *Boss Cermak of Chicago: A Study of Political Leadership*. Seattle: University of Washington Press, 1962.

Graham, Anderson, Probst and White. *The Architectural World of Graham, Anderson, Probst and White, Chicago, and Their Predecessors*. London: B. T. Batsford, 1933.

Graham, Jory. *Chicago, An Extraordinary Guide.* Chicago: Rand McNally, 1969.

Granger, Alfred Hoyt. *Chicago Welcomes You.* Chicago: A. Kroch, 1933.

Great Lakes Dredge and Dock Co. *Progress Photos South Water Street Improvement.* Chicago, 1925.

Grube, Oswald W., Peter C. Pran, and Franz Schulze. *100 Years of Architecture in Chicago: Continuity of Structure and Form.* Chicago: G. Philip O'Hara, 1973.

Halvorsen, David. *Chicago. A Profile of Greatness.* Reprinted from the *Chicago Tribune,* 5–20 March, 1966.

Hamlin, Talbot F. *The American Spirit in Architecture.* New Haven: Yale University Press, 1926.

Hammett, Ralph W., and Gerald Bradbury, eds. *Architectural Annual, Chicago 1930.* Chicago: Architectural Annual Co., 1930.

Harbeson, John F. *The Study of Architectural Design.* New York: Pencil Points Press, 1926.

Harper, William Hudson, ed. *Chicago: A History and Forecast.* Chicago: Chicago Association of Commerce, 1921.

Hauser, Arnold. *The Social History of Art.* New York: Alfred A. Knopf, 1952.

Haussmann, Georges-Eugène, Baron. *Mémoires du Baron Haussmann.* 3 vols. Paris: Victor Havard, 1890–93.

Heinz, Thomas A. *Frank Lloyd Wright.* New York: St. Martin's Press, c. 1982.

Herringshaw, Mae Felts, ed. *Herringshaw's City Blue Book of Biography.* Chicago: Clark J. Herringshaw.

Hines, Thomas S. *Burnham of Chicago: Architect and Planner.* New York: Oxford University Press, 1974.

Historic City: The Settlement of Chicago. Chicago: Chicago Department of Development and Planning, 1976.

A History of Chicago's Public Works. Chicago: Department of Public Works, 1973.

A History of the City of Chicago: Its Men and Institutions. Chicago: Inter-Ocean, 1900.

Hoagland, Henry E., and Leo D. Stone. *Real Estate Finance.* Homewood, Ill.: R. D. Irwin, 1969.

Hood, Raymond. *Contemporary American Architects: Raymond M. Hood.* New York and London: McGraw-Hill Book Co., 1931.

House Numbers: The Loop. Chicago: Chicago Historical Society.

Hoyt, Homer. *According to Hoyt: 53 Years of Homer Hoyt.* Washington, D.C.: Homer Hoyt Associates, 1970.

———. *One Hundred Years of Land Values in Chicago.* Chicago: University of Chicago Press, 1933.

———. *Population Facts for Planning Chicago.* Chicago: Chicago Plan Commission, 1942.

Hoyt, Homer, Arthur M. Weimer, and George F. Bloom. *Real Estate*. New York: Ronald Press Co., 1972.

Hubbard, Theodora Kimball, and Henry Vincent Hubbard. *Our Cities Today and Tomorrow: A Survey of Planning and Zoning Progress in the United States*. Cambridge, Mass.: Harvard University Press, 1929.

Hudnut, Joseph. *Architecture and the Spirit of Man*. Cambridge, Mass.: Harvard University Press, 1949.

Hutchinson, William Thomas. *Cyrus Hall McCormick*. New York and London: Century Co., 1930.

————. *Cyrus Hall McCormick: Harvest 1856–1884*. New York: D. Appleton-Century Co., 1935.

Illustrations of Greater Chicago. Chicago: Wing Co., 1875.

Industrial Chicago: The Commercial Interests. Vol. 4. Chicago: Goodspeed Publishing Co., 1894.

The International Competition for a New Administration Building for the Chicago Tribune, 1922. Chicago: Tribune Co., 1923.

Jacobs, Herbert Austin. *Frank Lloyd Wright: America's Greatest Architect*. New York: Harcourt, Brace, 1965.

Jacobs, Jane. *The Death and Life of Great American Cities*. New York: Random House, 1961.

Jacobsen, Hugh Newell, ed. *A Guide to the Architecture of Washington, D.C.* New York: Washington Metropolitan Chapter, American Institute of Architects, 1965.

James, Cyril F. *The Growth of Chicago Banks*. Vol. 2. *The Modern Age, 1897–1938*. New York and London: Harper and Bros., 1938.

Johannesen, Eric. *Cleveland Architecture, 1876–1976*. Cleveland: Western Reserve Historical Society, 1979.

Jones, Howard Mumford. *The Age of Energy: Varieties of American Experience 1865–1915*. New York, 1970.

Jones, John H., and Fred A. Britten, eds. *A Half Century of Chicago Building: A Practical Reference Guide—All Building Laws and Ordinances Brought to Date*. Chicago, 1910.

Kaufmann, Edgar, ed. *An American Architecture, Frank Lloyd Wright*. New York: Horizon Press, 1955.

Kilan, Michael, Connie Fletcher, and F. Richard Ciccone. *Who Runs Chicago?* New York: St. Martin's Press, 1979.

Kilham, Walter H., Jr. *Raymond Hood, Architect: Form through Function in the American Skyscraper*. New York: Architectural Book Publishing Co., 1973.

Kimball, Fiske. *American Architecture*. Indianapolis and New York: Bobbs Merrill, 1928.

Kimball, Theodora, ed. *Municipal Accomplishments in City Planning and Published City Plan Reports in the United States*. Boston, 1920.

Kinnard, William N., Jr. *Income Property Valuation: Principles and Techniques of Appraising Income-Producing Real Estate.* Lexington, Mass.: Heath Lexington Books, 1971.

Knudtson, Thomas. *Chicago, the Rising City: A Historical View of Chicago, One Hundred Years after the Great Fire.* Chicago: Chicago Publishing Co., 1975.

Koester, Frank. *Modern City Planning.* New York: 1914.

Kogan, Herman. *Yesterday's Chicago.* Miami, Fla.: E. A. Seeman, 1976.

Kostof, Spiro, ed. *The Architect: Chapters in the History of the Profession.* New York and London: Oxford University Press, 1977.

Krinsky, Carol Herselle. "Sister Cities: Architecture and Planning in the Twentieth Century." In *Chicago and New York: Architectural Interactions,* 52–76. Chicago: Art Institute of Chicago, 1984.

The Lakeside Annual Directory of the City of Chicago. Chicago: Chicago Directory Co., 1916, 1928–29.

Lane, George. *Chicago Churches and Synagogues: An Architectural Pilgrimage.* Chicago: Loyola University Press, 1981.

Lawrence, Michael G. *Make No Little Plans: Architectural Drawings from the Collections of the Cuyahoga County Archives and the Western Reserve Historical Society.* Cleveland: Western Reserve Historical Society, 1980.

Lewis, Lloyd, and Henry Justin Smith. *Chicago; The History of Its Reputation.* New York: Harcourt, Brace and Co., 1929.

Lewis, Nelson P. *The Planning of the Modern City: A Review of the Principles of Governing City Planning.* New York, 1916.

Lindell, Arthur G. *Trib Town on the Prairie.* Chicago: Chicago Tribune, 1965.

Lowe, David. *Lost Chicago.* Boston: Houghton Mifflin Co., 1975.

McCahan, David, ed. *Investment of Life Insurance Funds.* Philadelphia: University of Pennsylvania Press, 1953.

McGraw-Hill: The Story of Forty Years of Growth, 1909–1949. New York: McGraw-Hill Book Co., 1950.

McIlvaine, Mabel. *Chicago, Her History and Her Adornment.* Chicago: C. D. Peacock, 1927.

———. *Reminiscences of Chicago during the Great Fire.* Chicago: Lakeside Press, R. R. Donnelley and Sons, 1915.

McKelvey, Blake. *The Emergence of Metropolitan America: 1915–1966.* New Brunswick, N.J.: Rutgers University Press, 1968.

———. *The Urbanization of America, 1860–1915.* New Brunswick, N.J., 1963.

May, Earl C., and Will Ourseler. *A Story of Human Security: The Prudential.* Garden City, N.J.: Doubleday, 1950.

Mayer, Harold M., and Richard C. Wade. *Chicago: Growth of a Metropolis.* Chicago: University of Chicago Press, 1969.

285

Mendelsohn, Felix. *Chicago Yesterday and Today*. Chicago: F. Mendelsohn, 1932.

Mercantile Advancement Co. *Chicago on the Eve of the 20th Century*. Chicago, 1900.

Merriam, Charles E. *Chicago: A More Intimate View of Urban Politics*. New York: Macmillan Co., 1929.

Miller, Francesca Falk. *The Sands: The Story of Chicago's Front Yard*. Chicago: Valentine-Newman, 1948.

Monchow, Helen Corbin. *Seventy Years of Real Estate Subdividing in the Region of Chicago*. Evanston and Chicago: Northwestern University Press, 1939.

Montgomery, Royal E. *Industrial Relations in the Chicago Building Trades*. Chicago: University of Chicago Press, 1927.

Moody, Walter D. *Men Who Sell Things*. Chicago: A. C. McClurg and Co., 1908.

———. *Plan of Chicago: The World of the Chicago Plan Commission during 1911*. Chicago: R. R. Donnelley and Sons, n.d.

———. *Wacker's Manual for the Plan of Chicago*. Chicago: 1912.

———. *What of the City? America's Greatest Issue: City Planning*. Chicago: A. C. McClurg and Co., 1919.

Moore, Charles. *Daniel H. Burnham: Architect, Planner of Cities*. New York: Houghton Mifflin Co., 1921.

Morrison, Hugh. *Louis Sullivan: Prophet of Modern Architecture*. New York: W. W. Norton and Co., 1935.

Moses, John, and Joseph Kirkland, eds. *The History of Chicago, Illinois*. Vols. 1 and 2. Chicago and New York: Munsell and Co., 1895.

Mujica, Francisco. *History of the Skyscraper*. New York: Da Capo Press, 1977.

Mumford, Lewis. *The Brown Decades*. New York: Harcourt, Brace and Co., 1931.

———. *Sticks and Stones: A Study of American Architecture and Civilization*. New York: Dover Publications, 1955.

Muschamp, Herbert. *Man about Town: Frank Lloyd Wright in New York City*. Cambridge, Mass.: M.I.T. Press, 1983.

Muschenheim, Arthur. *A Guide to Chicago Architecture*. Chicago, 1962.

Musham, Harry A. *Report on the Location of the First Fort Dearborn*. Chicago: Fort Dearborn Memorial Commission, 1940.

Nelson, Richard, and Frederick T. Aschman. *Real Estate and City Planning*. Englewood Cliffs, N.J.: Prentice-Hall, 1957.

Nixon, H. K. *Principles of Advertising*. New York: McGraw-Hill Book Co., 1937.

Notable Men of Chicago and Their City. Chicago: *Chicago Daily Journal*, 1910.

Olcott's Land Values Blue Book of Chicago. Chicago: George C. Alcott and Co., 1925–31.

O'Mara, W. Paul. *Office Development Handbook*. Washington, D.C.: Urban Land Institute, 1982.

Orear, George Washington. *Commercial and Architectural Chicago*. Chicago, 1887.

Peets, Elbert. *On the Art of Designing Cities: Selected Essays of Elbert Peets*, ed. Paul D. Spreiregen. Cambridge, Mass., 1968.

Pegg, Betsy. *Dreams, Money, and Ambition: A History of Real Estate in Chicago*. Chicago: Chicago Real Estate Board, 1983.

Phillips, H. G. *America's Most Distinctive Club: Medinah Athletic Club*. Chicago, c. 1929.

Picturesque Chicago. Chicago: Chicago Engraving Co., 1882.

Pierce, Bessie Louise. *A History of Chicago*. Chicago: University of Chicago Press, 1957.

Pinkey, David H. *Napoleon III and the Rebuilding of Paris*. Princeton, N.J.: Princeton University Press, 1958.

The Plan of Chicago, 1909–1979: An Exhibition of the Burnham Library of Architecture. Chicago: Art Institute of Chicago, 1979.

Plumbe, George Edward. *Chicago: Its Natural Advantages as an Industrial and Commercial Market*. Chicago: Civic-Industrial Committee of the Chicago Association of Commerce, 1910.

Poole, Ernest. *Giants Gone: Men Who Made Chicago*. New York and London: McGraw-Hill Book Co., 1943.

A Portfolio of Fine Apartment Houses. Chicago: Baird and Warner, 1928.

Prior, J. H. *The Work of M. J. Faherty, Associates and Staff, 1915–1923: Report to the Board of Local Improvements*. Chicago, 1923.

Prominent Citizens and Industries of Chicago. Chicago: German Press Club of Chicago, 1901.

Quaife, Milo Milton. *Chicago's Highways, Old and New*. Chicago: D. F. Keller and Co., 1923.

Rae, John Bell. *The American Automobile*. Chicago: University of Chicago Press, 1965.

———. *The Road and Car in American Life*. Cambridge: M.I.T. Press, 1971.

Rand McNally and Co. *Bird's-Eye Views and Guide to Chicago*. Chicago and New York: Rand McNally and Co., 1898.

———. *One Hundred and Twenty-five Photographic Views of Chicago*. Chicago: Rand McNally and Co., 1916.

———. *Pictorial Chicago: Containing Views of Principal Buildings, Residences, Streets, Parks, Monuments, etc.* Chicago: Rand McNally and Co., 1901.

Randall, Frank A. *History of the Development of Building Construction in Chicago*. Urbana: University of Illinois Press, 1949.

Reps, John. *The Making of Urban America*. Princeton: Princeton University Press, 1965.

Reynolds, Donald Martin. "Alschuler, Alfred S." In *Macmillan Encyclopedia of Architects*, ed. Adolf K. Placzek. Vol. 1, p. 72. New York: Free Press, 1982.

Rex, F. *The Mayors of the City of Chicago*. Chicago: Chicago Public Library, 1933.

Robinson, Cervin, and Rosemarie Haag Bletter. *Skyscraper Style: Art Deco, New York*. New York: Oxford University Press, 1975.

Robinson, Charles Mulford. *The Improvement of Towns and Cities*, New York, 1902.

———. *The Improvement of Towns and Cities: Or the Practical Basis of Civic Aesthetics*. 3d rev. ed. New York and London, 1909.

———. *Modern Civic Art or the City Made Beautiful*. New York and London, 1903.

Roth, Leland M. *The Architecture of McKim, Mead and White, 1870–1920*. New York: Garland Press, 1978.

———. *A Concise History of American Architecture*. New York: Harper and Row, 1979.

Saalman, Howard. *Haussmann: Paris Transformed*. New York: George Braziller, 1971.

Saarinen, Aline B. *The Proud Possessors: The Lives, Times and Tastes of Some Adventurous American Art Collectors*. New York: Random House, 1958.

Saarinen, Eliel. *The City, Its Growth, Its Decay, Its Future*. New York: Reinhold, 1943.

Sanborn Map Company. *Atlas of Chicago*. Vol. 2. *Embracing Territory between Fullerton and Chicago Avenues and between North Branch of the Chicago River and Lake Michigan*. Chicago: Rascher Publishing Co., 1892.

———. *Insurance Maps of Chicago, Illinois*. Vol. 1. *South Division*. New York: Sanborn Map Co., 1906.

Schorske, Carl E. *Fin-de-Siècle: Vienna, Politics and Culture*. New York: Vintage Books, 1981.

Schultz, Earl, and Walter Simmons. *Offices in the Sky*. Indianapolis: Bobbs-Merrill Co., 1959.

Scott, Mel. *American City Planning since 1890*. Berkeley: University of California Press, 1969.

Scott, Walter Dill. *The Theory of Advertising*. Boston: Small, Maynard and Co., 1903.

Scully, Vincent Joseph. *Frank Lloyd Wright*. New York: G. Braziller, 1960.

———. *The Shingle Style: Architectural Theory and Design from Richardson to the Origins of Wright*. New Haven: Yale University Press, 1955.

Sexton, R. W. *American Commercial Buildings of Today*. New York: Architectural Book Publishing Co., 1928.

Shackleton, Robert. *Book of Chicagoans*. Philadelphia: Penn Publishing Co., 1920.

Sheahan, James W., and George P. Upton. *The Great Conflagration*. Philadelphia: Union Publishing Co., 1871.

Shurtleff, Flavell. *Carrying Out the City Plan: The Practical Application of American Law in the Execution of City Plans*. New York, 1914.

Siegel, Arthur S. *Chicago's Famous Buildings: A Photographic Guide to the City's Architectural Landmarks and Other Notable Buildings*. Chicago: University of Chicago Press, 1969.

Simon, Andreas. *Chicago, the Garden City: Its Magnificent Parks, Boulevards and Cemeteries*. Chicago: F. Gindele Printing Co., 1893.

———. *Chicago, die Gartenstadt*. Chicago: Forany Gindele Printing Co., 1893.

Sims, William Lee, II. *150 Years . . . and the Future! Colgate-Palmolive (1806–1956)*. New York: Newcomer Society of North America, 1956.

Siry, Joseph. *Carson Pirie Scott: Louis Sullivan and the Chicago Department Store*. Chicago and London: University of Chicago Press, 1988.

Sitte, Camillo. *The Art of Building Cities*, trans. Charles T. Stewart. New York: Reinhold, 1945.

Smith, Henry Justin. *Chicago: A Portrait*. New York and London: Century Co., 1931.

———. *Chicago's Great Century: 1833–1933*. Chicago: Consolidated Publishers, published for a Century of Progress, 1933.

Smith, Norris Kelly. *Frank Lloyd Wright: A Study in Architectural Content*. Watkins Glen, N.Y.: American Life Foundation Study Institute, 1979.

Smyers, R. C. *Invested Wealth of Chicago: A Collection of Real Estate Sales 1880–1887*. Chicago: R. C. Smyers, 1889.

Solomon, Ezda, and Zarko G. Bilbija. *Metropolitan Chicago: An Economic Analysis*. Glencoe, Ill.: Free Press of Glencoe, 1959.

Starrett, William Aiken. *Skyscrapers and the Men Who Build Them*. New York and London: C. Scribner's Sons, 1928.

Stern, Robert A. M. *George Howe: Toward a Modern American Architecture*. New Haven: Yale University Press, 1975.

———. *Raymond Hood*. New York: Rizzoli International Publications, 1982.

Stern, Robert A. M., Gregory Gilmartin, and John Montague Massengale. *New York 1900: Metropolitan Architecture and Urbanism 1890–1915*. New York: Rizzoli International Publications, 1983.

Stern, Robert A. M., Gregory Gilmartin, and Thomas Mellins. *New York 1930: Architecture and Urbanism between the Two World Wars*. New York: Rizzoli International Publications, 1987.

Storrer, William Allin. *The Architecture of Frank Lloyd Wright: A Complete Catalog*. 2d ed. Cambridge, Mass.: M.I.T. Press, 1978.

The Story of the Tower. Chicago: Tribune Co., 1968.

Strauss, J. B. "The Bascule Bridge in Chicago." In *A Half Century of Chicago Building*, 91–93. Chicago, 1910.

Sullivan, Louis, *Kindergarten Chats and Other Writings*. New York: Dover Publications, 1918.

Survey of Advertising, Publishing, Printing and Allied Lines. Chicago: Chicago Association of Commerce, 1925.

Tafel, Edgar. *Apprentice to Genius: Years with Frank Lloyd Wright*. New York: McGraw-Hill, 1979.

Tallmadge, Thomas. *Architecture in Old Chicago*. Chicago: University of Chicago Press, 1941.

———. *The Story of Architecture in America*. New York: W. W. Norton and Co., 1927.

Tatum, George B. *Penn's Great Town: 250 Years of Philadelphia Architecture*. Philadelphia: University of Pennsylvania Press, 1961.

Taussig, Frank William. *Principles of Economics*. New York: Macmillan Co., 1930.

Taut, Bruno. *Modern Architecture*. London: Studio Limited, 1929.

Taylor, Joshua C. *America as Art*. Washington D.C.: Smithsonian Institution Press, 1976.

Teegen, Otto John. *Contemporary American Architects: Ely Jacques Kahn*. New York and London: McGraw-Hill Book Co., 1931.

Thorpe, A. H. *Atlas of Real Estate in City and Chicago Owned by Potter Palmer*. Chicago, c. 1895.

Twombly, Robert C. *Frank Lloyd Wright: An Interpretive Biography*. New York: Harper and Row, 1973.

Unwin, Raymond. *Town Planning in Practice: An Introduction to the Art of Designing Cities and Suburbs*. London: T. Fisher Unwin, 1909.

Van Zanten, David. "Architectural Composition at the Ecole des Beaux-Arts from Charles Percier to Charles Garnier." In *The Architecture of the Ecole des Beaux-Arts*, ed. Arthur Drexler. New York: Museum of Modern Art, 1977.

Vidler, Anthony. "The Scenes of the Street: Transformations in Ideal and Reality, 1750–1871." In *On Streets*, ed. S. Anderson. Cambridge, Mass.: M.I.T. Press, 1978.

Wagenknecht, Edward Charles. *Chicago*. Norman: University of Oklahoma Press, 1967.

Wagner, Otto. *Die Baukunst unserer Zeit; Dem Baukunstjünger ein Führer auf diesem Kunstgebiete.* 4th ed. Vienna, 1914.

———. *Die Groszstadt: Eine Studie über diese.* Vienna, 1911.

Waldrop, Frank C. *McCormick of Chicago: An Unconventional Portrait of a Controversial Figure.* Englewood Cliffs, N.J.: Prentice-Hall, 1966.

Washburn, Walter A. *Chicago: The City Beautiful.* Chicago: S. W. Straus and Co., 1923.

Wendt, Lloyd. *Chicago Tribune: The Rise of a Great American Newspaper.* Chicago: Rand McNally and Co., 1966.

Wetten, Albert H., ed. *Statistical Data Showing the Activity in the Real Estate Market in the Downtown District of Chicago Covering the Period November 1892 to 1910.* Chicago: Chicago Historical Society Scrapbook.

Whiffen, Marcus, and Frederick Koeper. *American Architecture 1607–1976.* Cambridge, Mass.: M.I.T. Press, 1981.

Who's Who in Chicago. Chicago: A. N. Marquis Co., various years.

Who's Who in Chicago and Illinois. Chicago: A. N. Marquis Co., 1950.

Who's Who in New York: City and State, ed. Winfield Scot Downs. New York: Who's Who Publications, 1929.

Wiebe, Robert H. *Businessmen and Reform: A Study of the Progressive Movement.* Cambridge, Mass., 1962.

———. *The Search for Order.* New York: 1967.

Wille, Lois. *Forever Open, Clear and Free: The Historic Struggle for Chicago's Lake Front.* Chicago: Regency, 1972.

Williams, Frank Backus. *The Law of City Planning and Zoning.* New York: Macmillan Co., 1922.

Williams, Kenny J. *In the City of Men: Another Story of Chicago.* Nashville, Tenn.: Townsend Press, 1974.

Williamson, Harold F., ed. *The Growth of the American Economy.* New York: Prentice-Hall, 1955.

Wincell, Samuel Robertson. *Chicago, Past and Present.* Chicago: A. Flanagan Co., 1906.

———. *A Civic Manual for Chicago, Cook County and Illinois.* Chicago: A. Flanagan Co., 1910.

Wolf, Peter M. *Eugène Hénard and the Beginning of Urbanism in Paris 1900–1914.* The Hague: International Federation for Housing and Planning, 1968.

Wood, David Ward. *Chicago and Its Distinguished Citizens on the Progress of Forty Years.* Chicago: Milton George and Co., 1881.

Wright, Chester Whitney. *Economic History of the United States.* New York and London: McGraw-Hill Co., 1941.

Wright, Frank Lloyd. *An American Architecture,* ed. Edgar Kaufmann. New York: Horizon Press, 1955.

————. *The Future of Architecture*. New York: Horizon Press, 1953.

————. *In the Cause of Architecture, Frank Lloyd Wright: Essays by Frank Lloyd Wright for Architectural Record 1908–1952*, ed. Frederick Gutheim. New York: Architectural Record, c. 1975.

Wright, John S. *Chicago: Past, Present and Future*. Chicago: Horton and Leonard, 1868.

Young, William, ed. *A Dictionary of American Artists, Sculptors and Engravers*. Cambridge, Mass.: William Young and Co., 1968.

Zimmerman, William, Jr. *William Wrigley, Jr.: The Man and His Business*. Chicago: R. R. Donnelley and Sons, 1935.

Zorbaugh, Harvey Warren. *Gold Coast and the Slum: A Sociological Study of Chicago's Near North Side*. Chicago: University of Chicago Press, 1929.

Zueblin, Charles. *A Decade of Civic Improvement*. Chicago, 1905.

Zukowsky, John. *Architecture in Context: 360 North Michigan Avenue*. Chicago: Art Institute of Chicago, 1981.

————. "The Capitals of American Architecture: Chicago and New York." In *Chicago and New York: Architectural Interactions*. Chicago: Art Institute of Chicago, 1984.

Zukowsky, John, ed. *Chicago Architecture 1872–1922: Birth of a Metropolis*. Munich: Prestel-Verlag in association with the Art Institute of Chicago, 1987.

A R T I C L E S

Agrest, Diana. "Architectural Anagrams: The Symbolic Performance of Skyscrapers." *Oppositions* 2 (Winter 1977): 28–51.

"An Ideal Club District." *North Central Journal* (December 1927): 26.

Angle, Paul. "Fort Dearborn, 1803–1812." *Chicago History* 2 (Summer 1949): 97–102.

————. "Views of Chicago, 1866–1867." *Antiques* 63 (January 1952): 60–61.

"Architecture and Illumination: A Notable Example in the Wrigley Building, Chicago." *Architectural Forum* 35 (October 1921): 135.

Arnold, Isaac B. "William B. Ogden and Early Days in Chicago." *Fergus' Historical Series, no. 17* (1882): 5–40.

Bach, Ira J. "Chicago Development." *American Institute of Planners Journal* 20 (Winter 1954): 21–26.

————. "A Reconsideration of the 1909 'Plan of Chicago.'" *Chicago History* 2 (1973): 132–41.

Ball, Charles B. "What of the City, Chicago: Vision-Planning-Promotion Realizations." Reprint from *City Planning* (January and July 1926).

"Beautifying the Nation's Capitol: The New Bridges at Washington Should Not Be a Blemish to the City." *Inland Architect and Building News* 39 (March 1902): 14–17.

Behrendt, Walter Curt. "Skyscraper in Germany." *Journal of the American Institute of Architects* 2 (September 1923): 365–70.

Bennett, Edward H. "The Chicago River Bridges." *Architectural Record* 52 (December 1922): 458.

———. "Wacker Drive Plans: Building Projects May Mar or Make General Impressions." *Chicago Skyline* (10 April 1927): 8–9.

Blackall, Charles. "American Architecture since the War: A Decade of Development." *American Architect* 129 (5 January 1926): 1–11.

Bosson, Alfred C. "Fifty Year's Progress toward an American Style in Architecture." *American Architect* 129 (5 January 1926): 43–50.

Boyd, David Knickerbacker. "The Skyscraper and the Street." *American Architect and Building News* 94 (18 November 1908): 161–67.

Bruegmann, Robert. "Holabird and Roche and Holabird and Root: The First Two Generations." *Chicago History* 9 (Fall 1980): 130–65.

"Chicago's Prudential Building." *Architectural Forum* 97 (August 1952): 90–97.

Cohen, Stuart E. "The Tall Building Urbanistically Reconsidered." *Threshold: American Journal of the School of Architecture, University of Illinois at Chicago* 2 (1983): 6–13.

Condit, Carl. "The Triumph and Failure of the Skyscraper." *Inland Architect* 21 (January 1977): 14–25.

Corbett, Harvey Wiley. "The American Radiator Building, New York City." *Architectural Record* 55 (May 1924): 473.

———. "The Birth and Development of the Tall Building." *American Architect* 129 (5 January 1926): 37–40.

———. "Zoning and the Envelope of the Building." *Pencil Points* 4 (April 1923): 15–18.

Creese, Walter L. "Saarinen's Tribune Design." *Journal of the Society of Architectural Historians* 6 (July–December 1947): 1–5.

"The Crown of the Skyscraper." *Architectural Record* 27 (May 1910): 431–34.

Danger, Gerald A. "Chicago's First Maps." *Chicago History* 13 (Spring 1984): 12–22.

"Designs Awarded Honorable Mention—Chicago Tribune Building Competition." *American Architect* 123 (3 January 1923): 23–26.

Desmond, Harry W. "Rationalizing the Skyscraper." *Architectural Record* 17 (May 1905): 422–25.

Dixon, John Morris. "The Tall One." *Architectural Forum* 133 (July/August 1970): 37–44.

"Dunham Building." *Architectural Forum* 47 (July 1927): 61–64.

Eliot, Charles W. "A Study of the New Plans of Chicago." *Chicago: A Collection of Articles* (1910): 417–31.

Embury, Aymar, II. "Impressions of Three Cities: Chicago, Detroit, Pittsburgh." *Architecture* 31 (1915): 19–53, 77–80, 105–9.

Faherty, Robert. "Cyrano of the Gold Coast." *Townsfolk* 40 (April 1949): 19–31.

"Frank Lloyd Wright: After 36 Years, His Tower Is Completed," *Architectural Forum* 104 (February 1956): 106–13.

"The Fraternity Clubs Building, New York." *Architectural Forum* 41 (July 1924) 9–16.

"Fred M. Torrey's Decorative Panels for a Chicago Skyscraper." *American Magazine of Art* 19 (September 1928): 483–88.

Frohne, Henry W. "A New Idea in Hotel Decoration: The Drake Hotel." *Good Furniture* 16 (May 1921), n.p.

Gillette, D. H. "Best Laid Plans of Mice and Men." *American Architecture* (March 1933): 43–45.

Gorden, F. C. "The Skyscraper." *American Architect and Building News* 46 (8 December 1984): 100–101.

Granger, Alfred. "The Tribune Tower as a Work of Architecture." *Western Architect* (November 1925): 111–13.

"The Great Gateway." *American Architect* 119 (11 May 1921).

Grosscup, Peter S. "Who Shall Own America?" *Chicago: A Collection of Articles* (1910): 146–57.

"Group of Buildings for Potter Palmer, Esq., Chicago, Illinois." *American Architect and Building News* 27 (25 January 1890): 61, pl. 735.

Haig, Robert M. "Toward an Understanding of the Metropolis." *Quarterly Journal of Economics* 40 (1926): 179–208, 402–34.

Hamwatt, Edward S. "The Building and the Designing of the 'Skyscraper.'" *American Architect and Building News* 88 (11 November 1905): 158–60.

Harmon, Arthur Loomis. "The Design of Office Buildings." *Architectural Forum* 52 (June 1930): 819–20.

Haskins, Henry J. B. "The Stevens Hotel, Chicago." *Architectural Forum* 47 (August 1927): 97–102.

Hastings, Thomas. "How the Beaux-Arts Institute Has Helped Our Architectural Schools." *Architecture* 37 (May 1918): 116.

———. "Modern Architecture: An Address Delivered before the Royal Institute of British Architects." *Architectural Forum* 40 (May 1924): 189–94.

"History of the Woman's Athletic Club." *Townsfolk* 25 (April 1955): 19.

Hitchcock, Henry Russell. "Sullivan and the Skyscraper." *The Builder* 185 (7 August 1953): 197–200.

"The Home of a Progressive Life Insurance Company, The Central Life Building: A Pioneer among Modern Structures of the District." *North Central Journal* 5 (December 1927): 16–17.

Hood, Raymond M. "The American Radiator Company Building, New York." *American Architect and Architectural Review* 126 (19 November 1924): 466–474.

———. "Exterior Architecture of Office Buildings," *Architectural Forum* 41 (September 1924): 97–99.

———. "The News Building, New York." *Architectural Forum* 53 (November 1930): 531–32.

———. "The Tribune Tower—the Architect's Problem." *Western Architect* 34 (November 1925): 114–15.

Hooper, Parker Morse. "Modern Architectural Decoration." *Architectural Forum* 48 (February 1928): 153–60.

———. "Office Buildings of Today and Tomorrow." *Architectural Forum* 48 (January 1928): 5–8.

Hoskins, Henry J. B. "The Palmolive Building, Chicago: Holabird and Root, Architects." *Architectural Forum* 52 (May 1930): 655–66.

———. "Structure and Equipment of the Palmolive Building, Holabird and Root, Architects." *Architectural Forum* 52 (May 1930): 730–36.

Hostache, Ellow. "Reflections on the Exposition des Arts Décoratifs." *Architectural Forum* 44 (January 1926): 11–16.

Howells, John M., and Raymond M. Hood. "The Tribune Tower." *Architectural Forum* 43 (October 1925): 184–90.

"Inlandscape: 900 North." *Inland Architect* 25 (March 1981): 2–48.

Irving, Robert F. "Andrew Rebori, Dreamer and All-Around Doer." *Inland Architect* 20 (May 1976): 12–16.

———. "Benny Marshall: The Dreams That Money Could Buy." *Inland Architect* (January 1978): 14–17.

———. "Holabird and Root: Still Going Strong after 95 Years." *Inland Architect* 20 (July 1976): 8–13.

Jones, Basset. "Illuminating the Exterior of Buildings." *Architectural Forum* 42 (February 1925): 93–96.

Karl, Joseph I. "Wrigley Buildings Attract Anew." *Real Estate News: Chicago* 19 (January 1924): 1–5.

Kibbe, Louis G. "Present Status of Cooperative Apartment Promotion and Finance." *Architectural Forum* 48 (January 1928): 117–21.

Kingston, J. L. "The Possible Height of Skyscrapers." *Architect* 13 (October 1929): 37.

Klatt, Wayne. "The Battle of Streeterville." *Reader* 12 (6 May 1983): 1 ff.

Lee, Anne. "The Chicago Civic Opera Building: Graham, Anderson, Probst and White, Architects." *Architectural Forum* 52 (April 1930): 490–514.

———. "The Chicago Daily News Building: Holabird and Root, Architects." *Architectural Forum* 52 (January 1930): 21–59.

———. "Malabry Court, Chicago—a Remodeled Building." *Architectural Record* 63 (February 1928) 97–104.

Leonard, Louis. "What Is Modernism." *American Architect* 137 (November 1929): 22–25, 112.

"London Guarantee and Accident Building, Chicago." *American Architect* 126 (27 August 1924): plates and plan.

Loring, Charles G. "Office Buildings Now and Then." *Architectural Forum* 52 (June 1930): 821–24.

McCarthy, Michael P. "Chicago Businessmen and the Burnham Plan." *Journal of the Illinois State Historical Society* 63 (Autumn 1970): 228–56.

McLean, Robert Craig. "The Gookins' Plan for Chicago's Reconstruction." *Western Architect* (October 1927): 158.

McMillan, James. "The American Academy in Rome." *North American Review* 174 (May 1902): 625–31.

"Magnificent Mile for Windy City: City Plan Proposal for Upper Michigan Avenue, Chicago." *Architectural Record* 101 (June 1947): 96–99.

Magurn, E. A. "Modernism in Architecture as It Appears to a Layman." *The Architect* 13 (October 1929): 33–36.

"The Malls at Water Tower Place." *Architectural Record* 162 (October 1977): 94–104.

"Michigan Square Building, Chicago, Ill.: Holabird and Root, Architects." *Architectural Record* 70 (October 1931): 257–62.

"A Modern Pyramid—Is Chicago's Palmolive Building." *Through the Ages* (October 1931): 40–42.

Moody, Walter D. *"Chicago Destined to Be the Center of the Modern World," Bank Man* 7, no. 11 (November 1912).

———. "The Chicago Plan." *Municipal Engineering* 43 (September 1912).

Moore, Charles. "Beautifying the Nation's Capital: Report of the Commissioners of the District of Columbia." *Inland Architect and Building News* 39 (February 1902): 2–6.

———. "Lessons of the Chicago World's Fair: An Interview with the Late D. H. Burnham." *Architectural Record* 33 (January 1913): 34–44.

Moore, Harold A. "The Story of a Real Estate Gold Bond." *Fort Dearborn Magazine* (Midsummer 1922): 19 and 30.

Moulton, Robert H. "The Plan of Chicago." *Architectural Record* 46 (November 1919): 457–70.

Mumford, Lewis. "High Buildings: An American View." *American Architect* 126 (5 November 1924): 423–24.

———. "New York vs. Chicago in Architecture." *Architecture* 56 (November 1927): 241–44.

Murchison, Kenneth. "The Spires of Gotham." *Architectural Forum* 52 (June 1930): 786–818.

"New Boulevard Link's Traffic Almost Double That of London Bridge." *Fort Dearborn Magazine* (November 1922): 4–6.

Newcomb, Rexford. "Concerning Apartment Houses." *Western Architect* 35 (April 1926): 41.

"New Gateway of the Greater Chicago." *American Architect* 119 (1921): 552–53.

Newman, James B. "Factors in Office Building Planning." *Architectural Forum* 7 (June 1930): 881–85.

"New Wrigley Building: Chicago's Tallest Structure." *Fort Dearborn Magazine* 2 (March 1921): 15.

Nichols, W. A. "Fourth Presbyterian Church of Chicago." *Architectural Record* 36 (September 1914): 176–97.

Nimmons, George C. "The New Renaissance in Architecture as Seen in the Design of Buildings for Mail Order Houses." *American Architect* 134 (5 August 1928): 141–49.

———. "The Passing of the Skyscraper." *Journal of the American Institute of Architects* 10 (1922): 356–61.

———. "Skyscrapers in America." *Journal of the American Institute of Architects* 2 (September 1923): 370–72.

North, Arthur T. "The Passing Show." *Western Architect* 39 (January 1930): 11–12.

"The North Michigan Avenue, Chicago Development." *American Architect* 114 (11 December 1918): 690–94.

Ogden, Palmer H. "The Chicago Allerton House." *Architectural Forum* 42 (May 1925): 313–16.

Onderdonk, Holmes. "The Tribune Tower." *Journal of the Western Society of Engineers* 29 (December 1924): 443–446.

Paige, James W. "A Leading Hotel District." *North Central Journal* 5 (December 1927): 10–14.

Palmer, C. F. "Office Buildings from an Investment Standpoint," *Architectural Forum* 52 (June 1930): 891–96.

"That Palmolive Look." *Inland Architect* 26 (May/June 1982): 7–17.

Parker, William Stanley. "Skyscrapers Anywhere." *Journal of the American Institute of Architects* 2 (September 1923): 370–72.

Parsons, William E. "Burnham as a Pioneer in City Planning," *Architectural Record* 38 (July 1915): 13–31.

Perkins, Lucy Fitch. "The City Beautiful: A Study of the Artistic Possibilities of Chicago." *Inland Architect and Building News* 34 (September 1899): 10–14.

Peterson, Jon A. "The City Beautiful Movement: Forgotten Origins and Lost Meanings." *Journal of Urban History* 2 (August 1976): 415–34.

"Planning in Chicago." *American Society of Planning Officials Newsletter* 15 (March 1949): 1.

Plous, F. K., Jr. "The Dowager of Michigan Avenue." *Midwest Magazine of the Chicago Sun-Times* (23 July 1972).

Poesch, Jessie J. "The Progressive Spirit in Architecture, the Chicago School in Contemporary Literature," *American Association of Architectural Bibliographers*. Publication no. 13 (1958).

Pond, DeWitt Clinton. "Treatment of the 'Set-Back,'" *Architecture* 54 (October 1926): 293–97.

Pond, Irving K. "High Buildings and Beauty." *Architectural Forum* 38 (February 1923): 41–44.

———. "High Buildings and Beauty (Part II)." *Architectural Forum* 38 (April 1923): 179–82.

———. "Zoning and Architecture of High Buildings." *Architectural Forum* 35 (October 1921): 131–34.

Real Estate Department of the Equitable Life Assurance Society of the United States. "Analysis Established Owner Requirements: Home Office Building for Equitable Life." *Architectural Record* 131 (May 1962): 178–81.

Rebori, Andrew N. "South Water Street Improvement—Chicago." *Architectural Record* 58 (September 1925): 216–22.

———. "The Work of Burnham and Root, D. H. Burnham and Co. and Graham Burnham and Co." *Architectural Record* 38 (July 1915): 32–168.

———. "Zoning Skyscrapers in Chicago." *Architectural Record* 58 (July 1925): 88–90.

Reed, Earl H., Jr. "Some Recent Work of Holabird and Root, Architects." *Architecture* 61 (January 1930): 1–40.

"Re-Opening Chicago Building Height Problem." *Western Architect* 32 (January 1923): 1.

"Report of the Architect's Committee, North Michigan Avenue Development of the North Central Association, Chicago. Submitted November 1, 1918." *American Architect* 114 (11 December 1918): 690–94.

Robertson, Howard. "The American Businessman's Hotel." *Architect* 117 (10 June 1927): 987.

Robertson, Paul. "The Skyscraper Office Building." *Architectural Forum* 52 (June 1930): 879–80.

Robinson, Charles Mulford, ed. "The City Plan." *Charities and the Commons* 19 (1 February 1908): 1487–1562.

———. "Improvement in City Life: *Aesthetic Progress*." *Atlantic Monthly* 83 (April 1899): 524–37; (May 1899): 654–64; (June 1899): 771–85.

———. "New Dreams for Cities." *Architectural Record* 17 (May 1905): 410–21.

Saarinen, Eliel. "A New Architectural Language for America." *Western Architect* 32 (February 1923).

———. "Project for Lake Front Development of the City of Chicago." *American Architect* 124 (December 1923): 487–514.

Scammon, J. Young. "William B. Ogden." *Fergus' Historical Series*, no. 17 (1882): 41–72.

Schlereth, Thomas, "Burnham's *Plan* and Moody's *Manual*; City Planning as Progressive Reform." *American Planner* (1983): 75–99.

Schultz, Earle. "The Office Building and the City."*Architectural Forum* 41 (September 1924): 141.

Schuyler, Montgomery. "To Curb the Skyscraper." *Architectural Record* 24 (October 1908): 300–302.

———. "The Evolution of a Skyscraper." *Architectural Record* 14 (November 1903): 329.

"Sculptural Treatment of Four Michigan Avenue Bridge Houses." *American Architect* 119 (11 May 1921): 552–53.

"The Seven Level Shopping Mall at Water Tower Place: A Try for a Revolution in Retailing." *Architectural Record* 159 (April 1976): 136–40.

Shapiro, Benjamin B. "Structural Design of the Stevens Hotel." *Architectural Forum* 47 (August 1927): 103–20.

Shaw, Alfred. "The Chicago Union Station: Graham, Anderson, Probst and White, Architects." *Architectural Forum* 44 (February 1926): 85–88.

Sheridan, Leo J. "Economic Factors of the Office Building Project." *Architectural Forum* 41 (September 1924): 121–32.

Shreve, R. H. "The Economic Design of Office Buildings." *Architectural Record* 67 (April 1930): 341–59.

Sitzenstock, Robert P. "Evolution of the High-Rise Office Building." *Progressive Architecture* 44 (September 1963): 146–57.

"Skylines of Modern American Cities." *American Architect* 134 (5 December 1928): 743–50.

Solon, Leon V. "The Evolution of an Architectural Design: The Tribune Building Tower, Chicago." *Architectural Record* 59 (March 1926): 215–22.

Sparks, Edwin Erle. "The Beginnings of Chicago." *American Architect and Building News* 81 (26 September 1903): 101–4.

Sparling, Samuel Edwin. "Municipal History and Present Organization of the City of Chicago." *Bulletin of the University of Wisconsin* 2 (May 1898).

Sprague, Paul E. "The Origin of Balloon Framing." *Journal of the Society of Architectural Historians* 40 (December 1981): 311–19.

Stamper, John W. "Patronage and the City Grid: The High-Rise Architecture of Mies van der Rohe in Chicago," *Inland Architect* 30 (March/April 1986): 34–41.

———. "Shaping Chicago's Shoreline," *Chicago History* 14 (Winter 1985–86): 44–55.

Strauss, J. B. "The Bascule Bridge in Chicago," *A Half Century of Chicago Building*, Chicago (1910): 91–93.

Sullivan, Louis H. "The Autobiography of an Idea," *Journal of the American Institute of Architects* 11 (September 1923): 335–42.

————. "The Chicago Tribune Competition." *Architectural Record* 53 (February 1923): 151–57.

Tallmadge, Thomas. "American Architecture: Modernism, the International Style." *Building for the Future* (January 1930): n.p.

————. "A Critic of the Chicago Tribune Building Competition." *Western Architect* 32 (January 1923): 7–8.

Taylor, C. Stanley. "The Annual Forecast of Architecture and Building, 1931." *Architectural Forum* 38 (January 1923): 9–12.

————. "Financing the Office Building." *Architectural Forum* 41 (September 1924): 137–40.

Taylor, Eugene S. "Chicago Plan Progress." *Chicago Skylines* (20 November 1927): 11–14.

"333 North Michigan Avenue, Chicago: Holabird and Root Architects." *Architectural Record* 65 (February 1929): 157–62.

Tower, Matthew. "Tower 256 Ft. High Tops 24 Story Building." *Engineering News Record* (24 November 1927): 824–27.

"The Tribune Tower, Chicago." *Architectural Forum* 43 (October 1925): 187.

Turak, Theodore. "William LeBaron Jenney: Pioneer of Chicago's West Parks." *Inland Architect* (March 1981): 39.

Van Zanten, David. "Twenties Gothic." *New Mexico Studies in the Fine Arts* 7 (1982): 19–24.

"The Vertical Style." *Architectural Forum* 82 (July 1945): 104–14.

Wacker, Charles H. "The Plan of Chicago—Its Purpose and Development." *Art and Archaeology* 12 (October 1921): 101–10.

Wacker, Charles H., and Edward H. Bennett. "The Plan of Chicago and Technical Features of the Plan of Chicago." *American City* 1 (1909): 49–58.

Walker, Ralph Thomas. "The Relation of Skyscrapers to Our Life." *Architectural Forum* 52 (May 1930): 689–95.

Webster, J. Carson. "The Skyscraper: Logical and Historical Considerations." *Journal of the Society of Architectural Historians* 18 (December 1959): 126–39.

Wells, Alton L. "Financing the Large Building Project." *Architectural Forum* 52 (January 1930): 115–20.

Westfall, Carroll William. "Benjamin Henry Marshall of Chicago." *Chicago Architectural Journal* 2 (1982): 8–21.

Wight, Peter B. "Additions to Chicago's Skyline: A Few Recent Skyscrapers." *Architectural Record* 28 (July 1910): 15–24.

————. "The Case for the Skyscraper." *Architectural Forum* 71 (December 1939): 463–64.

————. "Daniel Hudson Burnham and His Associates," *Architectural Record* 38 (July 1915): 7–12.

————. "Memorial to the Late W. W. Boyington." *Inland Architect and News Record* 32 (November 1898): 32.

Wilson, Richard Guy. "International Style: The MOMA Exhibition." *Progressive Architecture* (February 1982): 92–105.

Wilson, William H. "J. Horace McFarland and the City Beautiful Movement." *Journal of Urban History* 7 (May 1981): 315–34.

Winkler, Franz. "Some Chicago Buildings Represented by the Work of Holabird and Roche." *Architectural Record* 31 (April 1912): 313–88.

"The World's Fair Buildings at Large and the Lessons to be Drawn from them." *American Architect and Building News* 40 (17 June 1893): 181–83.

Wright, Frank Lloyd. "The Logic of Contemporary Architecture as an Expression of This Age." *Architectural Forum* 52 (May 1930): 637–38.

———. "Sheet Metal and a Modern Instance." *Architectural Record* 64 (October 1928): 334–42.

Wright, Henry. "The Architect, the Plan, and the City." *Architectural Forum* 54 (February 1931): 217–23.

"The Wrigley Building." *Through the Ages* (October 1925): 34–38.

Wrigley, Robert L. "The Plan of Chicago: Its Fiftieth Anniversary." *American Institute of Planners Journal* 26 (February 1960): 31–38.

Young, Hugh E. "New Wacker Drive Supplants 'Rundown' Water-Front Street." *American City Magazine* (April 1926): 3–7.

OTHER

Akeley, R. P. "Implementation of the 1909 Plan of Chicago: An Historical Account of Planning Salesmanship." Master's thesis, University of Tennessee, 1973.

Aldis, Graham. "History and Trend of Office Rentals." *Proceedings of the Annual Convention of the National Association of Building Owners and Managers*, 58–69. Chicago, 1924.

Allerton Club Residence, New York, Chicago and Cleveland. New York, 1923.

Ayer, Benjamin Franklin. "Lake-Front Questions." Paper read before the Chicago Literary Club, 28 May 1888.

Baird and Warner. *A Portfolio of Fine Apartment Homes.* Chicago, 1928.

Bies, Susan Adair Schmidt. "Commercial Banking in Metropolitan Areas: A Study of the Chicago SMSA." Ph.D. diss., Northwestern University, 1972.

"A Brief History of National Boulevard Bank of Chicago 1921–1971." Unpublished paper. Chicago, 1971.

Brown, Edward O. "The Shore of Lake Michigan." Paper read before the Law Club of the City of Chicago, 25 April 1902.

Carbide and Carbon Building, Chicago. Chicago: Union Carbide and Carbon Corp., 1932.

Chicago and its Resources Twenty Years After, 1871–1891. Chicago: Chicago Times Co., 1892.

Chicago Association of Commerce. *Survey of Banking and Finance.* Chicago, 1925.

Chicago Municipal Reference Library. *The Government of the City of Chicago.* Chicago, 1976.

Chicago Park District. *Preliminary Report on Lake Shore Drive Improvements.* Chicago, 1956.

Chicago Plan Commission. *Chicago: America's Greatest and Most Attractive City.* Chicago, 1920.

————. *Chicago Land Use Survey: A Project for the Settlement of the City of Chicago.* Chicago, 1940.

————. *Chicago Plan Commission: A Historical Sketch, 1909–1960.* Chicago, 1961.

————. "The Chicago Plan in 1933: Twenty-five Years of Accomplishment." Unpublished paper. Chicago 1933.

————. *Chicago Plan Progress.* Chicago, 1927.

————. "Chicago's Greatest Issue: An Official Plan Prepared under the Direction of the Chicago Plan Commission." Unpublished paper. Chicago, 1911.

————. *Chicago's World-Wide Influence in City Planning.* Chicago, 1914.

————. *Creating a World Famous Street.* Chicago, 1913.

————. *Fifty Million Dollars for Nothing.* Chicago, 1912.

————. *Improve the Lakefront! Pending Ordinance Should Be Adopted by City Council.* Chicago, 1919.

————. *Industrial and Commercial Background for Planning Chicago.* Chicago, 1942.

————. "The Michigan Avenue Extension." An Address by Charles H. Wacker, 13 April 1918. Chicago, 1918.

————. *The Outer Drive Along the Lake Front, Chicago.* Chicago, 1929.

————. *The Plan of Chicago in 1925: Fifteen Years Work of the Chicago Plan Commission.* Chicago, 1925.

————. *Reclaim South Water Street for All the People.* Chicago, 1917.

Chicago Public Library, Art Department. *Chicago Architecture from its Beginning to the Present Day.* Chicago, 1972.

————. *Chicago Monuments, Memorials, Markers, etc.* Chicago, 1963.

Chicago Real Estate Board. *Pages from the History of Chicago: Land Values.* Chicago, 1931.

Chicago Tribune Co. *Glimpses of Tribune Tower: Presented as a Souvenir of Your Visit to the Home of the World's Greatest Newspaper.* Chicago, n.d.

302

Chicago 21: A Plan for the Central Area Communities. Chicago, 1973.

City Council of the City of Chicago. *Chicago Zoning Ordinance.* Chicago, 1923.

Commercial Club of Chicago. *Plan for a Boulevard to Connect the North and South Sides of the River on Michigan Avenue and Pine Street.* Chicago, 1908.

Commission on Chicago Historical and Architectural Landmarks. *East Lake Shore Drive District: Preliminary Summary of Information.* Chicago, 1984.

———. "Fourth Presbyterian Church." Unpublished paper. Chicago, 1981.

———. "Michigan Avenue Bridge District, Preliminary Summary of Information." National Register Nomination, 1982.

———. *900 North Michigan Avenue: A Preliminary Survey of Information.* Chicago, 1982.

———. *Site of the Beaubien Claim.* Chicago, 1975.

———. *Site of the DuSable/Kinzie House.* Chicago, 1977.

Creese, Walter L. "American Architecture from 1918 to 1933 with a Special Emphasis on European Influence." Ph.D. diss., Harvard University, 1949.

Culver, Frederic. "Co-operative Apartments." *Proceedings of the Sixteenth Annual Convention of the National Association of Building Owners and Managers,* 145–59. Chicago, 1923.

Cushman, Robert S. *The 1957 Chicago Zoning Ordinance of Chicago as It Affects the Central Business District of Chicago.* Chicago, 1958.

Deane, William. "Methods of Determining Depreciation for Income Tax Purposes." *Proceedings of the Sixteenth Annual Convention of the National Association of Building Owners and Managers,* 101–18. Chicago, 1923.

Delmonico, Charles C. "Advertising Office and Apartment Buildings." *Proceedings of the Annual Convention of the National Association of Building Owners and Managers,* 677–96. Chicago, 1926.

The Drake and the Blackstone, 1924: Shopping List Points of Interest Information Book. Chicago: Drake Hotel Co., 1924 and 1932.

Draper, Joan. "The San Francisco Civic Center: Architecture, Planning and Politics." Ph.D. diss., University of California at Berkeley, 1979.

Field, Cynthia. "The Chicago Tribune Competition of 1922," Master's thesis, Columbia University, 1968.

———. "The City Planning of Daniel Hudson Burnham." Ph.D. diss., Columbia University, 1974.

Ford, Larry Royden. "The Skyscraper: Urban Symbolism and City Structure." Ph.D. diss., University of Oregon, 1970.

Fourth Presbyterian Church. Chicago: Commission on Chicago Historical and Architectural Landmarks, 1981.

Fourth Presbyterian Church. Chicago, 1937.

Gerberding, Holly. "Tribune Tower." Unpublished paper for Northwestern University, Department of Art History, 1983.

Harris, Neil. "The Planning of the Plan." An Address given to the 695th Regular Meeting of the Commercial Club of Chicago, 27 November 1979.

Howells, John Mead. "The Production of High Class Office Space as Affected by Architectural Design." *Proceedings of the Sixteenth Annual Convention of the National Association of Building Owners and Managers,* 258–61. Chicago, 1923.

The Italian Court for the Chicago Historical Society. Chicago: Romanek-Golub and Co., 1968.

Johnson, Henry C. *North Chicago: Its Advantages, Resources, and Probable Future.* Chicago: Henry C. Johnson, 1873.

Johnson, Vilas. *A History of the Commercial Club of Chicago Including the First History of the Club by John J. Glessner.* Chicago, 1977.

Jones, Archie. "Construction of the Chicago Water Tower." Chicago Historical Society Pamphlet File.

Kunning, Paul. "Founding of Fort Dearborn." Paper for the Chicago Association of Commerce and Industry, 1953.

The Landis Award: Its Purpose and Accomplishments. Chicago: Chicago Historical Society, 1927.

Lengerke Kehoe, Susan von. *Samuel M. Nickerson House.* Chicago: Commission on Chicago Historical and Architectural Landmarks, 1980.

Leonard, H. Steward. "The History of Architecture in Chicago." Master's thesis, University of Chicago, 1934.

Loebl, Schlossman and Hackel, Architects. Chicago, 1982.

London Guarantee Pamphlet File, Chicago Historical Society.

McCarthy, Michael Patrick. "Businessmen and Professionals in Municipal Reform: The Chicago Experience, 1887–1920." Ph.D. diss., Northwestern University, 1970.

McClure, James G. K. "Historical Address." *Fourth Church* (November 1936): 7–10.

"Magnificent Mile—Streeterville Historic District." National Register Nomination," Chicago Landmarks Preservation Council of Illinois, 1982.

Medinah Athletic Club. Chicago, c. 1930.

Medinah Athletic Club. *The Scmitar* (official publ. of the Medinah Club) (4 April 1930).

The Merchants Club of Chicago, 1896–1907. Chicago: Commercial Club of Chicago, 1922.

"Michigan-Wacker Historic District." National Register Nomination, Illinois Department of Conservation, 1978.

New Rush Street Bridge, Chicago; A Brief Memoranda of Its Construction. Chicago: Department of Public Works, 1884.

The North and South Side Boulevard Improvement: Plan No. 3 of the Chicago Plan Commission. Chicago: North and South Side Boulevard Property Owners Association, n.d.

Oset, Jill. "Graham, Anderson, Probst and White: Architect of an Industrial Vision." Paper for Northwestern University Department of Art History, 1983.

The Outer Drive Along the Lakefront: Chicago. Chicago: Chicago Plan Commission, 1929.

Packard, George. *Argument on the Boulevard Link.* Chicago: Michigan Avenue Improvement Association, 14 May 1908.

———. *The Boulevard Link.* Chicago, 1908.

Palmolive Building Pamphlet File, Chicago Historical Society.

Pamphlet of the North Central Association, 1918. Collection of the Chicago Historical Society.

Pictorial Views of the Medinah Club. Chicago, c. 1930.

Potter Palmer Journal and Ledger Accounts, 1880–1920, 1–27. Chicago Historical Society Manuscript File.

"The Preservation of the Plan of Chicago." Proceedings of the Two Hundred and Eleventh Meeting of the Commercial Club of Chicago, January 1910.

Proceedings of the Chicago City Council (Municipal Reference Library). Various years.

Reiss, Winold. Pamphlet File, Ryerson Library, Art Institute of Chicago.

Rezoning Chicago. Chicago: City Council, Committee on Building and Zoning, 1952.

Rubloff, Arthur, Collection of. Chicago Historical Society Manuscript File.

Scrapbooks supposedly compiled by J. C. Ambler for the Citizen's Association of Chicago, Chicago Historical Society.

Sheridan, Leo J. "Renting and Advertising Policies for Office Buildings." *Proceedings of the Annual Convention of the National Association of Building Owners and Managers,* 192–215. Chicago, 1929.

Sloan, Tom L. B. "The Architecture of William W. Boyington." Master's thesis, Northwestern University, 1962.

Small, Sidney. "Proper Office Building Financing." *Proceedings of the Annual Convention of the National Association of Building Owners and Managers,* 148–54. Chicago, 1928.

Sprague, Paul. "Submission to Illinois Historic Sites Advisory Council—Magnificent Mile-Streeterville Historic District Nomination." August 1982.

"Streetscape 1980: A New Look for Greater North Michigan Avenue." Chicago: Greater North Michigan Avenue Association, 1980.

Taussig, Meredith. "North Michigan Avenue: A Story of a Chicago Street, 1918–1930." Class paper for University of Illinois at Chicago. March 1983.

To the Tower. Chicago: Chicago Tribune, 1924.

The Unveiling of the Fountain of Diana, Carl Milles, Sculptor, Diana Court, Michigan Square Building. Chicago, 6 November 1930.

Wacker, Charles. *Argument in Favor of Michigan Avenue Boulevard Link.* Chicago, 1913.

———. *Chicago's Financial Needs.* Chicago: Chicago Plan Commission, 1919.

———. *Creating a World Famous Street.* Chicago: Chicago Plan Commission, 1913.

———. "The Economic and Commercial Features of a City Plan." In *The Presentation of the Plan of Chicago.* Chicago: Commercial Club of Chicago, 1910.

———. *The Michigan Avenue Bond Issue.* Chicago: Chicago Plan Commission, 1918.

———. "The Michigan Avenue Extension: An Address in Commemoration of the Initial Work on the Extension of North Michigan Avenue (Chicago: Chicago Plan Commission, 13 April 1918). Collections of the Chicago Historical Society.

Westfall, Carroll William. "Shaping a City: Alfred S. Alschuler and Chicago Architecture 1900–1930." Unpublished manuscript. Chicago, 1981.

Winter, Cheryl. "Lake Shore Drive: A Report on Its Stages of Development." Chicago Municipal Reference Library, 1973.